유영국

탄생 100주년 기념전

절대와 자유

YOO YOUNGKUK 1916-2002

The 100th Anniversary Exhibition of a Korean Modern Master

유영국 탄생 100주년 기념전

유영국, 절대와 자유

국립현대미술관 덕수궁관
2016년 11월 4일 – 2017년 3월 1일

부산시립미술관
2017년 3월 29일 – 6월 25일

The 100th Anniversary Exhibition of a Korean Modern Master:

YOO YOUNGKUK 1916-2002

National Museum of Modern and Contemporary Art, Deoksugung
4 November 2016 – 1 March 2017

Busan Art Museum
29 March 2017 – 25 June 2017

| 국립현대미술관 |

전시총괄	강승완, 류지연
기획 및 진행	김인혜
코디네이션	안지숙
운송 및 설치	류원현
공간 디자인	김종성 김용주
그래픽 디자인	김동수
공간조성	한명희
보존수복	김은진 범대건 박소현 최점복 조인애 이하림 한예림
작품출납	권성오 주동일 박은해
홍보	이정민 이기석 김은아 황보경 김성희(인턴)
교육	조장은 문혜정 정상연
아카이브	박지혜 박나라보라 이지희 윤정인
사진촬영	M2 스튜디오 (황현만, 황정욱)
영상제작	이미지 줌
영상편집	류재하
영상설치	멀티텍
디지털 출력	㈜트리콤

| 부산시립미술관 |

전시총괄	박정구 정성준
학예업무 총괄	이진철
전시진행	박진희 강선주
공간조성	황서미
작품출납 및 관리	박효원 김재동
공간시설관리	유광춘 박민호 김귀교 임이수 김경민
홍보	윤영준 이강호 박경란 이수영
교육	이미영 김유겸 김주란
아카이브	류민주 이영빈

자문 위원

오광수, 이인범

감사의 말씀

가람화랑, 갤러리 현대, 권행가, 김병기, 김복기, 김영나, 김우창, 김윤경, 무라이 마사나리 기념관(Memorial Museum of Murai Masanari), 뮤지엄 산(Museum SAN), 미즈사와 츠토무(Mizusawa Tsutomu), 미호 사카쿠라 키다(Migo Sakakura Kira), 박명자, 박형국, 삼성미술관 리움, 서울미술관, 서울시립미술관, 서울옥션, 세타가야 미술관(Setagaya Art Museum), 오무카 토시하루(Omuka Toshiharu), 우에노 히사미(Ueno Hisami), 윤명로, 이미나, 이츠코 무라이(Itsuko Murai), 케이옥션, 하세가와 사부로 갤러리(Konan Highschool Hasegawa Saburo Memorial Gallery), 그리고 익명을 요청한 많은 개인 소장가분들에게 감사의 말씀을 드립니다.

주최

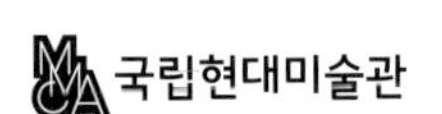

후원

유영국미술문화재단

Google Arts & Culture

미디어 후원

KBS 한국방송

유영국

탄생 100주년 기념전

절대와 자유

YOO YOUNGKUK 1916-2002

The 100th Anniversary Exhibition of a Korean Modern Master

일러두기

- 이 책에 나오는 인명 및 고유명사는 외래어 표기법에 준하여 표기하는 것을 원칙으로 한다.
- 작품은 〈 〉, 전시 제목은 《 》로 표시한다.
- 작품과 글의 영문 제목은 이탤릭체로 표시한다.
- 작품 제목의 경우, 작품이 처음 발표될 때의 제목을 확인할 수 있을 경우 이에 따랐으며, 그렇지 않은 경우 관습적으로 사용되는 제목을 사용한다.

Content

인사말

올해 한국 추상미술의 진정한 선구자로 널리 알려진 유영국(1916-2002)의 탄생 100주년을 맞이하여, 그의 회고전을 국립현대미술관 덕수궁관에서 개최하게 된 것을 매우 기쁘게 생각합니다.

유영국은 1916년 일제강점기 경상북도(당시의 행정구역상 강원도) 울진에서 태어나, 서울에서의 유학생활을 거쳐, 일본 도쿄 문화학원에서 본격적인 미술 공부를 시작했습니다. 놀랍게도 1935년 도쿄에서 처음 공부를 시작한 지 단 2년 후인 1937년, 그는 독립미술협회, N.B.G. 양화전, 자유미술가협회와 같은 여러 미술 단체에 작품을 발표하며 일약 작가로 등단했습니다. 갤러리나 사립 미술관이 없는 상황에서 이러한 기회를 통해 작가들은 자신의 작품을 대중에게 선보일 수 있었습니다. 그의 초기 작품은 한스 아르프(Hans Arp), 루이스 네벨슨(Louise Nevelson) 등을 연상시키는 부조 조각이 대부분을 이루었으며, 형태와 구성, 나무 표면의 재질적 특성만이 작품의 요소를 결정하는 '말없는' 추상을 실현해 나갔습니다.

20세기 초 유럽에서 추상은 '혁명'처럼 번져나갔지만, 일본의 문화는 구상화나 사실주의가 주를 이루었습니다. 제2차 세계 대전 당시 일본 정부가 장려한 미술 양식이나 전위예술에 반대하던 입장을 고려하면 작가의 이러한 과감한 선택은 특기(特記)할만한 것입니다. 1937년 독일에서도《퇴폐예술전(Entartete Kunst Ausstellung)》이 열리면서, 파시즘 정권의 전위예술에 대한 탄압이 본격화되던 시기였으니까요.

유영국은 1943년 한국으로 돌아온 이후 해방과 한국전쟁을 거쳐 1950년대 후반부터 다시 본격적인 작품 활동을 시작했으며, 이 시기 한국 화단의 가장 전위적인 그룹들을 이끌었습니다. 그러다가 돌연 그룹 활동의 종언을 선언한 그는, 1964년 그의 나이 만 48세에 첫 개인전을 개최한 이후 2002년 타계할 때까지 오로지 작업실에서 일평생 전업작가로 생활하며, 수많은 아름다운 작품들을 남겼습니다.

그의 선구자적인 결단은 많은 이들의 귀감이 되었습니다. 또한 완성도 높은 작품을 만들려는 그의 노력은 이후 세대 한국의 예술가에게도 많은 영향을 미쳤으리라 생각합니다. 그럼에도 불구하고 유영국의 예술 작품은 충분히 대중적인 관심을 끌지 못하고 있으며, 작가로서 그의 발자취를 이해하려는 관심도 부족한 면이 있었습니다. 그의 탄생 100주년을 기념한 이번 전시를 통해 유영국의 작품 세계가 좀 더 널리 알려지는 계기가 되기를 기대합니다.

이 전시는 서울전을 거쳐 부산시립미술관으로 순회합니다. 전시 준비 단계부터 적극적인 협력을 기울여준 부산시립미술관 측에 감사드립니다. 이 전시는 또한 유영국미술문화재단의 오랜 자료축적과 노력의 산물이기도 합니다. 이 자리를 빌려 유영국미술문화재단의 연구 협력과 아낌없는 후원에 깊이 감사드립니다. 마지막으로 전시에 귀중한 작품을 대여해 준 소장가 여러분, 그리고 전시의 대중적 접근을 위한 여러 가지 툴을 제안해주고 실현해준 구글과 KBS의 후원에도 깊은 감사의 말씀을 드립니다.

2016년 10월

국립현대미술관장

바르토메우 마리

Foreword

The National Museum of Modern and Contemporary Art, Korea(MMCA) is pleased to present the retrospective of Yoo Youngkuk, a true pioneer of abstract paintings in Korea, in MMCA Deoksugung in commemoration of the centennial of his birth.

Yoo was born in Uljin, North Gyeongsang Province (then-Gangwon Province), in 1916 during the Japanese colonial rule. He studied in Seoul, before starting to pursue his studies in art in Bunka-Gakuin University(文化學院). Only two years after he started to study art, did he present his artworks in several art exhibitions, such as the Independant Art Association, Neo Beaux-Arts Group, and the Association of Free Artist. In a context without private art galleries or museums, these were the occasions where artists could show their work to the public. His early works are mostly relief sculptures, which could be seen as under the influence of Hans Arp or Louise Nevelson. He tried to show his concept of "speechless" abstraction where forms, construction, and wood texture are the only factors that compose the artworks.

Abstraction sprouted like a revolution in the early 20th century in Europe, and yet the Japanese culture was dominated by figurative and realist representation. This bold move of Yoo Youngkuk is noteworthy given the anti-avantgarde positions and the official style promoted under Japan's Imperialist regime during World War II. In Germany, the fascist government also condemned avant-garde and abstract art movements when the Degenerate Art Exhibition(Entartete Kunst Ausstellung) opened in 1937.

Yoo came back to Korea in 1943, right before the country was liberated from Japanese colonial rule, and the Korean War broke out. It was in the late 1950s that he was able to start making artworks once again and led the most powerful avant-garde groups in the Korean art circles. However, after he abruptly put an end to his commitment to the group activities, the artist presented his first solo exhibition at the age of 48 in 1964 and dedicated the rest of his life to art only at his studio, leaving many outstanding artworks.

His decisiveness as a pioneer artist set a good example for many. As his works are done with a high level of perfection, Yoo had a great influence over Korean artists of next generation, as well. However, there has been not enough public attention and interest in his works of art until today to understand the steps this great artist took. Commemorating the 100th anniversary of his birth, I hope that this exhibition can be an opportunity for the public to understand him better.

This exhibition will be presented in the Busan Art Museum, after its presentation in Seoul. I would like to extend my sincere gratitude for the active collaboration of our partners in Busan since the early stage of preparation. This exhibition is also the product of the efforts to build the archives of the artist by the Yoo Youngkuk Art Foundation. I would like to take this opportunity to thank the family of the artist and collectors for their generous support to lend precious works for our exhibition. My gratitude also goes to Google for giving us many suggestions on tools for the public access. Finally, I would like to express my appreciation to KBS for their partnership.

October 2016

Bartomeu Mari
Director, National Museum of Modern and Contemporary Art, Korea

인사말

부산시립미술관은 국립현대미술관과 공동으로 기획한 유영국 탄생 100주년《유영국: 절대와 자유》전 개최를 뜻깊게 생각합니다.

1953년 피난시절, 부산 국립박물관에서 개최된《신사실파전》에 4점의 출품작을 들고 부산을 방문했던 고 유영국 선생님이, 2017년 봄 그의 예술적 생애를 망라하는 자료와 100여 점의 작품으로 부산을 찾아옵니다.

유영국은 1916년 경북 울진에서 출생하여, 서울의 제2고보를 거쳐, 1935년 일본의 자유, 지성, 예술의 상징이던 문화학원(文化學院, 분카가쿠인)에서 유학하였습니다. 그는 재학시절부터 공모전에 입선하는가 하면, 전위적인 신세대그룹전에 참여하고, 미술학교를 졸업하던 1938년에는 자유미술가협회상을 수상하였습니다. 부조, 사진, 콜라주가 과감하게 도입된 기하학적 추상과 생명의 포름을 추상화했던 유영국의 작품세계는 일본 전위미술사의 선구로 기록되어 있습니다. 당시 그의 전위적 실험은 중일전쟁에서 태평양전쟁으로 이어진 비상시국하에서 행해진 것이며, 그러한 성취는 표현이 다양화하고 서구추상회화 담론이 확산된 일본 추상미술화단에서의 평가라는 점에서 그 의미가 큽니다. 그러나 1943년 유영국의 전위정신을 길러낸 문화학원이 폐쇄명령을 받게 되자 울진으로 귀향합니다. 귀국 후 서울대학과 홍익대학 교수로 재직하며 후진을 양성하는 한편, 신사실파, 모던 아트협회, 신상회 등의 창립멤버, 국전의 추천작가로도 참여하여 한국 현대미술화단의 리더로 활약하였습니다. 생애 후반은 침묵의 자세로 일관하며 온전한 순수추상화가로서의 치열한 조형탐색에 몰입하였습니다.

그렇게 도달한 유영국의 추상회화는 미술 외의 요소를 철저히 배격하고 절대 순수미를 추구했던 20세기 미술혁신의 성취 그 자체였습니다. 하지만 그의 예술적 성취도나 한국현대미술사에서의 위치에 비하여 대중적 인지도가 낮은 모순을 안고 있습니다.

이번 전시에는 재제작된 초기 실험 작품과 관련 사료, 작가 주변 사진들이 함께 전시되어 모더니스트 유영국의 전위적 면모를 열어 보입니다. 그리고 귀국 후의 자연에 천착한 순수추상의 도정이 전시됩니다. 특히 그의 문화기억의 아르케라고 할 고향의 '산'과 우리의 '풍경'이 어떻게 미술의 국적을 취득하면서도 절대 보편의 순수미에 도달했는지를 밝혀줄 것입니다. 이 전시가 한국추상미술의 살아 있는 해석과 풍부한 의미를 생산할 출발점이 되고, 같은 문맥에서 부산의 추상미술에 관한 관심을 촉발하는 계기가 될 것을 기대합니다.

부산시립미술관이 공동기획자로, 새로운 정보를 공유하며 출품작과 자료에 대한 역사적 사실의 검증과 엄선작업을 수행할 기회를 제공해주신 국립현대미술관과 그간의 연구를 축적해온 유영국문화재단에 감사인사를 드립니다. 또한 이 전시를 위하여 귀중한 작품을 출품해주신 소장가분들에게 감사의 말씀을 드립니다.

2016년 10월

부산시립미술관장

김영순

Foreword

Busan Art Museum is proud to announce this special exhibition, co-organized with the National Museum of Modern and Contemporary Art, Korea, to commemorate the 100th anniversary of the birth of Yoo Youngkuk(1916-2002), one of the true pioneers of Korean abstract art.

Yoo Youngkuk visited Busan in 1953, amidst the flood of refugees who were fleeing the Korean War, when he brought four works for the exhibition *New Realism* at the National Museum in Busan. Now, in the spring of 2017, he is returning to Busan for this landmark exhibition, featuring about 100 works and materials that provide a comprehensive look at his entire artistic career.

Born in Uljin, North Gyeongsang Province, in 1916, Yoo Youngkuk attended Seoul Second High School. In 1935, he went to Tokyo to study at Bunka Gakuin University, which was then the center of freedom, intellectualism, and art in Japan. While at Bunka Gakuin University, Yoo joined various avant-garde groups of young artists and began showing his works at group exhibitions. After graduating in 1938, he was honored with the 2nd Association of Free Artists Award. Early in his career, Yoo Youngkuk freely indulged his passion for abstract art in various media, including painting, relief sculpture, photography, collage, and even organic life forms. Today, he is widely recognized as one of the leading innovators in the history of Japanese avant-garde art. Notably, these early avant-garde experimentations were carried out while Japan was in a state of emergency, during the Second Sino-Japanese War (1937-1945) and the Pacific War(1941-1945). In 1943, however, Bunka Gakuin University, the environment that had nurtured his spirit for abstraction, was shut down by the government, forcing him to return to Uljin. Upon his return to Korea, Yoo imparted his knowledge to younger artists as a professor at Seoul National University and Hongik University, while also working actively as a leader of the fledgling field of Korean contemporary art. He was a founding member of several Korean avant-garde art groups (including New Realism and the Modern Art Association) and also participated in the National Art Exhibition of Korea. In his later years, he lived mostly in solitude, remaining avidly devoted to his work as a free artist of pure abstraction.

Enacting a realm of absolute beauty solely through artistic elements, Yoo Youngkuk's abstract painting represents one of the foremost innovations and achievements of twentieth-century art. Unfortunately, however, despite these achievements and his seminal place in the history of Korean contemporary art, he remains relatively little-known among the public.

Hopefully, that status will change through this major exhibition, featuring works from throughout Yoo's career (including recreations of his early experimental works), as well as contemporaneous photos and other relevant materials. The ultimate goal is to unveil and investigate the avant-garde characteristics of Yoo Youngkuk as a modernist. Focusing on the trajectory of Yoo's work after his return to Korea, the exhibition shows how his fascination with nature—especially the mountainous landscape of Uljin—fueled his progression into pure abstraction. As the original constituents of Yoo's cultural memory, the mountains, trees, and waters of Uljin came to inhabit his art, eventually reaching the realm of pure and universal aesthetic. On behalf of all of the organizers, we hope that this exhibition will serve as the foundation for vibrant discussions and new interpretations of the profound meaning of Korean abstract art.

I wish to express my sincere gratitude to the National Museum of Modern and Contemporary Art, Korea and to the Yoo Youngkuk Art Foundation for giving Busan Art Museum the opportunity to co-organize this exhibition, and for their invaluable assistance in sharing new information, verifying historical facts, and selecting the exhibited works and materials. I also would like to extend my gratitade for the collectors who lend us valuable works and made this exhibition possible.

October 2016
Kim Youngsoon
Director, Busan Art Museum

유영국 탄생 100주년을 기념하여

김인혜
국립현대미술관 학예연구사

화가의 길

한때는 강원도였으나 지금은 경상북도로 편입된 울진(蔚珍). 몇 발자국만 안으로 들어가면 금세 한 길의 깊이가 되어버리는 검푸른 동해 바다가 있고, 조금만 내지로 들어가면 이내 해발 1,000미터의 높은 산을 맞닥뜨리게 되는 곳이다. 태백산맥의 준령들 사이사이로 급격하게 떨어지는 물줄기는 폭포를 이루다가 갑자기 해변을 만나 개천을 형성하기도 하는데, 그렇게 깊은 바다, 높은 산, 평온한 개천이 약속이나 한 듯이 한 지점에서 만나는, 바로 그곳 언저리에 유영국의 생가가 있다. 세계에 이러한 지형이 또 있을까 싶은, 그렇게 깊고도 깊으나 인간이 살기에도 적합한 묘한 장소에서 그가 태어났다.

그의 생가는 임진왜란도 일어나기 전 지금으로부터 약 400년도 더 전에 지어진 자그마한 한옥인데, 원래 원주에 터를 잡고 있던 조상들이 이 가옥을 울진으로 옮겨와서 오늘에 이르렀다고 전한다. 현재는 이 집안의 종부가 마치 오랜 역사의 증인처럼 여전히 이 집과 함께 살아 계신다.

울진에서 발행된 여러 책과 잡지에는, 유영국 스스로는 거의 얘기한 적이 없는 강릉 유씨 집안의 이야기가 전설처럼 기록되어 있다. 그의 집안은 조부 유재업(劉載業, 1845-1913)의 세대에 울진의 '말루' 지역에 정착하며 막대한 부를 이루었는데, 이는 유재업의 타고난 사업 수완에 힘입었을 뿐 아니라 시싯골이라는 깊은 골짜기 풍수지리상의 최고 길지(吉地)에 고조부의 묘소를 이장해 왔기 때문이라는 것이다. 유재업은 어느 날 사냥을 나가서 노루를 쫓아 산길을 따라 오르던 중 주위가 온통 눈으로 뒤덮인 산속 한가운데에서 기적같이 눈이 쌓이지 않는 따뜻하고 평평한 땅을 발견하게 되었다고 한다. 노루도 이 땅에서 잠시 놀다가 홀연히 사라졌는데, 다시 지세를 찬찬히 보니 주변의 산들이 병풍처럼 둘러쳐져 호위하는 듯한 기막힌 길지였다고 한다. 이후 그는 그의 조부의 묘소를 이곳으로 이장해 왔고, 이후 집안의 부가 일어났다는 설화 같은 이야기이다.

유재업이 쌓은 부는 유영국의 아버지인 유문종(劉文鐘, 1876-1946)의 세대에 이르러 좋은 일에 쓰이곤 했다. 평민 출신의 의병장이었던 신돌석 부대가 불영계곡 깊은 곳에 위치한 불영사(佛影寺)를 근거지로 의병활동을 할 때에 지역 유지였던 그는 거금을 흔쾌히 내놓았다. 일제 강점기 울진 지역의 민족 사학이라 할 수 있는 제동초등학교가 삼일운동 이후 정식 인가를 받고 1925년 개교할 때에는 일천 원의 거액을 기부하기도 했다. 제동초등학교는 제때 학교에 입학하지 못한 다양한 연령층의 지역민들과 가난한 이들을 위한 교육기관이었고, 고려혁명당 사건, 광주학생운동, 조선 독립공작당 사건 등 일제 강점기 수많은 사건에 휩싸이며 탄압을 받다가 1943년 울진공립보통학교에 강제 통합된 역사를 지닌 곳이다.[1]

교육열이 남달랐던 유영국의 부친은 셋째 아들인 유영국을 포함하여 대부분의 자녀들을 서울로, 도쿄로 유학하도록 지원했다. 유영국은 1931년 경성 제2고등보통학교(5년제)에 입학하여 학업에 열중하던 중 4년만 수료한 후 돌연 자퇴하고, 1935년 4월 도쿄 문화학원(文化學院)에 입학했다. 문화학원은 1921년 일본에서도 다이쇼 데모크라시가 한창이던 때에 우후죽순으로 생겨난 사립학교의 하나로, 한때 아나키즘과 사회주의 사상에 매료되었던 니시무라 이사쿠(西村伊作, 1884-1963)라는 건축가이자 교육사업가가 설립한 문예(文藝) 전문 학교였다. 원래 중학교로 시작했으나 1925년부터 대학부를 설립하여, 대학부 본과 외에 미술부, 문학부, 음악부, 여학부 등의 학과를 개설하고 있었다. 군국주의 시대 최후의 보루와 같이 자유로운 학원 분위기를 견지하다가 1943년 니시무라 이사쿠가 감옥에 끌려가면서 강제 폐교된 역사를 지니고 있다. 어찌 보면 시기적으로 울진 제동초등학교의 운명과 거의 유사한 경로를 거쳤다고도 볼 수 있다.

유영국은 이곳 문화학원의 입학 시기를 전후하여, 그의 예술가로서의 진로에 중대한 영향을 미쳤던 세 명의 일본인 화가를 만나게 된다. 바로 사토 쿠니오(佐藤九二男, 1897-1945), 무라이 마사나리(村井正誠, 1905-1999), 그리고 하세가와 사부로(長谷川三郎, 1906-1957)이다. 먼저 사토 쿠니오는 유영국의 경성 제2고등보통학교 재학 시절 미술교사로, 야마다 신이치(山田新一, 1899-1991)의 후임으로 1927년 이 학교에 부임하였다. 동경미술학교 출신으로 일본의 재야미술계와 네트워크를 유지하며 《독립미술협회전》에 꾸준히 작품을 발표했던 인물이다. 그는 야마다 신이치가 나중에 프랑스 유학 후 돌아와 군국주의에 동조하는 작품을 그릴 때조차 오로지 야수파적인 색채를 유지하며 우수에 찬 조선인의 모습을 화폭에 담곤 했다. 유영국은 경성 제2고보 시절 미술반 활동을 별도로 한 적이 없었다고 했지만,

사토 쿠니오의 자유로운 미술 교육에 감화를 받았음은 확실해 보인다. 사토 쿠니오는 유영국이 경성 제2고보를 4년만 마치고 문화학원에 입학할 수 있게 되기까지 일정한 역할을 했을 것으로 짐작된다. 1935년 4월 유영국이 도쿄에 정착한 직후, 사토 쿠니오가 유영국에게 보낸 엽서(도판 p. 30-31)를 통해 두 사제 간의 긴밀했던 관계를 새삼 확인할 수 있다.

문화학원 시기 유영국이 만났던 중요한 일본인 화가는 무라이 마사나리였다. 무라이는 문화학원 설립자인 니시무라 이사쿠와 동향(同鄕, 와카야마 현)으로 일찍부터 이들은 서로 잘 알고 지내는 사이였다. 1925년 문화학원이 대학부를 설립한 것은 동경미술학교 입학시험에 떨어진 무라이 마사나리를 문화학원에 진학시키기 위한 것이었다고 얘기될 정도이다.[2] 어찌 되었든 무라이 마사나리는 문화학원 대학부 제1회 입학생이 되었고, 3년제 학교를 재빨리 졸업하고 누구보다 먼저 프랑스 유학을 감행했으며, 귀국하자마자 곧바로 문화학원의 강사로 부임하였다. 무라이 마사나리는 동경미술학교의 아카데미즘적인 교육 방식을 탈피하여, 세계 미술의 '전위(前衛)'에서는 방편으로 '추상화'의 노선을 의도적으로 채택한 화가이다. 그는 1934년 '신시대양화전'이라는 소그룹의 결성을 거쳐, 1937년 자유미술가협회 창립의 주도적 인물이 되었다. 1937년 당시 문화학원 3학년에 불과했던 유영국은 무라이 마사나리 추종자들의 모임이었다고 해도 과언이 아닌 N.B.G.의 정식 멤버가 되었고 (이 단체는 문화학원 미술부 9회-11회 출신들이 주축이 되었다[3]), 곧바로 자유미술가협회에 작품을 발표하기 시작했으며, 1938년 문화학원을 졸업한 해에는 자유미술가협회상을 수상하며 회원 자격을 얻기까지 했다. 유영국의 이러한 갑작스런 '등단'에는 무라이 마사나리의 지원이 있었으리라 충분히 짐작할 수 있다. 무라이 마사나리는 태평양전쟁이 최고조에 달했을 때조차 끝까지 전쟁화를 그리지 않았으며, 스스로 창립했던 자유미술가협회를 자진 탈퇴하여 1950년 모던 아트협회를 결성하였다. 그 후 1999년 타계할 때까지 추상화의 개척자로 쉼 없는 작품 활동을 계속 했다.

마지막으로 하세가와 사부로는 유영국이 스스로 가장 존경하는 화가로 꼽았을 정도로, 그의 진로에 중요한 역할을 했던 인물이다. 하세가와는 동경제국대학 문학부 미학과 출신의 엘리트이며, 탁월한 미술평론가이자 예술가였다. 유럽 여행을 자유자재로 할 수 있는 재력을 가졌던 그는 유럽의 최신 미술 동향을 『미즈에(みづゑ)』, 『비노쿠니(美の国)』 등에 끊임없이 소개하며, 당대 미술계 최고의 지식인으로 활약했다. 무라이 마사나리와 함께 자유미술가협회의 초창기 리더였던 그는 조선인 예술가들에게 특히 우호적인 편이었다. 1938년 유영국이 협회상을 받을 때에도 그

의 작품에 대한 호평을 『비노쿠니(美の国)』에 실었으며[4], 김환기, 문학수, 이중섭 등에 대해서도 애정 어린 평론을 많이 남겼다. 유영국은 사진을 공부했던 그의 친구 주현(본명 이범승)과 함께 하세가와 사부로의 집에 드나들었던 것 같다. 그는 1937년 『アブストラクトアート(Abstract Art)』라는 책을 발표하며 추상미술의 최고 이론가로 활약하다가, 군국주의 시대 전위예술을 탄압하는 분위기 속에서 1941년에 감옥 신세를 지기도 했다. 1942년 이후에는 미술창작가협회(자유미술가협회의 개칭) 전시에도 더 이상 출품하지 않았으며, 1944년에는 시가 현 나가하마(長浜)에서 농사를 지으며 은둔생활을 하다가 종전을 맞았다.[5] 하세가와 사부로의 강한 리더십, 타협하지 않는 생활태도, 추상미술에의 경도, 사진에 대한 관심 등은 유영국과 여러 지점에서 일맥상통하는 면을 지니고 있다. 무엇보다도, '예술'을 통해 일종의 유토피아적 '삶'을 '실천'하고자 했던 하세가와 사부로의 철저한 신념은 유영국의 생애 전체에 심대한 영향을 미쳤으리라 짐작된다.

유영국은 어떤 점에서 매우 경제적으로 '효율적인' 인생을 살지 않았나 생각된다. 그는 엄청난 직관력의 소유자로서, 그 직관력을 통해 그토록 험난했던 시대를 관통하면서도 오로지 훌륭한 사람들과만 교류하는 놀라운 능력을 지녔던 것 같다. 그것이 개인적으로는 매우 '고독한' 삶을 자처하는 결과를 낳았지만, 동시에, 다른 이들이 대부분 고생스러운 삶의 격정에 휘말릴 때에도 홀로 우뚝 서서 불행을 피해간 것처럼 보이는, 그런 종류의 삶을 영위할 수 있었던 이유가 되기도 했다.

추상의 길

이렇게 그의 출생과 가계, 그리고 화가로의 등단 시기 주변 인물들까지 다소 장황하게 설명하는 이유는, 필자 스스로 여전히 풀리지 않는 두 가지의 질문에 대해 나름대로의 답을 찾으려는 과정이라고 할 수 있다.

첫 번째 질문은 유영국은 애초에 어떻게 그토록 전격적으로 '추상미술'이라는 선택지를 찾아갈 수 있었을까 하는 것이다. 미술을 공부하기 시작한 지 불과 2년 만에 그는 곧바로 나무판자 조각을 화면에 구성하여 붙인 부조 작품을 일본의 그룹전에 출품하였다. 첩첩산중과 망망대해가 교차하는 시골에서 갑자기 코즈모폴리턴(cosmopolitan)의 도시 도쿄로 와서 세계 미술의 가장 앞선 경향을 단번에 선택하고 섭취하는 그 '비약'이야말로 일종의 신화적인 요소를 지닌 것처럼 느껴질 정도이다.

두 번째 질문은 어떤 면에서 더욱 답하기 어려운 것인데, 유영국은 어떻게 그러한 선택을 일평생 그토록 일관되게 그리고 '지속적으로' 유지할 수 있었을까 하는 것

이다. 그의 '예술'과 '추상'에 대한 신념, 그리고 그러한 신념을 지속할 수 있었던 원동력은 대체 무엇이었을까. 그저 추상미술이 가장 최신의 트렌드였기 때문에 좇았다거나 단순히 가장 앞서가겠다는 자기인식이 지배적이었다고 치부하기에는, 그가 추상을 내걸고 한 시대를 지내오며 감내해야 했을 희생이 너무 컸을 것이다. 지금도 '추상'이라는 단어가 많은 이들에겐 그저 생소할 뿐인데, 더구나 과거에 그의 '추상'을 이해하는 이는 한국 사회에 극소수에 불과했을 것이다. 그렇다고 대학교수를 오래하거나 화단정치를 하는 식의 협소한 권력에 현혹되지도 않은 채,[6] 일평생 전업작가로서 매일매일 침실과 아틀리에 사이를 정시 출퇴근하며 끊임없이 작품 제작에 몰두했던 그가 평생 매달린 화두는 과연 무엇이었을까?

언제나 그의 대답은 단순했다. "간섭받지 않고 자유롭고 싶었다." 그는 미술을 처음 선택했던 이유에 대해 이렇게 간명하게 말했다. 일제 강점기 무엇을 해도 자유로울 수 없었던 시대의 한계 속에서 그는 그나마 '미술'을 통해 자신만의 자유로운 세계에 빠져들 수 있는 가능성을 발견하고, 차라리 일본 본토로 가버렸던 것이다. 그리고 그 미술 중에서도 어떠한 객관적인 법칙이나 의무(데생을 한다든지, 똑같이 그린다든지 하는 식의 규칙)로부터 완전히 자유로운 '추상'의 세계에 빠르게 접근했던 것 같다.

'추상'은 20세기 초 유럽에서 하나의 '양식'이 아니라 '이념'으로써 대두된 것이다. 1917년 몬드리안이 처음 '신조형주의(Neo-Plasticism)' 이론을 발표하고, '추상-실제(Abstract-Real)' 회화의 기치를 내걸었을 때, '추상'은 새로운 시대, 새로운 예술이 걸어가야 할 당연한 경로라고 주장되었다. 인류는 지금까지 헛되이 '비극'으로 얼룩진 세계 속에서 살아왔다. 그러나 이제 "새로운 삶을 위한 예술", 즉 추상의 세계에서는 어떠한 비극적 요소도 제거된 완전한 평형상태를 추구하게 될 것이다. 인간은 정신성을 더욱 고양함으로써, "조화로움의 순수한 표현"을 찾아나가야만 한다. 예술은 '추상'이라는 새로운 조형을 통해, 정확한 질서를 드러내고 완벽하게 동등한 평형상태를 시각화하게 되는데, 바로 그러한 동등성의 관계는 새로운 사회가 추구해야 하는 바이기도 하다. 그런 점에서 예술은 인류가 보다 나은 삶과 사회를 창출할 수 있는 시각을 일깨워준다. 그것이 바로 새로운 시대 예술의 역할이자 소명인 것이다.

이러한 혁명적 생각은 제1차 세계대전의 혼돈을 통과하며 인류가 꾸며낸 갖가지 드라마로 인해 지긋지긋한 비극을 경험했던 몬드리안의 세대가, 예술을 통해 도달하고자 했던 완벽한 정신적 평온의 상태였다. 어떠한 극적 요소로부터도 자유로운, 완전하게 '순수한' 조형의 세계! 유영국의 표현대로라면, "말없는" 세계인 것이

다. 그렇게 제1차 세계대전 후의 몬드리안에게서나 제2차 세계대전 중의 일본 화가들 혹은 유영국에게 있어 '추상'의 세계가 지니는 의미는 오늘날 우리가 상상하는 것보다 훨씬 더 엄중한 것이었다.

유영국의 삶과 예술

유영국 탄생 100주년을 기념하여, 100년 전 식민지 조선에서 태어난 그가 화가의 길을 선택하고 또한 추상화의 선구자가 되는 경로를 추적해 보는 작업은 의미 있는 일일 것이다. 이번 전시는 그런 점에서 그의 전반기 작업에 특히 주목하면서, 크게 다음의 두 시기로 구분되어 있다.

첫 번째는 1937년 일본에서의 유학기 작품에서부터 1964년 신문회관에서 첫 개인전을 열기 전까지의 시기에 해당한다. 그는 일본에서도 가장 전위적인 재야 그룹에서 활동했던 것처럼, 한국으로 돌아와서도 1947년부터 1963년까지 신사실파, 모던 아트협회, 현대작가초대전, 신상회 등 당대 한국의 가장 전위적인 미술 그룹들을 차례로 이끌며 일종의 '미술 운동'에 헌신했다.[7] 예술의 사회적 역할에 대한 신념에 기초하여, 척박한 예술계에서 예술인들의 소모임을 활성화하는가 하면, 공모제를 통해 젊은 예술가들의 참된 등용문을 여는 데에도 열의를 보였다. 그는 새로운 전시에 참여할 때마다 조금씩 달라지는 화풍을 구사하며, 사람, 도시, 노을, 언덕, 계곡, 바다, 산맥 등이 순수한 조형의 요소들로 축약되는 과정을 작품에서 보여주었다.

두 번째는 1964년 이후 그가 돌연 그룹 활동의 종언을 고하며 개인전을 개최한 이후 2002년 타계할 때까지, 사회 활동을 그만둔 채 홀로 작업에만 몰두하던 시기에 해당한다. 1964년 그의 첫 개인전은 깊은 숲 속에 빠져든 것 같은 착각을 불러일으키는 거대한 화면들로 구성되어 있는데, 숭엄한 자연의 울림이 점차적으로 고양되는 정신성에 융해되어 가는 느낌을 준다. 이후 그는 1970년대 전반까지 끊임없는 '자기부정'을 계속하는데, 점, 선, 면, 형, 색 등 각각의 조형 요소들을 통해 할 수 있는 모든 종류의 조형실험을 스스로 다 해본 것 같은 인상을 준다. "창작과정에서 막다른 골목에 이르렀을 때에 나는 항상 뚫고 나갈 길이 있다고 생각한다. 그래서 한 작품은 다음 작품을 위한 과정이고 계속적으로 작품을 해야 되는 근거가 된다."[8] 그는 그렇게 작업을 계속해 나갔던 것이다.

특히 1970년대 초 그의 작품에 "라라라"라는 부제를 붙였을 때에는 작가 스스로 일종의 클라이맥스를 경험하지 않았을까 하는 생각이 들 정도이다. 그러나 일종의 '정점'에 도달하자마자 급격한 건강상의 문제가 찾아온 것은 우연일까? 그는

1977년 심장박동기를 달기 시작한 이후 2002년 타계할 때까지 8번의 뇌출혈, 37번의 입원생활을 겪어야 했다. 그러니까 1970년대 후반 이후 그의 작품이 강렬도가 떨어지고 밀도나 옅어지며, 대신 서정(抒情)이 등장하고 평온한 기분이 생겨나는 데에는 신체적인 이유가 일차적이라고 할 수 있다. 원래 신체와 정신은 분리될 수 없는 것이다. 이 시기 그의 작품들에는 여러 차례의 죽을 고비를 넘어선 이의 안도와 위안, 그리고 생(生)에 대한 예찬이 담겨있는 것처럼 보인다.

그럼에도 불구하고 그의 작품은 언제나 '아름답다.' 무엇보다도 강렬한 색채들이 상호 작용을 일으키며 발산하는 에너지는 유례를 찾아볼 수 없는 그만의 특징이다. 빨간 형상 하나가 그 뒤에 조금 더 옅은 빨간 형상을 불러오고, 이들은 그 뒤에 놓인 보라색 형상과 긴장관계를 형성한다. 이들의 대결을 또 다른 밝은 빨간 형상이 끼어들면서 균형을 유지하는 식이다. 유영국은 이러한 작업에 평생 끈질기게 매달려 지내며 스스로 지복(至福)을 누린다고 느꼈을 것이다.

그는 1916년에 태어나서 식민지, 해방, 전쟁, 전후 혼란기를 모두 겪었으며, 1975년 그의 나이 만 59세에 처음으로 작품이 팔리기 시작했는데도 오로지 전업작가로 일평생을 살았다. 실제로 그에게만 행운이 찾아왔을 리가 없는, 그런 시대 속에서 그는 살았던 것이다. 그러나 그는 마치 경험해 보지 않아도 선험적으로 어떤 지식을 습득한 사람처럼, 그의 작품에서 보듯 항공기 위에서 촬영한 것 같은 조감도적 시선으로 일생을 초월한 듯 살아갔다.

그렇게 삶의 태도에 있어서도 작품의 경향에 있어서도, 그는 어쩐지 대중에게 일종의 거리감을 주는 것이 사실이다. 그래서 '유영국'이라는 이름은 한국 사회에 상대적으로 덜 알려져 있다. 그렇기에 이번 전시가 유영국을 좀 더 일반적으로 널리 알리는 계기가 되었으면 하는 바람이 있다. 한국의 근대 미술사에서 유영국이라는 작가가 있었다는 사실은 우리에게 일종의 자부심이 될 수도 있지 않을까. 그는 그 험난한 시대를 관통하면서도, 삶에서도 예술에서도 최대한 '비극'을 제거한 채 완전한 행복을 향해 나아갈 수 있었던 작가였다. 그것은 그에게만 주어졌던 행운 때문이 결코 아니다. 그가 어떠한 보이지 않는 고통과 고독 속에서도 삶과 예술의 순수한 아름다움을 찾아나갈 수 있는 능력을 지녔기 때문이다. 그런 작가가 우리 근대 역사에도 있었다는 사실은 다행스러운 일이 아닐까.

조각가 최종태는 2002년 유영국의 부고를 듣고 빈소를 다녀와서 다음의 편지를 고인에게 바쳤다. "세월이란 참으로 묘한 것이어서 어떤 시대고 간에 꼭 있을만한 사람을 반드시 심어놓고 지나갑니다. 그 시대 그가 아니면 있을 수 없는 그런 일을 하

는 사람들을 역사는 빠뜨리지 않는다는 것입니다. (중략) 선생님의 빈소에서 그분의 영정을 바라보는데 문득 '아, 한 시대가 마감하는구나' 하는 생각이 나는 것이었습니다."[9]

1 울진초등학교 편, 『울진초등백년사』, 2012, p. 19.

2 무라이 마사나리 미망인과의 인터뷰 중에서 (2016년 2월 1일, 무라이 마사나리 기념관에서)

3 N.B.G. 회원으로 문화학원 9회 졸업생은 오카모토 테츠시로(岡本鉄四郎), 10회 졸업생은 가메야마 토시코(亀山敏子), 츠시모토 사사무(津志本貞), 나가미 요타카(永見胖), 11회 졸업생은 유영국이 있다.

4 長谷川三郎, 「第二回自由美術展入選作品評」, 『美の国』, 14-7, 1938, p. 24.

5 『長谷川三郎とその時代』, 下関市立美術館, 1988, pp. 150-151.

6 유영국은 1948-50년 약 2년간 서울대학교에, 1966-70년 약 4년간 홍익대학교에 재직하였으나, 두 번 다 스스로 사임하였다.

7 그는 일본 유학 후 한국으로 돌아와서는 상황이 허락하지 않을 때는 때로 어부로 살았고, 양조장을 운영하며 술을 빚었다. 그 외에는 가능한 모든 시간을 마치 시간에 쫓기는 사람처럼 작품 제작에 매달렸다.

8 임영방, 「유영국: 자연을 조형공간으로 내면화시키려는 탐구와 노력」, 『공간』, vol. 147, 1979, p. 34에서 작가의 말 재인용.

9 최종태, 「고인에게 바치는 편지」, 『미술세계』, vol. 217, 2002, p. 217.

Commemorating the 100th Anniversary Exhibition of a Korean Modern Master: Yoo Youngkuk (1916-2002)

Kim Inhye

Associate Curator, National Museum of Modern and Contemporary Art, Korea

Path of a Painter

Yoo Youngkuk was born in Uljin(present-day North Gyeongsang Province), which was formerly part of Gangwon Province. Uljin lies along the dark blue waters of the East Sea, where just a few steps from the shore, the depth is already greater than a person's height. Inland, Uljin is backed by the steep peaks of the Taebaek Mountains, with an altitude of more than 1,000 meters, where rapidly descending streams form waterfalls and creeks that flow out to the sea. Anyone who sees this place, where the deep sea, high mountains, and quiet creeks converge as one, must wonder if there is anywhere else like it on earth. In this unique landscape, ideal for human habitation, Yoo Youngkuk was brought into the world.

He was born a small *hanok* (traditional Korean house), which was more than 400 years old, having survived even the devastating Imjin War (a series of Japanese invasions of Korea, 1592-1598). It is said that his ancestors originally settled in Wonju, Gangwon Province, before moving the house to Uljin. The house is still there, now occupied by an elder member of the family who serves as the witness of the long history.

Yoo was a descendant of the legendary Gangneung Yoo clan. Although stories of this clan fill the pages of books and magazines published in Uljin, Yoo himself rarely talked about such things. The Gangneung Yoo clans settled in Mallu in Uljin at the time of Yoo's grandfather, Yoo Jae-eop(劉載業, 1845-1913), who made a great fortune. According to the records, Yoo Jae-eop's success was due not only to his natural business acumen, but also thanks to his decision to relocate the grave of his grandfather to the deep valley of Sisitgol, which was a most auspicious spot according to the principles of feng shui. As the story goes, Yoo Jae-eop was out hunting one winter's day, when he pursued a roe deer up a mountain path. The deer led him to a warm, flat spot that was miraculously untouched by snow, even in the midst of the snow-covered mountains. After a brief frolic on the exposed ground, the deer quickly disappeared, and Yoo Jae-eop realized that he had discovered a truly auspicious place, which the mountains protected like a folding screen. He had his grandfather's grave moved to the spot, and according to the fable-like story, the wealth of his family soon rose.

Yoo Jae-eop's fortune was handed down to his son Yoo Munjong(劉文鐘, 1876-1946), Yoo Youngkuk's father, with

the condition that it be used for public good. It was near the beginning of the Japanese colonial period, and in Uljin, the Uibyeong (Righteous Army), a venerated militia unit led by Shin Dol-seok, was fiercely battling the Japanese army. The Uibyeong were stationed in Buryeongsa Temple, deep in Buryeong Valley. As a community leader, Yoo Munjong gladly supported the cause with large amounts of money. He also generously donated one thousand won(present-day USD 100,000) to Jaedong Elementary School, an independent (i.e., Korean) private school that the Japanese had allowed to be established in Uljin in 1925. Jaedong Elementary School immediately became an invaluable educational institution for the Uljin community, giving poor and underprivileged people of all ages their first real chance for an education. The school was also a hotbed for various independence movements, such as the Korean Revolutionary Party, Gwangju Student Independence Movement and Korean Independence Party.[1] Thus, the Japanese colonial government continuously harassed and suppressed Jaedong Elementary School, until it was forcibly merged into Uljin Public Elementary School in 1943.

Being very passionate about education, Yoo Munjong sent all of his children—including his third son, Yoo Youngkuk—to study in Seoul and Tokyo. In 1931, Yoo Youngkuk entered Seoul Second High School, a public school for students grades 8 through 12. After studying diligently for four years, he left the school early to attend Bunka Gakuin University(文化學院) in Tokyo, where he enrolled in April 1935. Founded in 1921, Bunka Gakuin University was one of several new private schools that had been established in Japan at the peak of the so-called "Taisho Democracy." This school of liberal arts was founded by Nishimura Isaku(西村伊作, 1884-1963), an architect, and educational official, who was known to have some interest in anarchism and socialism. After starting out as a middle school, Bunka Gakuin was established as a university in 1925 . In the era of Japanese militarism, Bunka Gakuin University held out for many years as one of the last bastions of liberalism in the country. In 1943, however, it was finally shut down by the government, and the founder and principal Nishimura Isaku was sent to prison. Thus, the school's history and fate closely mirrors that of Jaedong Elementary School in Uljin.

Around the time that he entered Bunka Gakuin University, Yoo Youngkuk met three Japanese painters who would have a profound influence on his artistic career: Sato Kunio(佐藤九二男, 1897-1945), Murai Masanari(村井正誠, 1905-1999), and Hasegawa Saburo(長谷川三郎, 1906-1957). First, Sato Kunio was Yoo Youngkuk's art teacher at Seoul Second High School. Sato Kunio started teaching at Seoul Second High School in 1927, succeeding Yamada Shinichi(山田新一, 1899-1991). As a graduate of the Tokyo School of Fine Arts, Sato maintained a close network with the independent art field in Japan, and he continually showed his works in Japan at exhibitions of the Independent Art Association. Even when some of his fellow artists, such as Yamada Shinichi, began making pro-militarist paintings, Sato Kunio maintained his fauvist style in paintings that depicted downtrodden Koreans under colonial rule. Although Yoo later said that he was not a member of Sato's student art club at Seoul Second High School,

he certainly seems to have been influenced by Sato's liberal views and teachings. Indeed, Sato Kunio likely played a key role in Yoo's decision to leave Seoul Second High School before graduation to enter Bunka Gakuin University. Their close relationship is evinced by a postcard that Yoo Youngkuk received from Sato Kunio in April 1935, just after he had settled in Tokyo (refer to pp. 30-31.).

At Bunka Gakuin University, Yoo Youngkuk studied under Murai Masanari, an important Japanese artist who would also have a powerful impact on Yoo's artistic development. Murai Masanari was from Wakayama Prefecture(和歌山県), the same hometown as Nishimura Isaku, the founder of Bunka Gakuin University, and the two had known each other for a long time. In fact, it was rumored that Nishimura had established Bunka Gakuin as a university in 1925 in order to accommodate Murai Masanari, who had recently failed the entrance exam for the Tokyo School of Fine Arts.[2] In any case, Murai entered Bunka Gakuin University in its inaugural year as a three-year university. After graduation, he left to study in France, becoming the first member of his class to study abroad. Upon his return to Japan, he immediately became a lecturer at Bunka Gakuin University. Breaking away from the emphasis on academism that dominated art education at the time, as represented by the Tokyo School of Fine Arts, Murai Masanari intentionally pursued and promoted abstract art as a way to stand at the forefront of the international art scene. In 1934, he formed a small art group that held an exhibition entitled *Paintings of the New Age*(新時代洋畫展). Then in 1937, he became one of the founding leaders of the Association of Free Artists(自由美術家協会).

In 1937, Yoo Youngkuk was in his third year at the university. He became a member of the N.B.G.("Neo Beaux-Arts Group"), a group that primarily consisted of Murai Masanari's students and followers, most of whom had entered the Art Department of Bunka Gakuin University from 1933 through 1935.[3] Shortly thereafter, Yoo began submitting his works to the exhibitions of the Association of Free Artists. In 1938, after graduating from Bunka Gakuin University, Yoo received the Association of Free Artists Award and officially joined the ranks of the group. Yoo's rapid ascension into the group was likely made possible by the support of Murai Masanari. Even at the peak of Japanese militarism, Murai Masanari persistently refused to make paintings glorifying or supporting the Pacific War. He voluntarily stepped down from the Association of Free Artists, the group that he himself had founded. He would then go on to establish the Modern Art Association(モダンアート協会) in 1950. Until his death in 1999, Murai Masanari diligently pursued his own style as one of the pioneers of abstract painting in Japan.

Finally, the person who may have had the deepest impact on Yoo's art career was Hasegawa Saburo. Indeed, Yoo himself named Hasegawa Saburo as the figure he most admired among his mentors and colleagues. A graduate of the Aesthetics Department in the College of Literature at Tokyo Imperial University, Hasegawa Saburo was a highly renowned intellectual, art critic, and artist. Being from an affluent family, he was able to travel freely in Europe, allowing him to keep in touch with the latest European

art trends. His resulting articles in magazines such as *Mizue*(みづゑ) and *Binokuni*(美の国) established him as the most important art critic of the time. Along with Murai Masanari, Hasegawa Saburo was one of the leaders of the Association of Free Artists in its early days, and he was particularly supportive of Korean artists. When Yoo Youngkuk received the Association of Free Artists Award in 1938, Hasegawa wrote a favorable review of Yoo's works in *Binokuni*.[4] Furthermore, he also wrote many positive reviews for Kim Whanki, Moon Haksoo, and Lee Jung-Seob. It seems that Yoo Youngkuk frequented Hasegawa Saburo's house, often accompanied by his friend Lee Beomseung(aka Ju Hyeon), who studied photography. In 1937, Hasegawa published *Abstract Art*(アブストラクトアート), establishing himself as Japan's leading theorist of abstract art. But he also suffered under the militaristic regime, which condemned all forms of avant-garde art, such that he was eventually sent to prison in 1941. After 1942, he stopped submitting his works to exhibitions of the Association of Art Creators (i.e., the Association of Free Artists, as it had been renamed in 1940). In 1944, he withdrew from the art world and moved to Nagahama in Shiga Prefecture, where he lived as a farmer until the end of the World War II.[5] Hasegawa and Yoo Youngkuk had a great deal in common, including strong leadership skills, an uncompromising attitude, an admiration for abstract art, and an interest in photography. Above all, Hasegawa Saburo's determination to practice a type of utopian life through art had a profound influence on Yoo Youngkuk throughout his life.

Above all, Yoo Youngkuk strived to live a life of great efficiency. Through his keen insight, he was somehow able to surround himself with the most gifted and intelligent people, even in the most turbulent times. On a personal level, however, his determination to associate with such people must have been quite lonely. But that solitude and detachment may have helped him to evade the misfortune that plagued many of his fellow artists in those difficult times.

Path of Abstraction

Throughout his career, Yoo remained deeply committed to abstract art. To understand the origin and strength of that commitment, it is necessary to examine the conditions of his birth, his family, and his professional colleagues, particularly from the very beginning of his career.

Just two years after he had begun his formal study of art, Yoo submitted an abstract work to a group exhibition in Japan. This work consisted of geometric forms that he creatively arranged and pasted onto wooden panels. How did a young man from the remote countryside of Uljin, surrounded by mountains and the desolate open sea, adapt so quickly to life in Tokyo, one of the most cosmopolitan cities in the world? Furthermore, how did Yoo immediately choose and assimilate to abstract art, the most advanced movement in world art? Such a leap must have involved some truly remarkable circumstances.

Even more impressively, Yoo Youngkuk doggedly maintained his commitment to

abstract art throughout his entire career. What was the source of this amazing resolve? Some might say that he wanted to stay at the cutting-edge of the art world, as represented by abstract art. But this simple answer fails to explain the great sacrifices that Yoo made throughout his career, particularly in his early years. Even today, the term "abstract art" is unfamiliar to most people, so imagine the situation sixty or seventy years ago, when almost no one in Korean society had any idea what "abstract art" was. It is particularly notable that Yoo was never tempted by positions of superficial power in politics or as a long-tenured professor in academia.[6] He preferred his everyday life of artistic creation, persistently commuting between his bedroom and his workshop. What principles or priorities drove him to pursue such a lifestyle?

Faced with such questions, Yoo always had a simple response. When asked why he chose to become an artist, he replied, "I didn't want to be interfered with; I wanted to be free." Having been raised under Japanese colonial rule, Yoo yearned for a taste of freedom, and he saw the potential for personal liberation in art. Thus, he left the strict colonial rule of Korea to study in Tokyo, where the atmosphere was more liberal. Among all of the styles of art that he could have chosen, he was immediately drawn to the world of abstraction, which seemed to be completely free from objective rules or obligations, unlike classical or realist art, which involved intensive and repetitive training in drawing.

Abstraction emerged in early twentieth-century Europe, not as a single unified style but as a new kind of concept on art, or ideology. In 1917, after Piet Mondrian introduced the theory of Neo-Plasticism and promoted the value of "Abstract-Real" painting, abstraction was celebrated as the natural path to create a new art for the new era. According to Mondrian, humanity had thus far been struggling in vain to subsist in a world characterized by tragedy. But abstraction, as the new art for a new life, opened the door to a perfect equilibrium devoid of tragic elements. In order to reach a higher spirituality, people must find pure and harmonious expressions. The art of abstraction, with its openness and "plasticity," can unveil and visualize the precise order and consistent equilibrium that the new society should aspire to. As such, the role of art is to awaken humanity's vision for creating a better life and society.

Thus, Mondrian and his fellow theorists sought to use art as a means for attaining the mental serenity and purity required to exist in a world defined by chaos. Notably, this was the generation that had experienced the horror and confusion of World War I and other major conflicts. Abstract art was seen to embody the pure and perfect world of plasticity, free from such conflict or drama, or the "silent" world, in the words of Yoo Youngkuk. For Mondrian after World War I and for Yoo Youngkuk and the Japanese painters of the World War II era, the meaning of the world of abstraction was much more profound and severe than we can now imagine.

Life and Art of Yoo Youngkuk

To properly commemorate Yoo Youngkuk on the 100th anniversary of his birth,

it is absolutely necessary to trace the trajectory of his life and career, from his birth and childhood under Japanese colonial rule through his decision to become a painter and his firm dedication to abstract painting. This exhibition is divided into two sections, but places special focus the first half of Yoo's career.

The first section roughly covers the first half of Yoo's career, featuring works from 1937, while he was a student in Japan, until 1964, when he held his first solo exhibition at the Korea Press Center. In Japan, Yoo was an active member of the country's leading avant-garde and independent art group. After World War II, he returned to Korea, where he remained dedicated to the avant-garde movement. From 1947 to 1963, he served as a leader of several Korean avant-garde art groups, including New Realism(신사실파), Modern Art Association(모던아트협회), Contemporary Artists Exhibition(현대작가초대전), New Form Group(신상회, 新象展).[7] Motivated by his strong beliefs in the social role of art, he organized many gatherings of artists, during a time when the Korean art field was relatively dormant. He also opened doors for many young artists by inviting them to participate in public contests. As for his own work, he continually modified his style over time, such that his works from successive exhibitions always show slight differences and progressions. In particular, his works show his ongoing efforts to reduce specific objects (e.g., people, cities, sunsets, hills, valleys, seas, mountains) into pure forms.

The second part of the exhibition covers the second half of his career, from 1964, when he pronounced the end of his involvement with art groups, until his death in 2002. Notably, during these years, he withdrew almost completely from society to focus solely on his own artistic creation. His first solo exhibition in 1964 consisted of huge canvases, which gave the viewers the illusion of being lost in a deep forest. Resonating with the sublimity of nature, these works eventually generated feelings of spiritual elation. But from that point until the early 1970s, Yoo's art was characterized by self-denial, as he persistently experimented with various formal elements, such as dots, lines, planes, shapes, and colors. Yoo once said that "Whenever I hit a dead end in my creative work, I think that there must be a way to get through it. So each work is nothing more than a process for the next work, which serves as the foundation for me to continue."[8] In this way, he continued his art.

Interestingly, starting in the early 1970s, he added the subtitle of "Lalala" to his works, seemingly indicating a type of climax or revelation. But soon after he reached this climax, his physical health began to severely decline. Can this be a mere coincidence? In 1977, Yoo had to have a pacemaker inserted in his heart. Then from 1977 until his death in 2002, Yoo suffered eight cerebral hemorrhages which caused him to be hospitalized 37 times. Not surprisingly, starting in the late 1970s, his art became less severe and intense, in favor of a more lyrical and serene style. As we all know, it is impossible to separate the body from the spirit, and the changes in Yoo's artistic style and spirit would certainly seem to be related to the changing condition of his body. His later works seem to be infused with the relief of a person who escaped the throes of death on

several occasions.

Nonetheless, throughout his career, Yoo created works of astonishing *beauty*. In all of his works, the interaction of strong colors produces an almost unparalleled energy. For example, a deep red form entices a lighter red form, so that they come together to produce a purple form. Another form with an even lighter tone of red interferes with their confrontation, but the interference yields a type of balance. Immersing himself in such works throughout his life, Yoo Youngkuk must have felt the utmost bliss.

Born in 1916, Yoo lived through colonial rule, independence, the Korean War, and the post-war confusion. Although his artworks did not begin to sell until 1975, when he was almost sixty years old, he was still able to live as a full-time artist throughout his life. Given the time period in which he lived, it is not possible to say that he had luck or fortune on his side. But like a novice relying solely on intuition, rather than experience, he allowed his transcendental attitude to guide him through life. This attitude can be seen in the bird's-eye view in some of his works, which seem to have been captured from an airplane.

In both his social attitude and his artistic style, Yoo Youngkuk kept a certain distance from the public, which is probably why he is not as well-known as some of his colleagues. Hopefully, this exhibition will serve to introduce him to a wider audience. The people of Korea should take great pride in having a figure like Yoo Youngkuk in Korean modern art history. Despite living through one of the most traumatic periods of our nation's history, he was able to use his art to overcome tragedy, as much as possible, and to live a life of happiness and fulfillment. His personal success and well-being was not a matter of good fortune, but instead came from his capacity to find the pure beauty of life and art, even in the midst of suffering and solitude.

In 2002, after visiting Yoo's mortuary, the sculptor Choi Jong Tae dedicated a letter to Yoo, in which he wrote: "Time periods are such a strange thing. No era passes without the presence of someone who must be there. History never misses those people who are needed to perform certain tasks… At your mortuary, I see the portrait of *the person*. Then I think, 'Ah…it's the end of that era.'"[9]

1. *100-Year History of Uljin Elementary School*(울진초등백년사), (Uljin: Uljin Elementary School, 2012), p. 19.
2. From an interview with the widow of Murai Masanari on February 1, 2016 at Murai Masanari Memorial Museum of Art in ToKyo.
3. N.B.G. members included Okamoto Tetsushiro(岡本鉄四郎), who entered Bunka Gakuin University in 1933; Kameyama Toshiko(亀山敏子), Tsushimoto Sasamu(津志本貞), and Nagami Yutaka(永見胖) from 1934; and Yoo Youngkuk from 1935.
4. Hasegawa Saburo, "Review of Selected Works of the 2nd Association of Free Artists Exhibition"(第二回自由美術展入選作品評), Binokuni(美の国) vol. 14-7, 1938, p. 24.
5. *Hasegawa Saburo and His Era*(長谷川三郎とその時代), (Shimonoseki: Shimonoseki City Art Museum, 1988), pp. 150-151.
6. Yoo Youngkuk briefly taught at Seoul National University(1948-50) and at Hongik University(1966-70), but in both cases he chose to resign.
7. After completing his study in Japan, Yoo returned to Korea, where he occasionally worked as a fisherman and also brewed and sold his own liquor, to supplement his income. But for the most part, he was completely devoted to his art, working feverishly like a man living on borrowed time.
8. Quote from Yim Yeongbang, "Yoo Youngkuk: Explorations and Efforts to Internalize Nature into Aesthetic Space"(유영국: 자연을 조형공간으로 내면화시키려는 탐구와 노력), Space(공간), vol. 147, 1979, p. 34.
9. Choi Jong Tae, "Letter to the Late Yoo Youngkuk"(고인에게 바치는 편지), Misul Segye(미술세계), vol. 217, 2002, p. 217.

YOO YOUNGKUK 1916-2002

The 100th Anniversary Exhibition of a Korean Modern Master

아카이브 1935–1942

Archives 1935-1942

경성 제2고등보통학교

1921년 개교한 5년제 공립학교로 현재 경복고등학교의 전신이다. 경성 제1고등보통학교와 함께 명문으로 널리 알려져 있다. 유영국은 이 학교에서 1931년부터 1935년 2월까지 약 4년간 수학하였으며, 졸업을 1년 앞두고 자퇴하였다.
이 학교의 미술교사로는 동경미술학교 출신의 야마다 신이치(山田新一)가 있었는데, 그의 후임으로 1927년부터 사토 쿠니오(佐藤九二男)가 부임하여 미술부를 이끌었다. 사토 쿠니오는 조선미술전람회뿐 아니라 일본의 독립전에도 출품하는 등 일본 미술계와 친밀하게 교류했다. 또한 자유로운 미술교육을 지향하여 한국인 학생들의 신망을 얻었던 것으로 보인다. 그의 미술 수업을 받았던 경성 제2고보의 제자들, 유영국, 장욱진, 이대원 등은 후에 제2고보의 '2', 쿠니오(九二男)의 '9'를 따서, 2·9 동인을 결성, 1961년부터 1964년까지 전시회를 가진 바 있다.

Seoul Second High School

Seoul Second High School (now Kyungbock High School) opened in 1921 as a public school for students grades 8 through 12. It was quickly established as one of the most prestigious schools in the country, along with Seoul First High School (now Kyunggi High School). Yoo Youngkuk studied at Seoul Second High School from 1931 to 1935, before dropping out one year prior to graduation.
The first art teacher at the school was Yamada Shinichi(山田新一) from the Tokyo School of Fine Arts. He was succeeded in 1927 by Sato Kunio(佐藤九二男), who became the leader of the school's student art group. Having participated in the Joseon Art Exhibition and other independent exhibitions in Japan, Sato Kunio was in close contact with the Japanese art field. He also promoted free art education, which earned him the trust of his Korean students, including Yoo Youngkuk, Chang Uc-chin, and Lee Daewon. The students including these three would later form the "2·9 Group": "2" from Seoul "Second" High School and "9" from "ku," the first syllable of their teacher's name. This group held exhibitions from 1961 to 1964.

경성 제2고보 시절 유영국의 사진 1935년 2월, 유영국미술문화재단 소장

Yoo Youngkuk at Seoul Second High School February 1935, Photo: courtesy of Yoo Youngkuk Art Foundation.

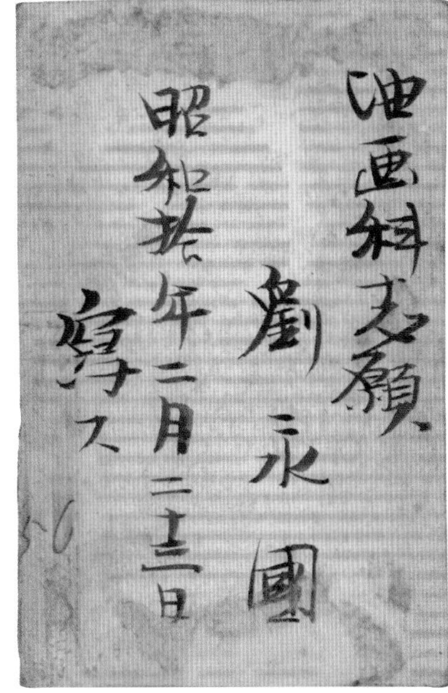

1935년 2월 23일 일본 문화학원에 지원할 당시 사진으로 보인다.

This is probably the photo that was used for Yoo Youngkuk's application to Bunka Gakuin University in Tokyo, dated February 23, 1935.

경성 제2고보 시절 유영국의 사진 1935년 2월, 유영국미술문화재단 소장

Yoo Youngkuk at Seoul Second High School February 1935, Photo: courtesy of Yoo Youngkuk Art Foundation.

1935년 2월 4일 강남스튜디오에서 유영국이 경성 제2고보 친구들과 함께 찍은 사진으로, 그가 일본으로 유학을 가기 직전에 촬영된 것이다. 뒷줄 맨 오른쪽이 유영국.

This photo was taken in Gangnam Studio with Yoo Youngkuk's friends at Seoul Second High School on February 4, 1935 right before his departure to Japan for study. Yoo Youngkuk is the first on the right in the back row.

사토 쿠니오가 유영국에게 보낸 엽서 1935년 4월, 유영국미술문화재단 소장

Postcard by Sato Kunio sent to Yoo Youngkuk April 1935, courtesy of Yoo Youngkuk Art Foundation.

경성 제2고보 시절 유영국의 미술교사였던 사토 쿠니오가 1935년 4월 유영국이 도쿄에 정착하자마자 보낸 이 엽서를 통해, 둘 사이의 친밀했던 관계를 확인할 수 있다.

Sato Kunio was Yoo Youngkuk's art teacher at Seoul Second High School. Soon after Yoo Youngkuk settled in Tokyo, he received this postcard from Sato Kunio, showing their close relationship.

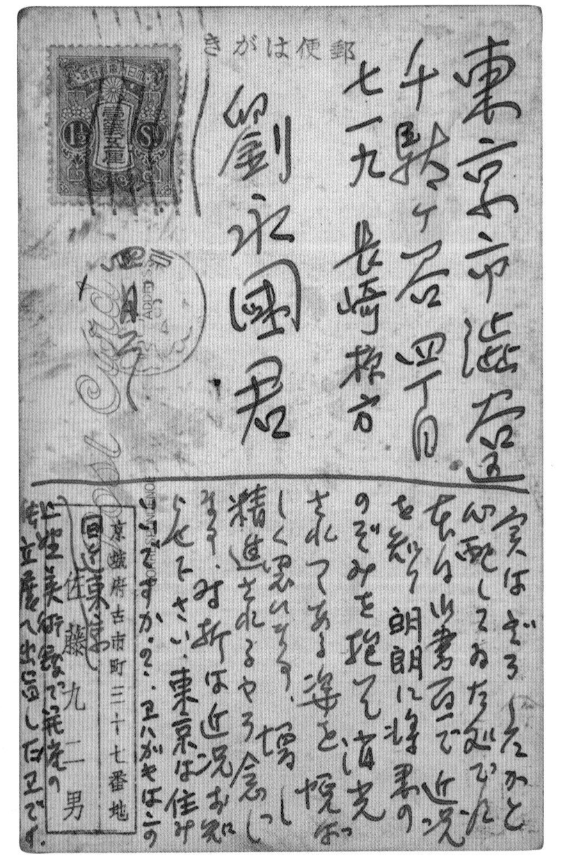

東京市渋谷区千駄ヶ谷四丁目719　長崎様方　劉永國君

実はどうしたかと心配していたところでした。
本日小書面で近況を知り明朗に将来ののぞみを抱いて
消光されつつある姿を悦ばしく思います。
増々精進されるよう念じます。
時折は近況お知らせください。東京は住み良いですか？
エ(絵)はがきはこの間迄東京上野美術館で開催の独立展へ出品した
エです。

京城府古市町37番地　佐藤九二男

4-719, Setagaya, Shibuya-ku, Tokyo, Mr. Nagasaki

Dear Mr. Yoo Youngkuk,
I was actually concerned about how you've been doing.
I received your letter today, so now I know how you've been.
I'm very happy that you're spending your time there dreaming of a bright future.
I hope that you continue to devote yourself to your dream.
Also, let me know how you're doing there. How is life in Tokyo?
This postcard shows the painting that I recently submitted to the Independent Art Exhibition held at the Ueno Museum in Tokyo.

37, Goshi-jung, Seoul
Sato Kunio

도쿄시 시부야구 센다가야 욘쵸메 719 나가사키님 댁

유영국 군
실은 어떻게 된 건지 걱정하고 있었어요.
오늘 편지로 근황을 알게 되었네요.
명랑한 미래에 대한 꿈을 품고 시간을 보내고 있는 모습을 기쁘게
생각했습니다.
점점 더 정진하시길 바랍니다. 가끔씩 근황을 알려 주세요. 도쿄는
살기 괜찮은가요?
그림엽서는 요전까지 도쿄 우에노미술관에서 개최한 독립전에
출품한 그림입니다.

경성부 고시정 37번지 사토 쿠니오

문화학원

문화학원(文化學院, 분카가쿠인)은 1921년 건축가이며 교육사업가인 니시무라 이사쿠(西村伊作)가 설립한 사립학교이다. 남녀공학으로 교복을 입지 않았으며 가족적인 분위기의 학교로 유명했다. 학교령의 지배를 받지 않는 자유로운 학풍을 유지하였으나, 1943년 '천황에 대한 불경죄'로 니시무라 교장이 감옥에 가고 학교가 강제 폐교된 바 있다. 미술교사로는 이과회의 핵심멤버였던 이시이 하쿠테이(石井柏亭)가 설립 때부터 관여하였으며, 높은 수준의 교수진과 강사진이 수업을 이끌었다. 무라이 마사나리의 경우, 1925년 대학부가 처음 설립될 때 문화학원에 입학하였고, 프랑스 유학을 거쳐 1930년대 후반부터 강사로 출강했다. 한국인 학생의 수는 그리 많지 않았지만, 유영국, 김병기, 문학수, 이중섭, 김종찬, 박성환 등 훌륭한 화가들을 배출했다.

Bunka Gakuin University

Bunka Gakuin University(文化學院) was a private co-ed school founded in 1921 by Nishimura Isaku(西村伊作), an architect and educational official. The school, which was not bound by the Imperial Rescript on Education, became famous for its liberal and familial atmosphere. For example, the students were not required to wear uniforms. The school attracted many renowned professors and lecturers, such as Ishii Hakutei(石井柏亭), a core member of the Nikakai (or Second Section Association), who began teaching art classes from the year of the school's establishment. Also, Murai Masanari(村井正誠) studied there starting in 1925 (the year that the school first became a university), then left to study abroad in France, before returning to serve as a lecturer in the late 1930s. In 1943, however, the school was shut down and Principal Nishimura was arrested and sent to prison for lèse-majesté (i.e., disrespecting the Emperor). Although Bunka Gakuin University did not have very many Korean students, several of Korea's top modern artists graduated from there, including Yoo Youngkuk, Kim Byunggi, Moon Hak-soo, Lee Jung Seob, Kim Jongchan, and Park Seonghwan.

문화학원신문에 수록된 미술부 신입생 소개기사 1935. 6. 15, 국립현대미술관 미술연구센터 김복기 컬렉션

Article from the campus newspaper of Bunka Gakuin University about the new students of the Art Department

June 15, 1935, courtesy of Kim Boggi Collection from MMCA Art Research Center

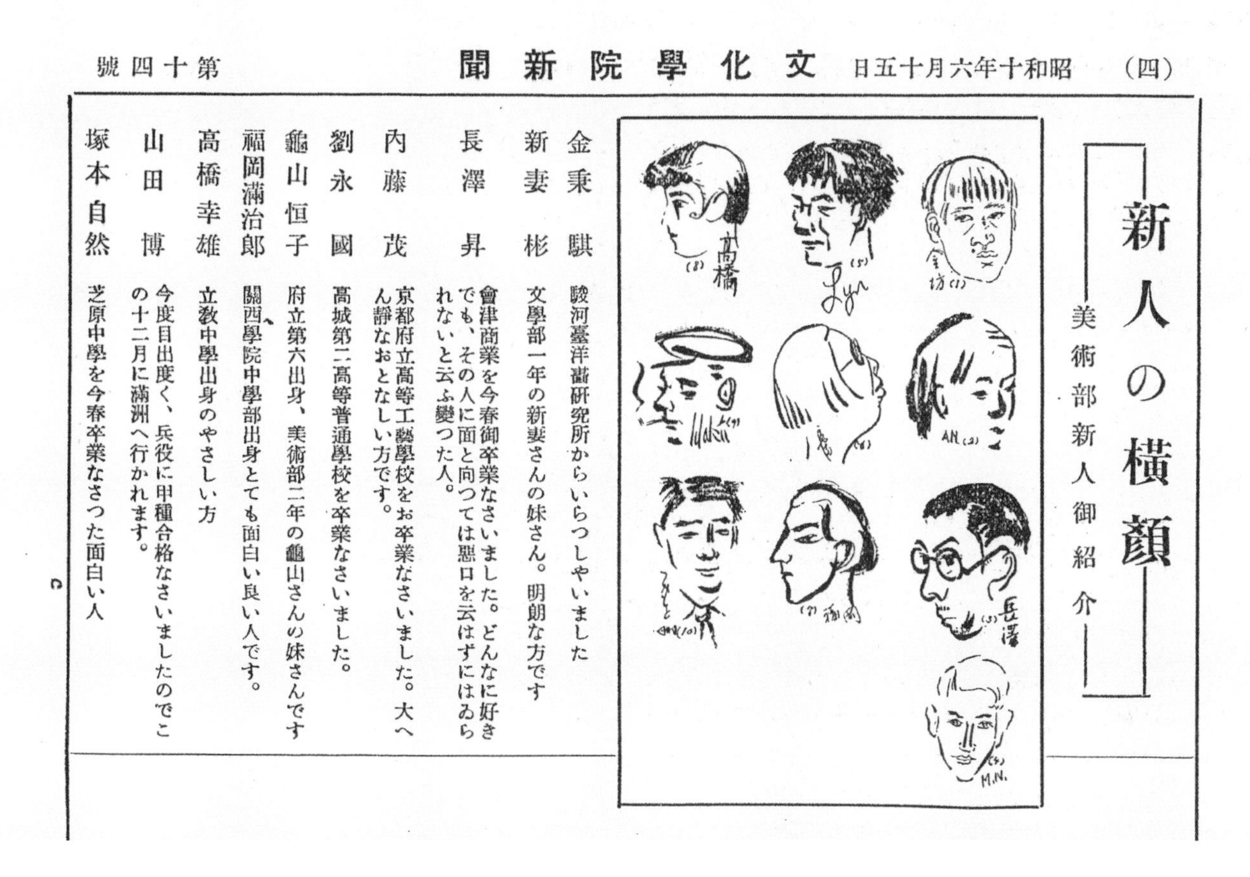

(四) 昭和十年六月十五日 文化學院新聞 第十四號

新人の横顔

美術部新人御紹介

金秉騏 駿河臺洋畫研究所からいらつしやいました

新妻彬 文學部一年の新妻さんの妹さん。明朗な方です

長澤昇 會津商業を今春御卒業なさいました。どんなに好きでも、その人に面と向つては悪口を云はずにはゐられないと云ふ變つた人。

内藤茂 京都府立高等工藝學校をお卒業なさいました。大へん静なおとなしい方です。

劉永國 高城第二高等普通學校を卒業なさいました。

龜山恒子 府立第六出身、美術部二年の龜山さんの妹さんです

福岡滿治郎 關西學院中學部出身とても面白い良い人です。

高橋幸雄 立教中學出身のやさしい方

山田博 今度目出度く、兵役に甲種合格なさいましたのでこの十二月に滿洲へ行かれます。

塚本自然 芝原中學を今春卒業なさつた面白い人

문화학원 발행 신문에 실린 신입생의 캐리커처와 소개문이다.
캐리커처 윗줄 가운데 (5)번이 유영국이다.
유영국의 오른쪽 (1)번은 김병기이며, 맨 아랫줄 왼쪽에 있는 (10)번은 후에 유영국을 모델로 한 실험적 사진을 남겼던 츠카모토 시젠이다.

유영국에 대한 설명에는 "경성 제2고등보통학교를 졸업하였습니다"라고 되어 있다.

Caricatures and introductions of new students of the Art Department from the campus newspaper.
Yoo Youngkuk is in the top row, center (number 5).
To the right of Yoo Youngkuk is Kim Byunggi (number 1); in the lower left corner is Tsukamoto Shizen (塚本自然, number 10), who took experimental photos with Yoo Youngkuk as the model.

Yoo Youngkuk is introduced as having "graduated from Seoul Second High School.

문화학원 교정 사진 1935-38년경, 유영국미술문화재단 소장

Campus photos of Bunka Gakuin University c.1935-38, courtesy of Yoo Youngkuk Art Foundation

문화학원의 행사 사진으로 추정된다. 화면 중앙에는 문화학원 미술부 1회 입학생이며, 당시 강사로 출강하고 있었던 무라이 마사나리의 모습이 보인다.

This photo was taken at an unknown event at Bunka Gakuin University. The figure in the center is Murai Masanari, a lecturer at Bunka Gakuin University at that time.

문화학원 재학 당시 유영국의 모습이다.
오른쪽이 유영국.

Yoo Youngkuk (on the right) as a student at Bunka Gakuin University.

제11회 문화학원 미술과 졸업사진 1938년, 유영국미술문화재단 소장

Photo of the 11th graduating class of the Art Department at Bunka Gakuin University 1938, courtesy of Yoo Youngkuk Art Foundation

1938년 제11회 문화학원 미술과 졸업식 사진이다.
1 유영국, **2** 요사노 아키코(与謝野晶子), **3** 라티프 사프타리타(サプタリタ, Latip Saptarita), **4** 니시무라 소노(西村ソノ, Mrs. C. F. Begert), **5** 가메야마 츠네코(亀山恒子), **6** 이시이 미후유(石井三冬, 결혼 후 마츠무라 미후유(松村三冬)), **7** 츠카모토 시젠(塚本自然), **8** 아카기 야스노부(赤城泰舒), **9** 호리 타다요시(堀忠義), **10** 나카고메 쥰지(中込純次), **11** 이시이 하쿠테이(石井柏亭), **12** 니시무라 이사쿠(西村伊作) 교장, **13** 가와사키 나츠(河崎なつ), **14** 니시무라 아야(西村アヤ, 결혼 후 이시다 아야(石田アヤ)), **15** 도가와 슈코츠(戸川秋骨)이다.
사진 앞줄 손에 꽃을 들고 있는 이들이 졸업생이며, 그 외는 교수진이다. (사진해독: 김복기)

The graduating class of 1938 from the Art Department at Bunka Gakuin University.
Front row, from the left: **1** Yoo Youngkuk; **2** Yosano Akiko(与謝野晶子), **3** Latip Saptarita(サプタリタ), **4** Mrs. C. F. Begert(西村ソノ), **5** Kameyama Tsuneko(亀山恒子), **6** Ishii Mifuyu(石井三冬, married name Matsumura Mifuyu〔松村三冬〕), **7** Tsukamoto Shizen(塚本自然), **8** Akagi Yasunobu(赤城泰舒), **9** Hori Tadayoshi(堀忠義), **10** Nakagome Junji(中込純次), **11** Ishii Hakutei(石井柏亭), **12** Principal Nishimura Isaku, **13** Kawasaki Natsu(河崎なつ), **14** Nishimura Aya(西村アヤ, married name Ishida Aya〔石田アヤ〕), **15** Togawa Shukotsu(戸川秋骨). The students in the front row who are holding flowers are the graduates, while the rest of the people are teachers or faculty (annotations by Kim Boggi).

독립미술협회 獨立美術協會

독립미술협회는 1930년 11월 사토미 가츠조(里見勝蔵), 가와구치 키가이(川口軌外), 미기시 코타로(三岸好太郎), 후쿠자와 이치로(福澤一郎) 등이 결성한 미술협회로, 1931년 첫 전람회를 시작으로 지금까지도 명맥을 이어오고 있는 일본의 미술단체이다. 상당히 큰 규모의 재야단체로, 관전에 비해 처음부터 야수파 및 초현실주의 경향이 강했으며, 추상미술도 수용하였다. 1930-40년대 많은 한국인이 《독립미술협회전》에 출품하여 입선하였으며, 유영국은 1937년 제7회전에 처음으로 작품을 발표한 바 있다.

Independent Art Association

The Independent Art Association is a large independent art organization formed in November 1930 by Satomi Katsuzo(里見勝蔵), Kawaguchi Kigai(川口軌外), Migishi Kotaro(三岸好太郎) and Fukuzawa Ichiro(福澤一郎). The group, which held its first exhibition in 1931, remains active to this day. In its early years, the group showed a strong preference for fauvist, surrealist, and abstract art and activities, diverging from the mainstream art presented at government-sponsored exhibitions. Many Korean artists submitted their works for exhibitions of the Independent Art Association, and many were accepted and shown in the 1930s and 40s. Yoo Youngkuk showed his work for the first time at the 7th exhibition of the Independent Art Association in 1937.

제7회 《독립미술전람회》 출품기념 엽서 1937년, 유영국미술문화재단 소장

Postcard to commemorate the 7th exhibition of the Independent Art Association 1937, courtesy of Yoo Youngkuk Art Foundation

유영국, 〈랩소디〉, 1937, 제7회 《독립미술협회전》 출품작
Yoo Youngkuk, *Rhapsody*, 7th exhibition of the Independent Art Association

제7회 《독립미술전람회》 리플릿 1937년, 국립현대미술관 미술연구센터 소장

Leaflet from the 7th exhibition of the Independent Art Association 1937, courtesy of MMCA Art Research Center

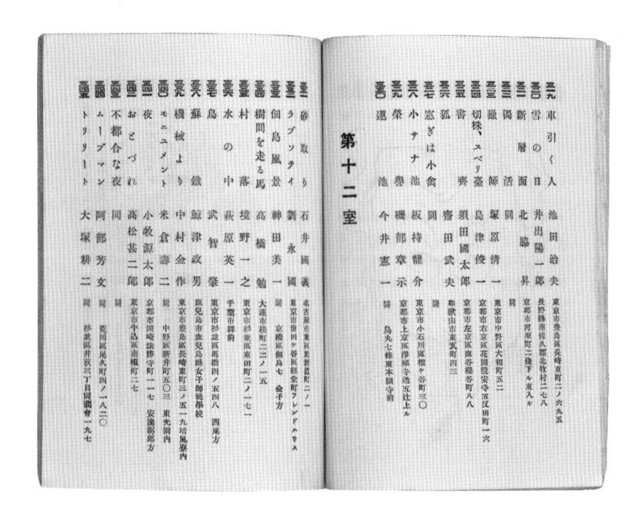

三一九	車引く人	池田治夫	東京市豊島區長崎東町二ノ六九五
三二〇	雪の日	井出陽一郎	長野縣南佐久郡北牧村二七八
三二一	新層面	北脇昇	京都市河原町二條下ル東入ル
三二二	獨活	同	同
三二三	獵師	塚原清一	東京市中野區大和町五二
三二四	切株、スベリ臺	島津俊一	京都市右京區花園龍安寺五反田町一六
三二五	書齋	須田國太郎	京都市左京區鹿ヶ谷櫻谷町八八
三二六	狐	齋田武夫	和歌山市東長町四三
三二七	窓ぎは小禽	同	同
三二八	小サナ池	板持龍介	東京市小石川區指ヶ谷町三〇
三二九	榮譽	磯部章示	京都市上京區淨福寺通五辻上ル
三三〇	選池	今井憲一	同 烏丸七條東本願寺前

第十二室

三三一	砂取り	石井國義	名古屋市東區東新道町二ノ一
三三二	ラプソディ	劉永國	東京市世田ヶ谷區經堂町フレンドハウス
三三三	佃島風景	神田美一	同 京橋區佃島七 金子方
三三四	樹間を走る馬	高橋勉	大連市桂町二二ノ一五
三三五	村落	境野一之	東京市杉並區東田町二ノ一七一
三三六	水の中	萩原英一	千葉市驛前
三三七	鳥	武智肇	東京市杉並區馬橋四ノ五四八 西尾方
三三八	蘇鐵	鯨津政男	鹿兒島市鹿兒島縣女子師範學校
三三九	機械より	中村金作	東京市豊島區長崎東町三ノ五一九 培風寮內
三四〇	モニユメント	米倉壽二	同 中野區新井町五〇三 東光園內
三四一	夜	小牧源太郎	京都市岡崎法勝寺町一一七 安達彬郎方
三四二	おとづれ	高松甚二郎	東京市牛込區南榎町二七
三四三	不都合な夜	同	同
三四四	ムーブマン	阿部芳文	同 荒川區尾久町四ノ一八二〇
三四五	トリリート	大塚耕二	同 杉並區井荻三丁目岡瀾會一九七

유영국은 문화학원 3학년에 재학 중이던 1937년에 일본의 대표적인 재야미술단체인 독립미술전에 출품하였다. 제12실 두 번째에 〈랩소디〉라는 작품명, 작가이름과 주소를 확인할 수 있다.

In 1937, while he was a third-year student at Bunka Gakuin University, Yoo Youngkuk submitted his work for the 7th exhibition of the Independent Art Association, Japan's representative independent art group. This leaflet from the exhibition shows his name and address, and lists his work *Rhapsody* as the second work on display in the 12th Gallery.

N.B.G.

N.B.G.는 프랑스어로 "Neo Beaux-Arts Group"의 약자로 1936년 가메야마 토시코(亀山敏子), 나카이 야스유키(中井康之), 나가미 요타카(永見胖), 오카모토 테츠시로(岡本鉄四郎), 츠시모토 사사무(津志本貞) 등이 함께 결성한 그룹이다. 대부분의 회원은 문화학원 미술과 제10회 동기생이었으며, 제11회 학생이었던 유영국은 1938년 1월 제2회 N.B.G. 전시 때부터 작품을 출품하기 시작했다. 유영국 외에 세이노 가츠미(清野克己), 오가와 타다시(小川貞彦) 등의 회원이 후에 추가되었다. 처음부터 추상미술을 강력하게 표방한 청년화가 단체로, 1937-1939년까지 총 7회에 걸쳐 동경 긴자의 기노쿠니야 화랑(紀伊國屋畫廊)에서 의욕적으로 전시회를 가진 것으로 확인된다. 전시회 내역은 다음과 같다.

제1회: 1937. 9. 28-30
제2회: 1938. 1. 26-28 (이후 유영국 참가)
제3회: 1938. 4. 13-15
제4회: 1938. 9. 22-24
제5회: 1938. 11. 23-25
제6회: 1939. 3. 27-29
제7회: 1939. 10. 19-24

N.B.G.

N.B.G. (which stands for "Neo Beaux-Arts Group") was an art group formed in 1936 by Kameyama Toshiko (亀山敏子), Nakai Yasuyuki (中井康之), Nagami Yutaka (永見胖), Okamoto Tetsushiro (岡本鉄四郎), and Tsushimoto Sasamu (津志本貞). Most members of the group were classmates who entered the Art Department of Bunka Gakuin University in 1934. Yoo Youngkuk, who entered the school in 1935, began to submit his works for the second N.B.G. exhibition in January 1938. He would later join the group, along with Seino Katsumi (清野克己) and Ogawa Tadashi (小川貞彦). From its outset, the N.B.G. group of young artists strongly favored abstract art. The group was very prolific, holding seven exhibitions from 1937 to 1939 at Kinokuniya Gallery in Ginza, Tokyo. The details of those exhibitions are as follows:

1st N.B.G. exhibition: September 28-30, 1937
2nd N.B.G. exhibition: January 26-28, 1938 (Yoo Youngkuk's first exhibition; he participated in all of the subsequent N.B.G. exhibitions)
3rd N.B.G. exhibition: April 13-15, 1938
4th N.B.G. exhibition: September 22-24, 1938
5th N.B.G. exhibition: November 23-25, 1938
6th N.B.G. exhibition: March 27-29, 1939
7th N.B.G. exhibition: October 19-24, 1939

《N.B.G. 양화전》 엽서 1937-39년, 유영국미술문화재단 소장

Postcards to commemorate the N.B.G. exhibitions 1937-39, courtesy of Yoo Youngkuk Art Foundation

제2회 《N.B.G. 양화전》 엽서 1938. 1. 26-28
Postcard for 2nd N.B.G. exhibition (January 26-28, 1938).

제4회 《N.B.G. 양화전》 엽서, 1938. 9. 22-24
Postcard for 4th N.B.G. exhibition (September 22-24, 1938).

제6회 《N.B.G. 양화전》 엽서 1939. 3. 27-29
Postcard for 6th N.B.G. exhibition (March 27-29, 1939).

《N.B.G. 양화전》 엽서 1938년, 유영국미술문화재단 소장

Postcard to commemorate the 5th N.B.G. exhibition
1938, courtesy of Yoo Youngkuk Art Foundation

제5회 《N.B.G. 양화전》 엽서
1938. 11. 23-25
유영국의 작품이 실려 있다.
E. LYU. 는 유영국의 이름이다.
E는 '영'의 일본식 발음인 '에이'의 약자이다.

Postcard for 5th N.B.G. exhibition (November 23-25, 1938).
This postcard shows a work by Yoo Youngkuk. In the center is his signature: "E. LYU." The "E" stands for "*ei*", the Japanese word for "young," which Yoo Youngkuk adopted for his signature in Japan.

제5회 《N.B.G. 양화전》 설치 사진(기노쿠니야 화랑) 1938년, 유영국미술문화재단 소장

5th N.B.G. exhibition, held at Kinokuniya Gallery in 1938 1938, courtesy of Yoo Youngkuk Art Foundation

제5회 《N.B.G. 양화전》 회원들 사진(기노쿠니야 화랑) 1938년, 유영국미술문화재단 소장

Participants of the 5th N.B.G exhibition, held at Kinokuniya Gallery in 1938

1938, courtesy of Yoo Youngkuk Art Foundation

제10회 문화학원 미술과 졸업사진 속의 N.B.G. 회원들 1937년, 국립현대미술관 미술연구센터 김복기 컬렉션

N.B.G. members from the 1937 graduating class of the Art Department at Bunka Gakuin University

1937, Kim Boggi Collection from MMCA Art Research Center

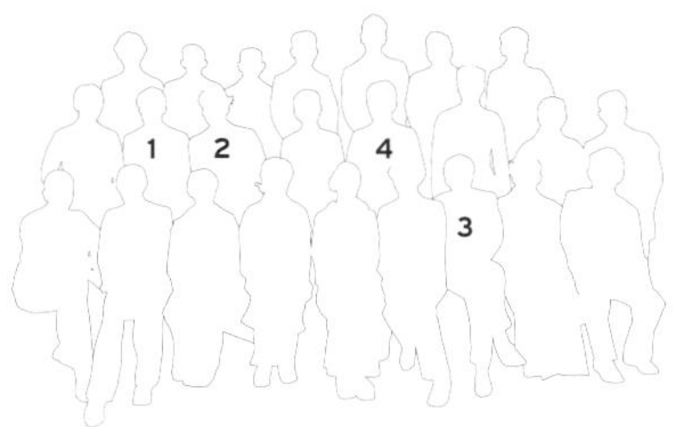

유영국의 문화학원 1년 선배들인 제10회 문화학원 졸업생 사진에 N.B.G. 회원들로 추정되는 인물들(**1-3**)이 보인다. 한편, 한국인 화가 이철이(**4**)의 모습이 주목된다.

The 1937 graduates of the Art Department at Bunka Gakuin University were one year ahead of Yoo Youngkuk. As marked in the photo, several of them were members of N.B.G. (**1-3**) Another notable figure is the Korean artist Lee Cheul-yi (**4**).

유영국의 《N.B.G. 양화전》 출품기념 엽서 1938-39년, 유영국미술문화재단 소장

Postcards to commemorate Yoo Youngkuk's works from N.B.G. exhibitions

1938-39, courtesy of Yoo Youngkuk Art Foundation

〈릴리프 오브제〉, 1938, 제2회 《N.B.G. 양화전》 출품기념 엽서
Relief Object, 1938, postcard for 2nd N.B.G. exhibition.

〈습작(習作)〉, 1938, 제3회 《N.B.G. 양화전》 출품기념 엽서
Study, 1938, postcard for 3rd N.B.G. exhibition.

〈작품〉, 1938, 제2회 《N.B.G. 양화전》 출품기념 엽서
Work, 1938, postcard for 2nd N.B.G. exhibition.

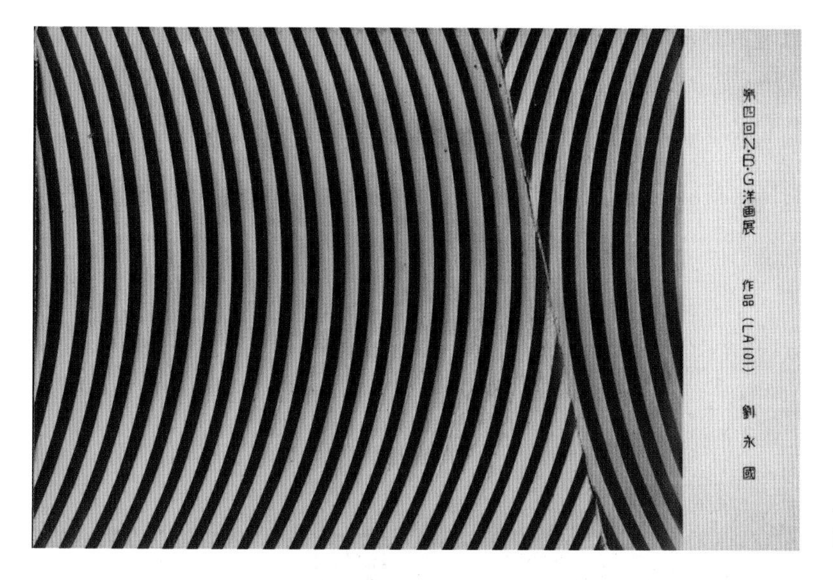

〈작품 (LA-101)〉, 1938, 제4회 《N.B.G. 양화전》 출품기념 엽서
Work LA-101, 1938, postcard for 4th N.B.G. exhibition.

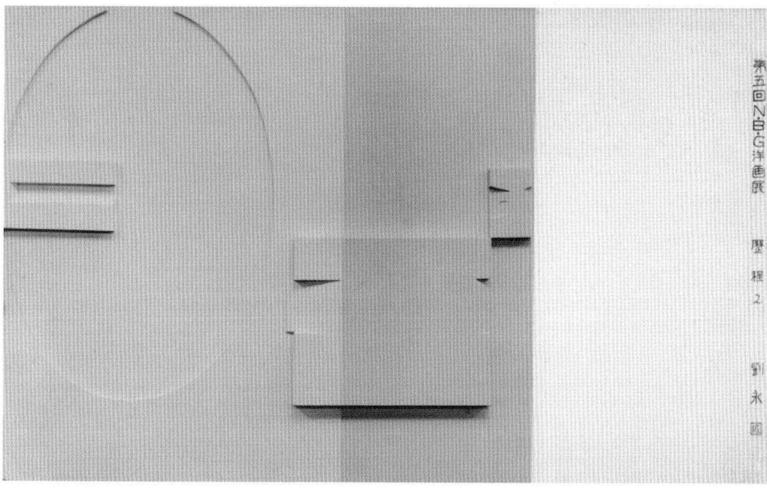

〈역정(歷程) 2〉, 1938, 제5회 《N.B.G. 양화전》 출품기념 엽서
Journey 2, 1938, postcard for 5th N.B.G. exhibition.

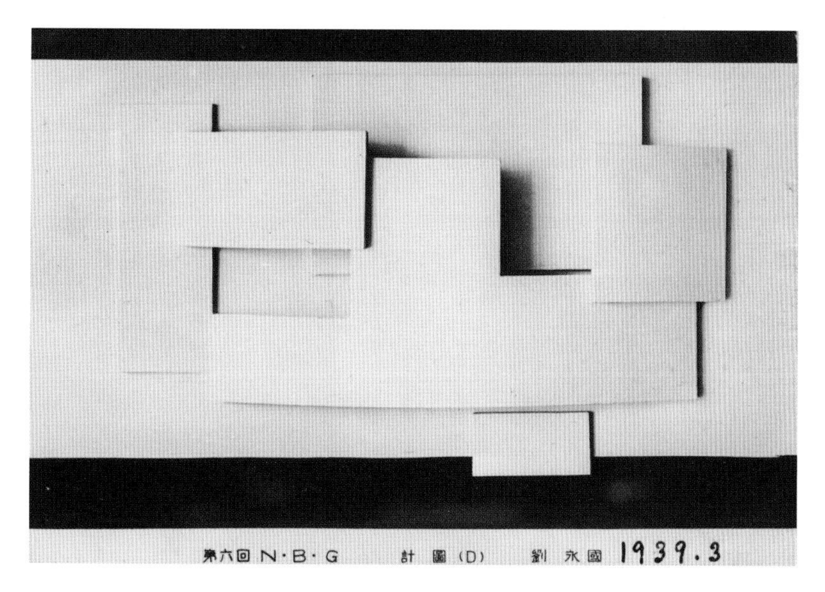

〈계도(計圖) D〉, 1939, 제6회 《N.B.G. 양화전》 출품기념 엽서
Design D, 1939, postcard for 6th N.B.G. exhibition.

N.B.G. 양화전 회원들의 출품기념 엽서 1937-39년, 유영국미술문화재단 소장

Postcards to commemorate works by other members of N.B.G. from the group's exhibitions

1937-39, courtesy of Yoo Youngkuk Art Foundation

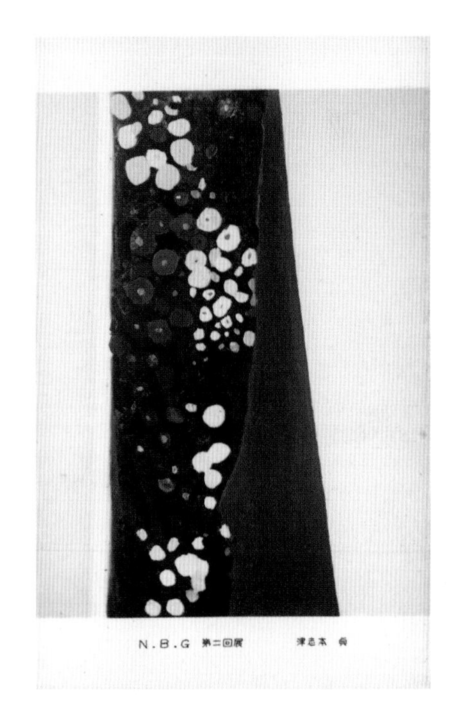

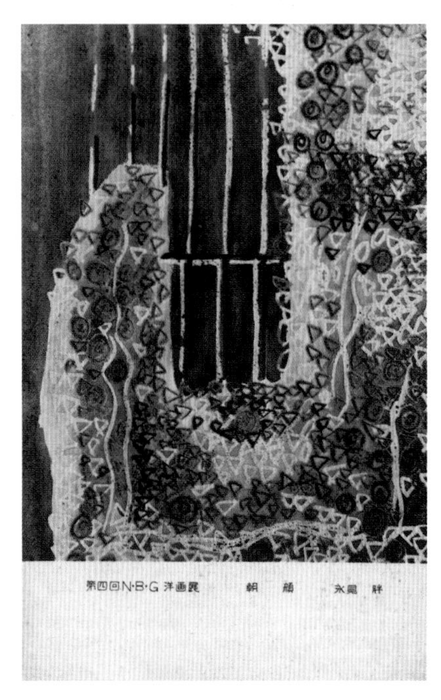

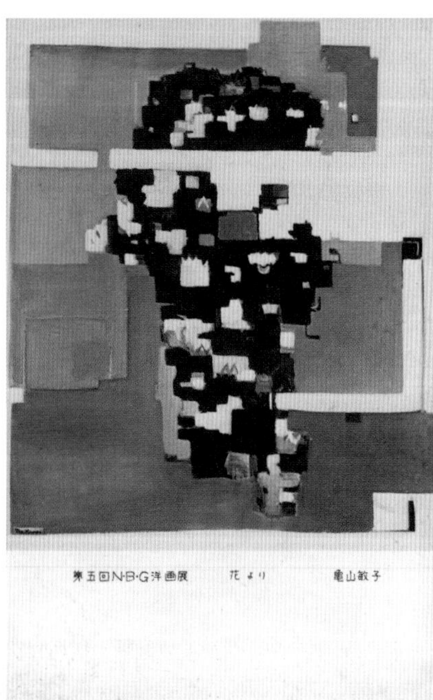

第六回 N・B・G　金魚鉢　永見 胖

第三回N・B・G洋画展　珊瑚礁　津志本 貞

第三回N・B・G洋画展　花　永見 胖

第六回N・B・G　夜の花　亀山 敏

第三回N・B・G洋画展　花　亀山敏子

자유미술가협회 自由美術家協會

자유미술가협회는 하세가와 사부로(長谷川三郎), 무라이 마사나리(村井正誠), 야바시 로쿠로(矢橋六郎), 야마구치 카오루(山口薫) 등 신시대양화전 조직 멤버에 양화그룹 '포름(フォルム)'의 남바타 타츠오키(難波田龍起), 흑색양화전의 오노사토 토시노부(小野里利信), 신자연파협회 등이 합류하여 1937년 결성되었다(1940년 미술창작가협회로 개칭). 유화, 수채화, 판화, 소묘, 콜라주, 오브제, 사진(포토그램) 부문에서 작품을 공모, 전위적 표현을 지향하는 젊은 미술가들의 호응을 얻었다.

1944년 제8회까지 개최한 본전시 외에도 오사카, 나고야, 삿포로 등 타 지방에서도 전시가 열렸으며, 1940년에는 경성전을 부민회관에서 열기도 했다. 이 협회에 한국인으로는 유영국 외에도 김환기, 이중섭, 문학수 등이 활동하였다.

Association of Free Artists

This association was formed in 1937, before being renamed the Association of Art Creators in 1940. The association was composed of different artists and art groups who participated in major exhibitions of Western-style paintings. Some notable members included Hasegawa Saburo(長谷川三郎), Murai Masanari(村井正誠), Yabashi Rokuro(矢橋六郎), and Yamaguchi Kaoru(山口薫) from the Paintings of the *New Age exhibition*; Nambata Tatsuoki(難波田龍起) from *Forum*(フォルム), a Western painting group; Onozato Toshinobu(小野里利信) from *Black and White Paintings*; and members of the *Association of New Naturalism*. Inviting a wide range of works, such as oil paintings, watercolors, prints, drawings, objects, photography, and photograms, the Association of Free Artists was very popular among young artists seeking an outlet for their avant-garde expressions.

The association held eight primary exhibitions until 1944, as well as regional exhibitions in Osaka, Nagoya, and Sapporo. The group also held a 1940 exhibition in Korea at Seoul Public Hall. Active members of the association included Korean artists Yoo Youngkuk, Kim Whanki, Lee Jung Seob, and Moon Haksoo.

자유미술가협회 회우들 사진 1940년

Members of the Association of Free Artists 1940

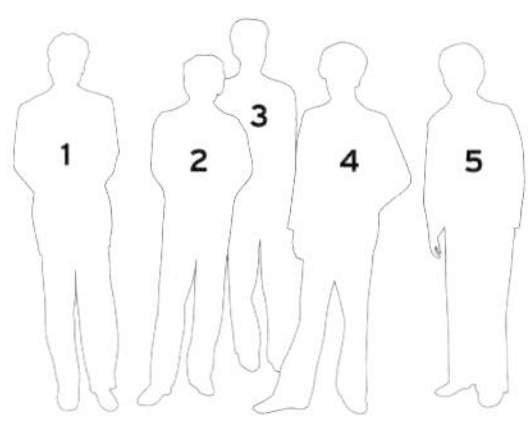

1940년 7월 삿포로 미스코시백화점에서 열린 《자유미술가협회회원 소품전》의 전시장 모습이다. **1** 우에키 시게루(植木茂), **2** 코야마 노보루(小山昇), **3** 유영국, **4** 아라이 타츠오(荒井龍男), **5** 남바타 타츠오키(難波田龍起)이다. (출처: 目黒美術館, 『荒井龍男作品集』, 美術出版, 1991, p. 163)

This photo was taken at the Association of Free Artists exhibition, held in July 1940 at the gallery of Sapporo Mitsukoshi Department Store. **1** Ueki Shigeru(植木茂), **2** Koyama Noboru(小山昇), **3** Yoo Youngkuk, **4** Arai Tatsuo(荒井龍男), **5** Nambata Tatsuoki(難波田龍起). (From *Collected Works of Arai Tatsuo*〔荒井龍男作品集〕, Tokyo: Bijutsu publisher, 1991, p. 163).

『미술창작(美術創作)』에 실린 《자유미술가협회 오사카전》 전시장 설치사진 1940년, 국립현대미술관 미술연구센터

Installation of the Association of Free Artists, Osaka, published in *Art Creation*(美術創作)

1940, courtesy of MMCA Art Research Center

1940년 5월 제4회 《자유미술가협회전》 이후 6월에 오사카에서 순회전시를 가졌다. 사진 왼쪽 벽에 걸린 부조 작품이 유영국의 것으로, 그중 가장 오른쪽 작품은 〈작품 404-D〉이다. 자유미술가협회(1940년 6월 이후 '미술창작가협회'로 개칭)의 기관지였던 『미술창작(美術創作)』(3호, 1940)에 수록된 전시장 사진이다.

After the 4th Association of Free Artists exhibition in May 1940, the association went to Osaka for a traveling exhibition in June. Yoo Youngkuk's *Work 404-D* is the third work from the left on the wall. This photo originally appeared in the group's journal *Art Creation*(美術創作), which they began publishing in June 1940, shortly after the group had been renamed as the *Association of Art Creators*.

『자유미술(自由美術)』에 실린 유영국의 작품 1940년

Free Art(自由美術) Yoo Youngkuk's work introduced in the journal 1940

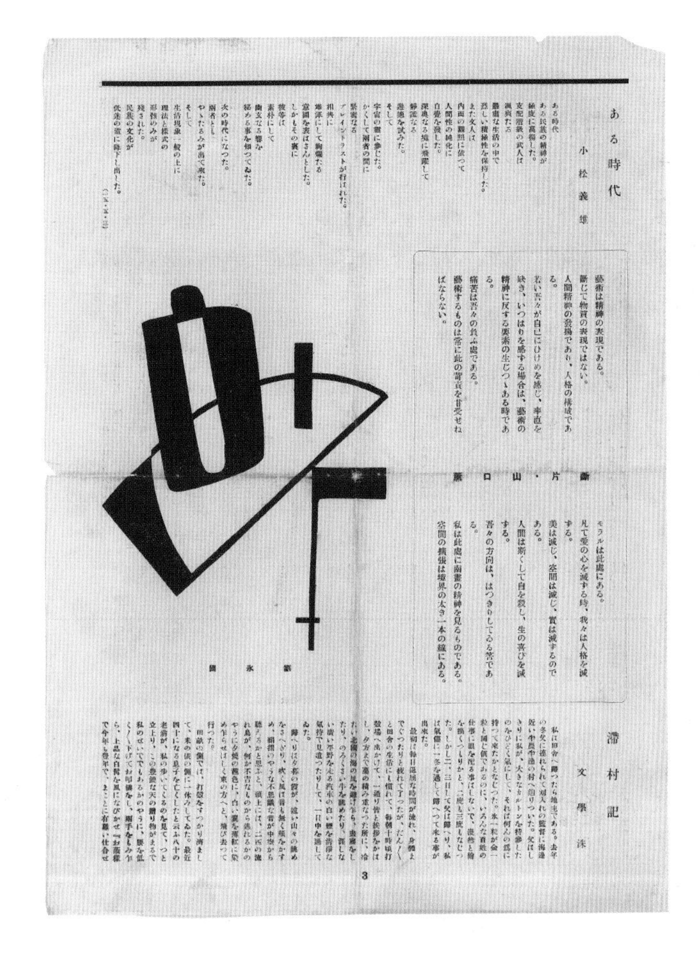

ある時代

小松義雄

ある時代
ある民族の精神が
極度に高揚した。
支配階級の武人は
颯爽たる
豪壮な生活の中で
烈しい積極性を保持した。
また文人は
內面の纖細に依つて
人間性の純化に
自覺を發した。
深奧なる境に飛躍して
靜謐なる
逍遙を試みた。
そして
宇宙の靈に參じた。
かくして兩者の間に
緊密なる
ブレイントラストが行はれた。
相共に
雄渾にして絢爛たる
意圖を表はさんとした。
しかもその裏に
彼等は
素朴にして
幽玄なる響を
秘める事を知つてゐた。
次の時代になつた。
兩者とも
やゝたるみが出て來た。
そして
生活現象一般の上に
理法と樣式の
形骸のみが
殘された。
民族の文化が
低迷の淵に降下し出した。

（一五・五・三）

斷片・山口薰

藝術は精神の表現である。

斷じて物質の表現ではない。

人間精神の發揚であり、人格の構成である。

若い吾々が自己にひけめを感じ、率直を缺き、いつはりを感ずる場合は、藝術の精神に反する要素の生じつゝある時である。

痛苦は吾々の負ふ處である。

藝術するものは常に此の苛責を甘受せねばならない。

モラルは此處にある。

凡て愛の心を滅する時、我々は人格を滅する。

美は滅じ、空間は滅じ、實は滅するのである。

人間は斯くして自を殺し、生の喜びを滅する。

吾々の方向は、はつきりしてゐる筈である。

私は此處に繪畫の精神を見るものである。

空間の擴張は境界の太き一本の線にある。

劉永國

滯村記

文學洙

3

자유미술가협회 기관지였던 『자유미술(自由美術)』(2호, 1940)에 유영국의 드로잉이 실렸다. 그 아래 문학수의 에세이도 함께 실려 주목된다.

This drawing by Yoo Youngkuk, accompanying an essay by Moon Haksoo, was published in *Free Art* (自由美術), the journal of the *Association of Free Artists*.

제2회 자유미술가협회전 상장 1938년, 유영국미술문화재단 소장

Certificate for winning the 2nd Association of Free Artists Award 1938, courtesy of Yoo Youngkuk Art Foundation

賞

第二回自由美術家協會展覽會

自由美術家協會賞

右贈呈ス

昭和十三年五月

自由美術家協會

劉永國殿

유영국은 1938년 제2회《자유미술가협회전》협회상을 수상했고, 이후 협회의 회우 자격을 얻었다.

In 1938, Yoo Youngkuk received the 2nd Association of Free Artists Award and became an official member of the association.

유영국의 《자유미술가협회전》 출품기념 엽서 1937년, 1938년, 유영국미술문화재단 소장

Postcards to commemorate Yoo Youngkuk's works from exhibitions of the Association of Free Artists

1937, 1938, courtesy of Yoo Youngkuk Art Foundation

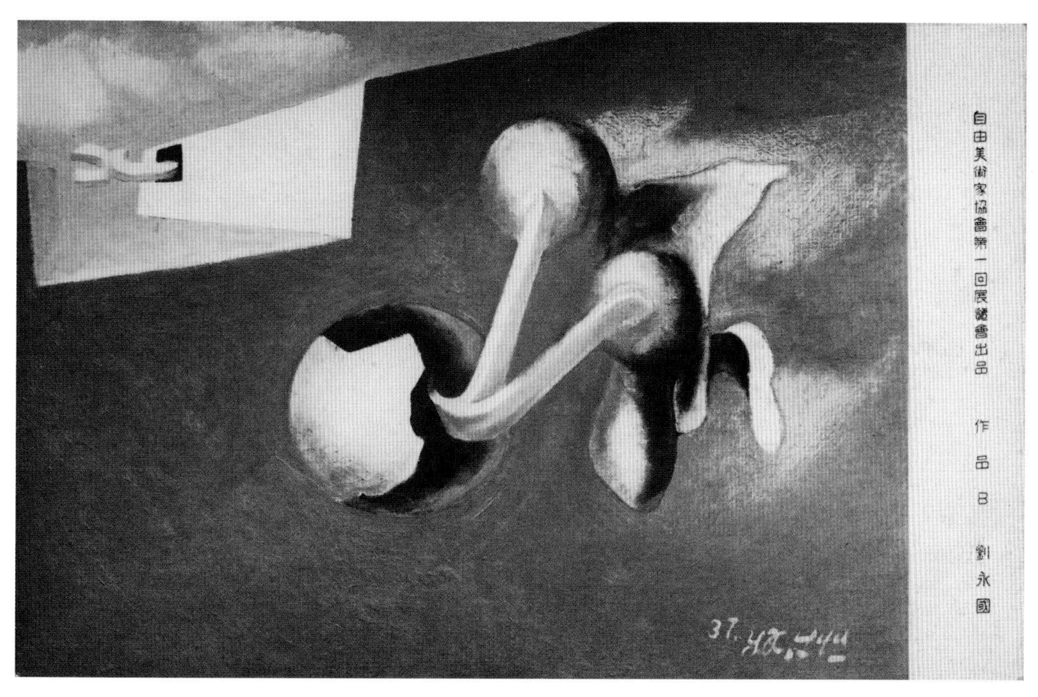

〈작품 B〉, 1937. 7. 10-19, 제1회 《자유미술가협회전》 출품 기념 엽서
Work B, postcard for 1st Association of Free Artists exhibition (July 10-19, 1937).

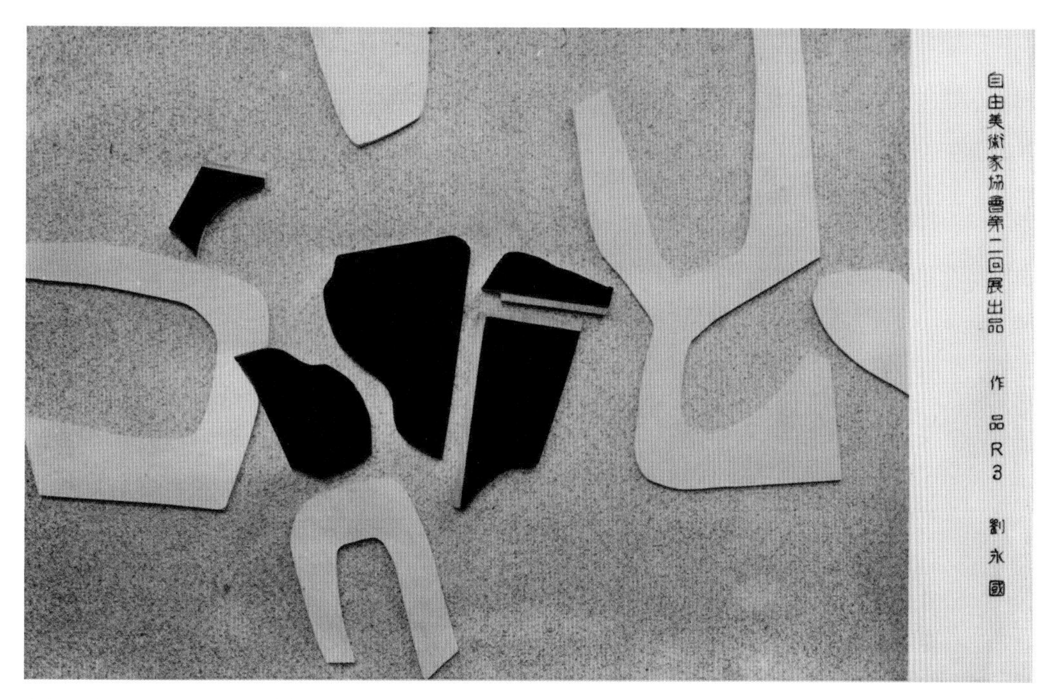

〈작품 R3〉, 1938. 5. 22-31, 제2회 《자유미술가협회전》 출품 기념 엽서
Work R3, postcard for 2nd Association of Free Artists exhibition (May 22-31, 1938).

유영국의 《자유미술가협회전》 출품기념 엽서 1939-1942년, 유영국미술문화재단 소장

Postcards to commemorate Yoo Youngkuk's works from the exhibitions of the Association of Free Artists

1939-1942, courtesy of Yoo Youngkuk Art Foundation

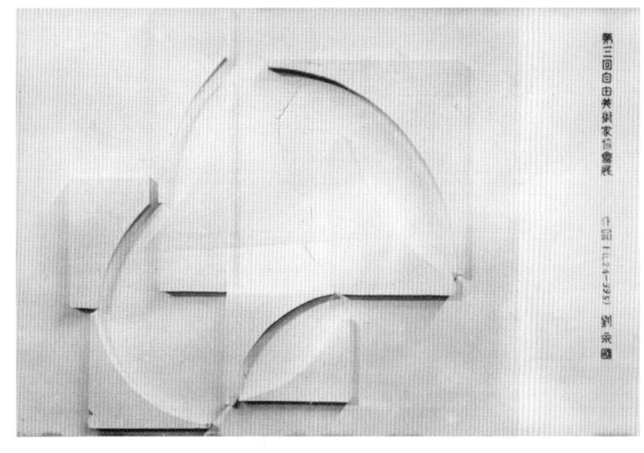

〈작품 1(L24-39.5)〉, 1939. 5. 21-30, 제3회 《자유미술가협회전》 출품기념 엽서
Work 1(L24-39.5), postcard for 3rd Association of Free Artists exhibition (May 21-30, 1939).

〈작품 4(L24-39.5)〉, 1939. 5. 21-30, 제3회 《자유미술가협회전》 출품기념 엽서
Work 4(L24-39.5), postcard for 3rd Association of Free Artists exhibition (May 21-30, 1939).

〈작품 404-C〉, 1940. 5. 22-31, 제4회 《자유미술가협회전》 출품기념 엽서
Work 404-C, postcard for 4th Association of Free Artists exhibition (May 22-31, 1940).

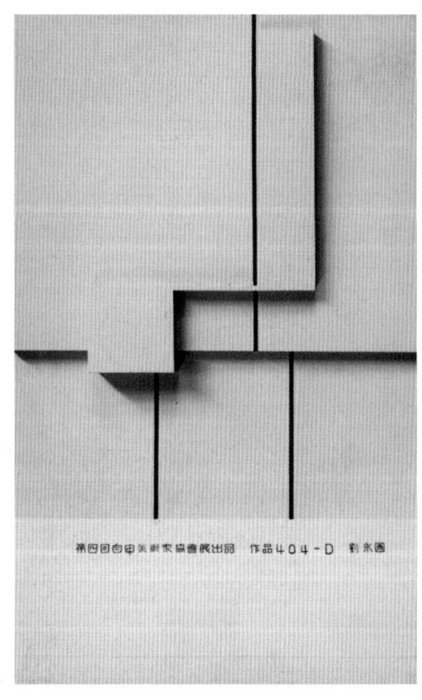

〈작품 404-D〉, 1940. 5. 22-31, 제4회 《자유미술가협회전》 출품기념 엽서
Work 404-D, postcard for 4th Association of Free Artists exhibition (May 22-31, 1940).

〈10-4〉, 1941. 4. 10-21
제5회《미술창작가협회전》출품기념 엽서
10-4, postcard for 5th Association of Art Creators exhibition
(April 10-21, 1941).

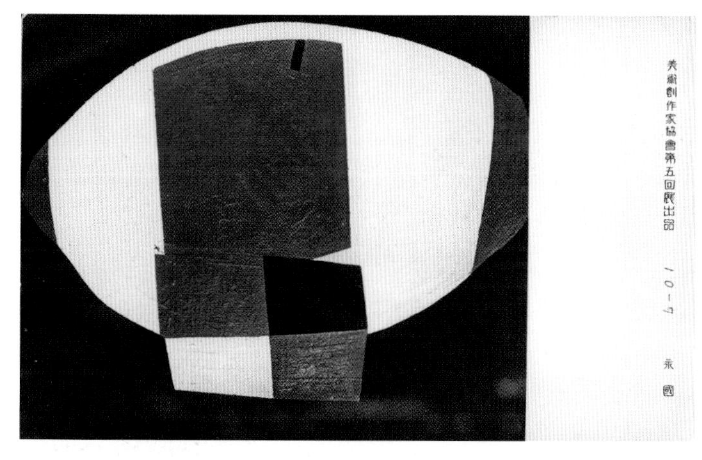

〈10-7〉, 1941. 4. 10-21
제5회《미술창작가협회전》출품기념 엽서
10-7, postcard for 5th Association of Art Creators exhibition
(April 10-21, 1941).

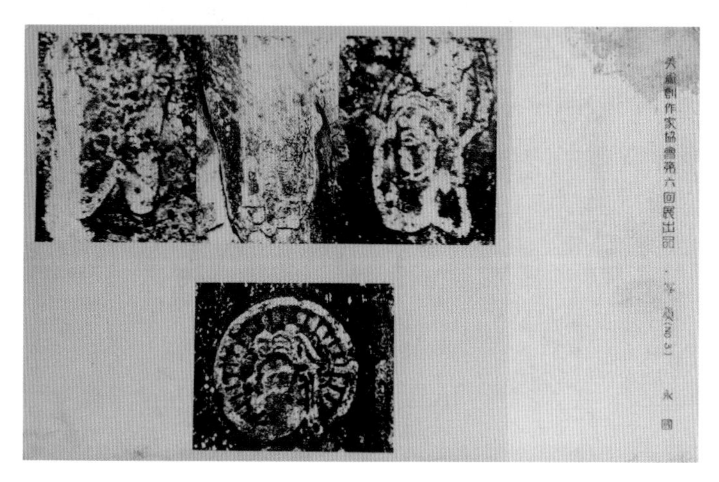

〈사진 No.3〉, 1942. 4. 4-12.
제6회《미술창작가협회전》출품기념 엽서
Photography No.3, postcard for 6th Association of Art Creators exhibition (April 4-12, 1942).

자유미술가협회는 '자유'라는 명칭을 사용하지 못하게 되면서, 1940년 6월부터 협회명을 미술창작가협회로 변경하였다. 전위예술에 대한 탄압이 계속되는 가운데 유영국은 1942년 제6회전에 사진 작품을 출품하였다.
In June 1940, the Association of Free Artists was renamed as the Association of Art Creators, because the word "free" had been banned from such usage. Due to the ongoing suppression of avant-garde art, Yoo Youngkuk switched to photography for the 6th exhibition of the association in 1942.

자유미술가협회원들의 전시 출품기념 엽서 1938-40년, 유영국미술문화재단 소장

Postcards to commemorate other members' works from the Association of Free Artists exhibitions

1938-40, courtesy of Yoo Youngkuk Art Foundation

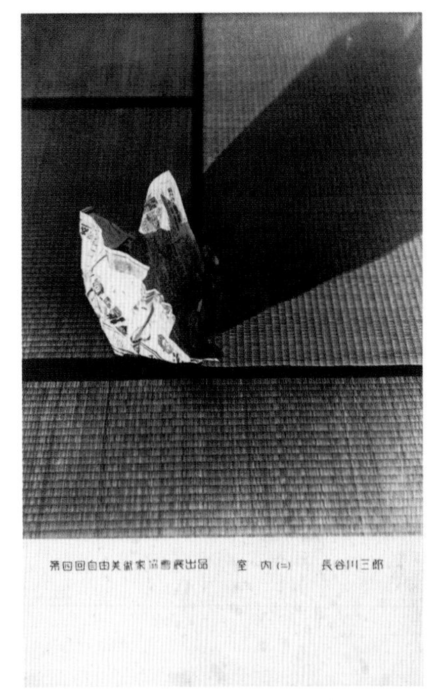

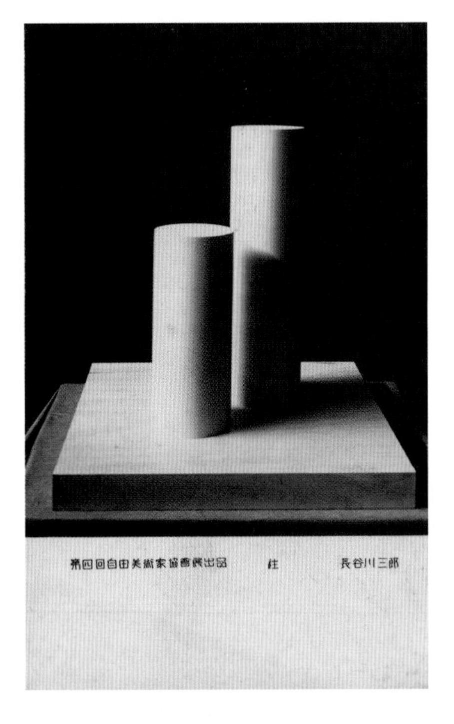

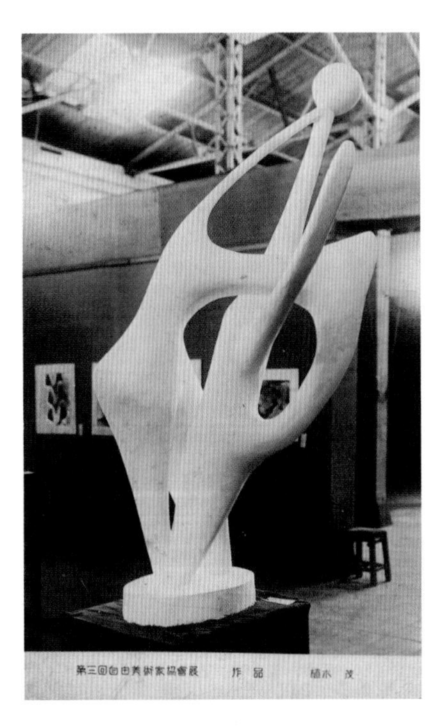

自由美術家協會第二回展出品 天 蓋 尚 津志本 貞

第三回自由美術家協會展
作品
植木 茂

第三回自由美術家協會展
山百合
亀山 敬

第三回自由美術家協會展 鐘 矢橋六郎

自由美術家協會第二回展出品 母 子 永良 胖

자유미술가협회의 리더였던 무라이 마사나리(村井正誠)의 사진 1940년경, 유영국미술문화재단 소장

Photos of Murai Masanari(村井正誠), one of the leaders of the Association of Free Artists

c.1940, courtesy of Yoo Youngkuk Art Foundation

유영국이 촬영한 것으로 보이는 무라이 마사나리의 사진. 뒤에 그의 작품 〈9개의 형상〉이 보인다.

This photo of Murai Masanari is believed to have been taken by Yoo Youngkuk. On the wall behind Murai are his works entitled *Nine Types of Images*.

무라이 마사나리와 유영국이 함께 찍은 사진, 1940년경, 유영국미술문화재단 소장
1 무라이 마사나리의 부인, **2** 유영국, **3** 무라이 마사나리이다.

Photo of Murai Masanari and Yoo Youngkuk c.1940, courtesy of Yoo Youngkuk Art Foundation.
1 Wife of Murai Masanari, **2** Yoo Youngkuk, **3** Murai Masanari.

『미즈에(みづゑ)』, 414호, 428호

1939년 6월호(표지: 하세가와 사부로), 국립현대미술관 미술연구센터 소장
1940년 7월호(표지: 무라이 마사나리), 국립현대미술관 미술연구센터 소장

Mizue (みづゑ), Vol. 414, 428

June 1939, cover by Hasegawa Saburo, courtesy of MMCA Art Research Center
July 1940, cover by Murai Masanari, courtesy of MMCA Art Research Center

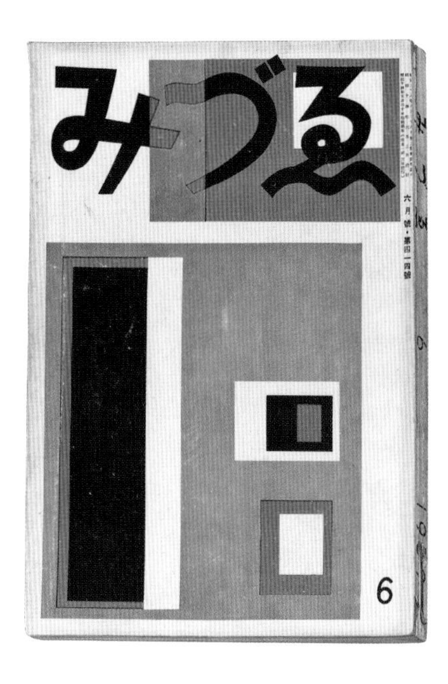

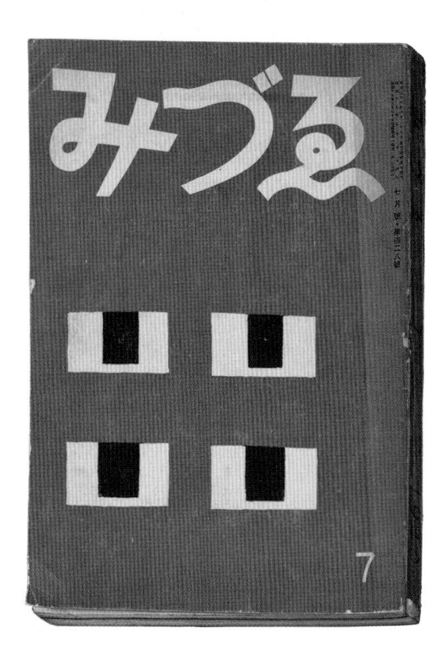

하세가와 사부로와 무라이 마사나리는 당대 일본의 추상미술계를 이끈 대표적인 작가들이었다. 특히 동경제국대학 문학부 미학과 출신이었던 하세가와 사부로는 평론가로도 맹활약하였으며, 그의 글은 『미즈에(みづゑ)』, 『비노쿠니(美の国)』 등의 잡지에 자주 실렸다. 유영국은 자유미술가협회의 리더격이었던 두 작가와 상당히 가까운 관계였으며, 자주 그들의 집을 드나들곤 했다.

The Association of Free Artists was led by Hasegawa Saburo and Murai Masanari, two of the most renowned figures at the forefront of Japanese abstract art at the time. In particular, after graduating from the Aesthetics Department of the College of Literature at Tokyo Imperial University, Hasegawa Saburo became an active and prominent critic. His articles were frequently published in magazines, including Mizue(みづゑ) and Binokuni(美の国). Yoo Youngkuk was close with both of these two artists and frequently visited their homes.

무라이 마사나리(村井正誠)의 작품

무라이 마사나리, 〈9개의 상형(像型)〉, 1940년경, 캔버스에 유채,
27.6×21.8cm, 세타가야 미술관 소장
Murai Masanari, *Nine Types of Images,* c. 1940, Oil on canvas,
27.6×21.8cm, Setagaya Art Museum.

무라이 마사나리, 〈9개의 상형(像型), No. 9〉, 1940, 캔버스에 유채,
27.5×22cm, 세타가야 미술관 소장
Murai Masanari, *Nine Types of Images, No. 9*, 1940, Oil on canvas,
27.5×22cm, Setagaya Art Museum.

무라이 마사나리, 〈9개의 상형(像型)(노란 태양)〉, 1940년경, 캔버스에
유채, 27.1×22.2cm, 세타가야 미술관 소장
Murai Masanari, *Nine Types of Images (Yellow Sun)*, c. 1940, Oil on
canvas, 27.1×22.2cm, Setagaya Art Museum.

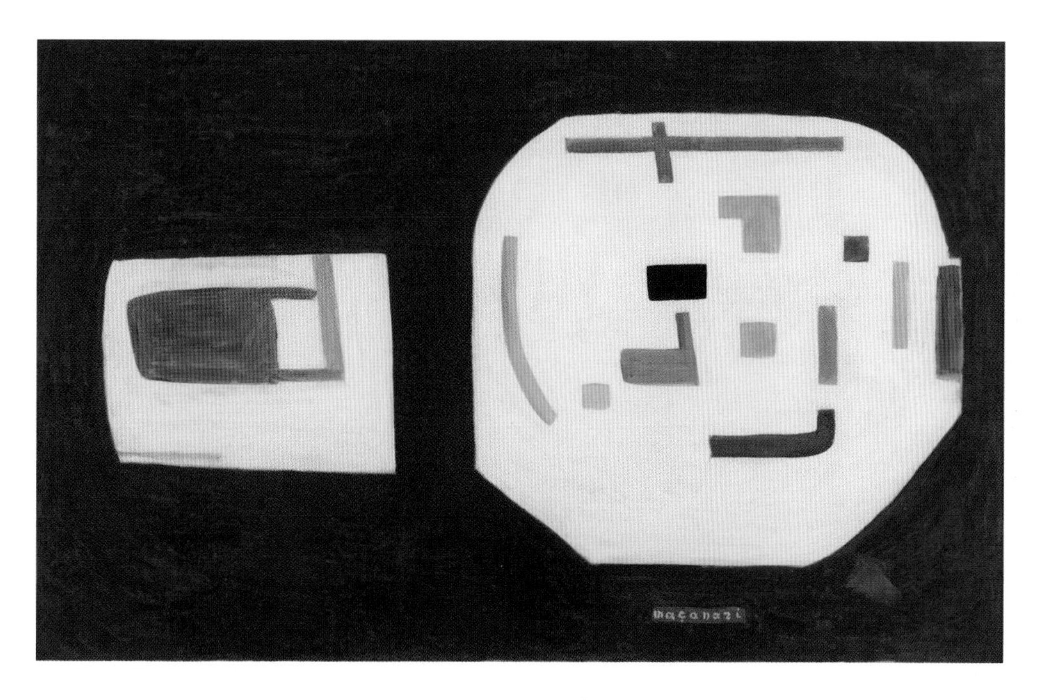

무라이 마사나리, 〈백령묘(百靈廟)〉, 1938, 캔버스에 유채, 72.4×116.6cm, 세타가야 미술관 소장
Murai Masanari, *Bailing Miao*(百靈廟), 1938, Oil on canvas, 72.4×116.6cm, Setagaya Art Museum.

무라이 마사나리, 〈도시(Cité)〉, 1940년경, 캔버스에 유채, 80.5×100.1cm, 세타가야 미술관 소장
Murai Masanari, *Cité*, c. 1940, Oil on canvas, 80.5×100.1cm, Setagaya Art Museum.

하세가와 사부로(長谷川三郎)의 작품

하세가와 사부로, 〈형태(形態)〉, 1937, 57×69×5cm, 코난학원갤러리 소장
Hasegawa Saburo, *Forms*(形態), 1937, 57×69×5cm, Konan Gakuin Gallery.

하세가와 사부로, 〈주(柱)〉, 1940, 55×55.2×56.1cm, 코난학원갤러리 소장
Hasegawa Saburo, *Column*(柱), 1940, 55×55.2×56.1cm, Konan Gakuin Gallery.

YOO YOUNGKUK 1916-2002

The 100th Anniversary Exhibition of a Korean Modern Master

도판과 에세이

Plates and Essays

우리는 외적인 것에 대한 집착으로부터 자유로워질 필요가 있다.
그래야만 비극을 극복하고 일어서서 모든 것 속에 있는 평온함을
의식적으로 관조할 수 있게 된다.

- 몬드리안, 「신조형주의: 조형적 등가가치의 일반이론」 중에서, 1920

릴리프 오브제 *Relief Object*
1937(유리지 재제작 Reproduced by Yoo Lizzy 2002), 혼합재료 Mixed media, 53×40cm

습작(習作) ***Study***
1937(유리지 재제작 Reproduced by Yoo Lizzy 2003), 혼합재료 Mixed media, 49.5×37cm

작품 ***Work***

1938(유리지 재제작 Reproduced by Yoo Lizzy 2003), 혼합재료 Mixed media, 40×52.5cm

작품 LA-101 ***Work LA-101***
1938(유리지 재제작 Reproduced by Yoo Lizzy 2003), 혼합재료 Mixed media, 40×51cm

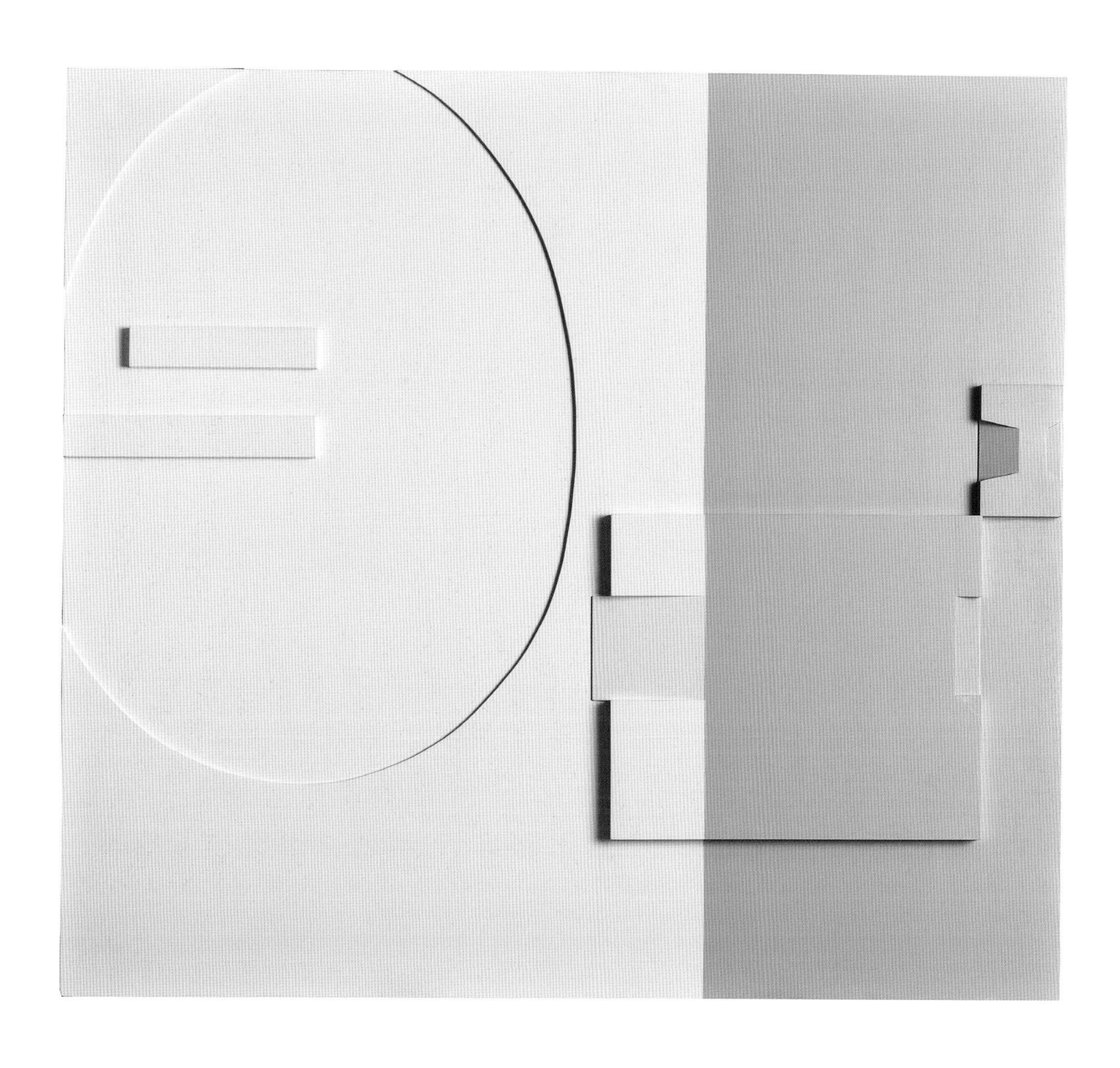

역정(歷程) 2 ***Journey 2***
1938(유리지 재제작 Reproduced by Yoo Lizzy 2002), 혼합재료 Mixed media, 81×90.5cm

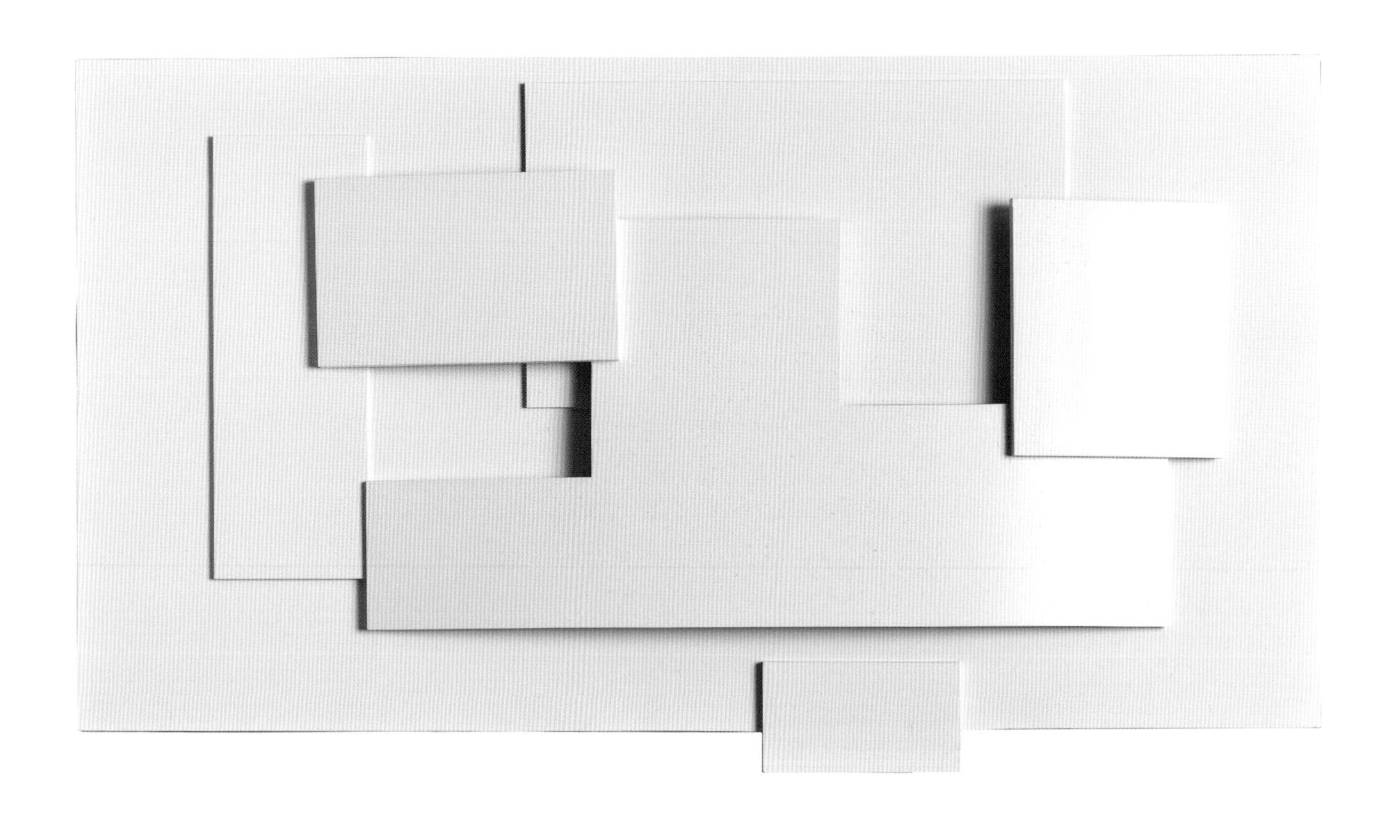

계도(計圖) **D** ***Design D***
1939(유리지 재제작 Reproduced by Yoo Lizzy 2002), 혼합재료 Mixed media, 51×90cm

작품 R3 ***Work R3***
1938(유리지 재제작 Reproduced by Yoo Lizzy 1979), 혼합재료 Mixed media, 65×90cm

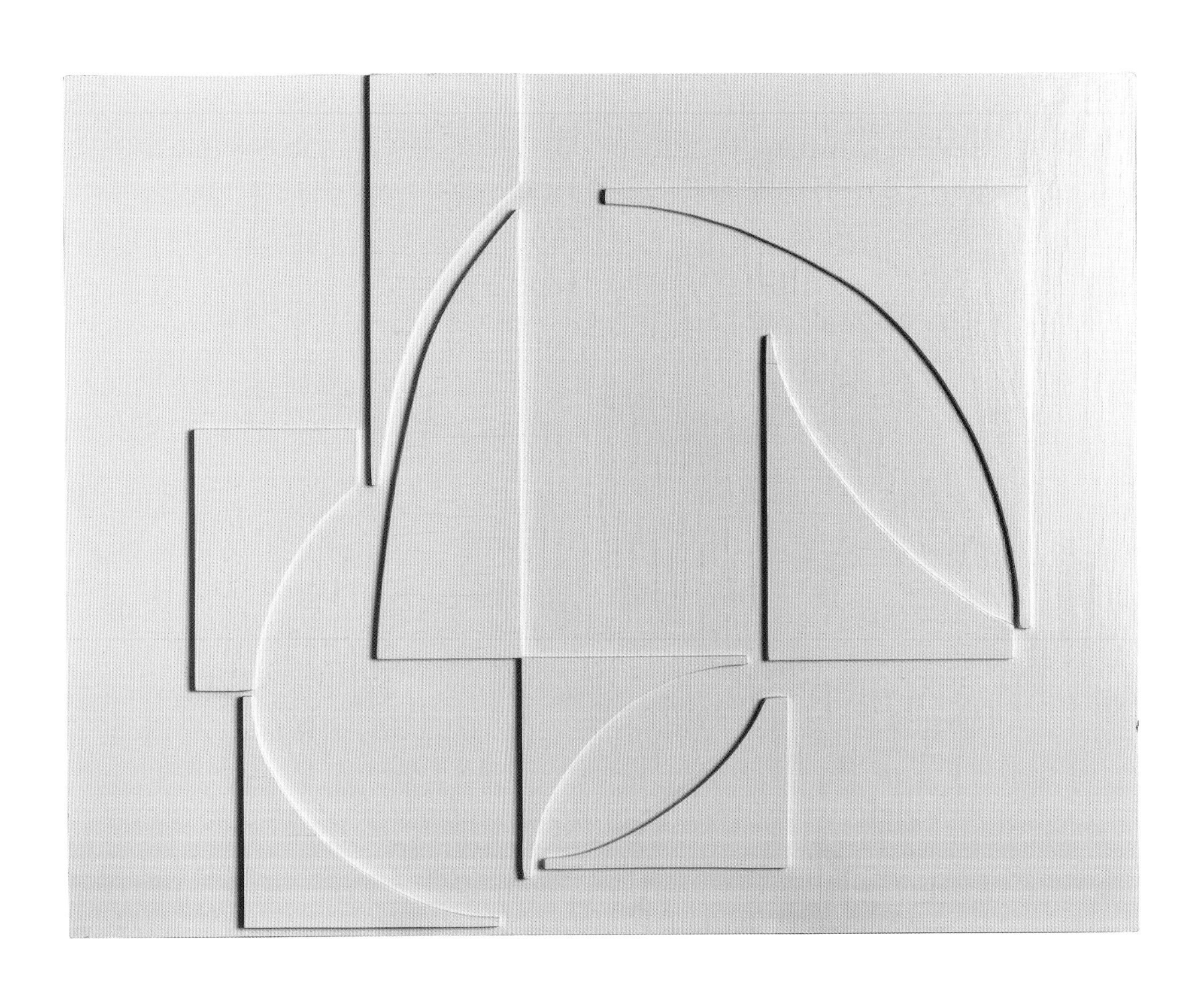

작품1(L24-39.5) ***Work 1(L24-39.5)***
1939(유리지 재제작 Reproduced by Yoo Lizzy 1979), 혼합재료 Mixed media, 70×90cm

작품 4 (L24-39.5) ***Work 4 (L24-39.5)***
1939(유리지 재제작 Reproduced by Yoo Lizzy 2003), 혼합재료 Mixed media, 62×90cm

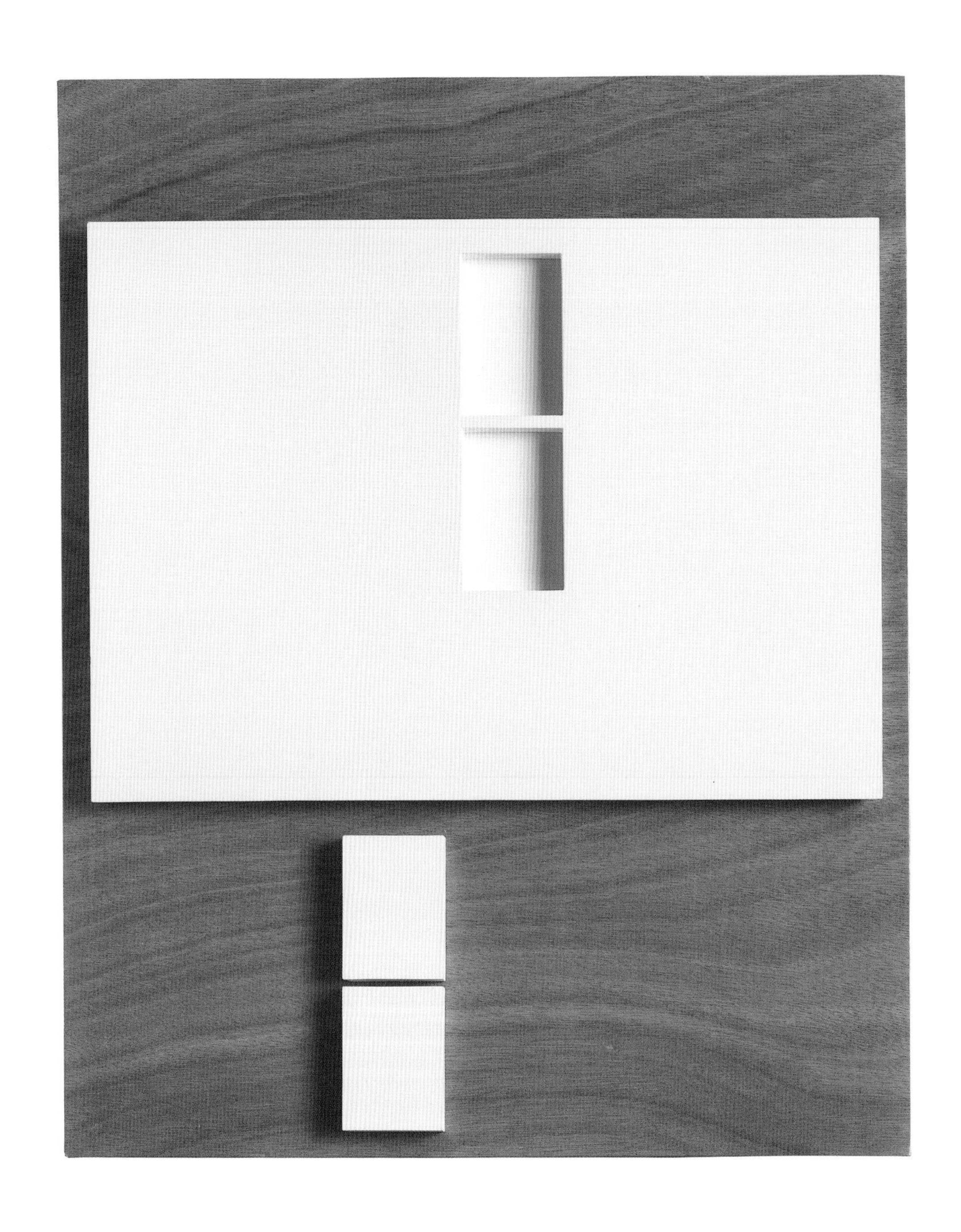

작품 404-C *Work 404-C*
1940(유리지 재제작 Reproduced by Yoo Lizzy 2003), 혼합재료 Mixed media, 48×40cm

작품 404-D *Work 404-D*

1940(유리지 재제작 Reproduced by Yoo Lizzy 2002), 혼합재료 Mixed media, 90×74cm

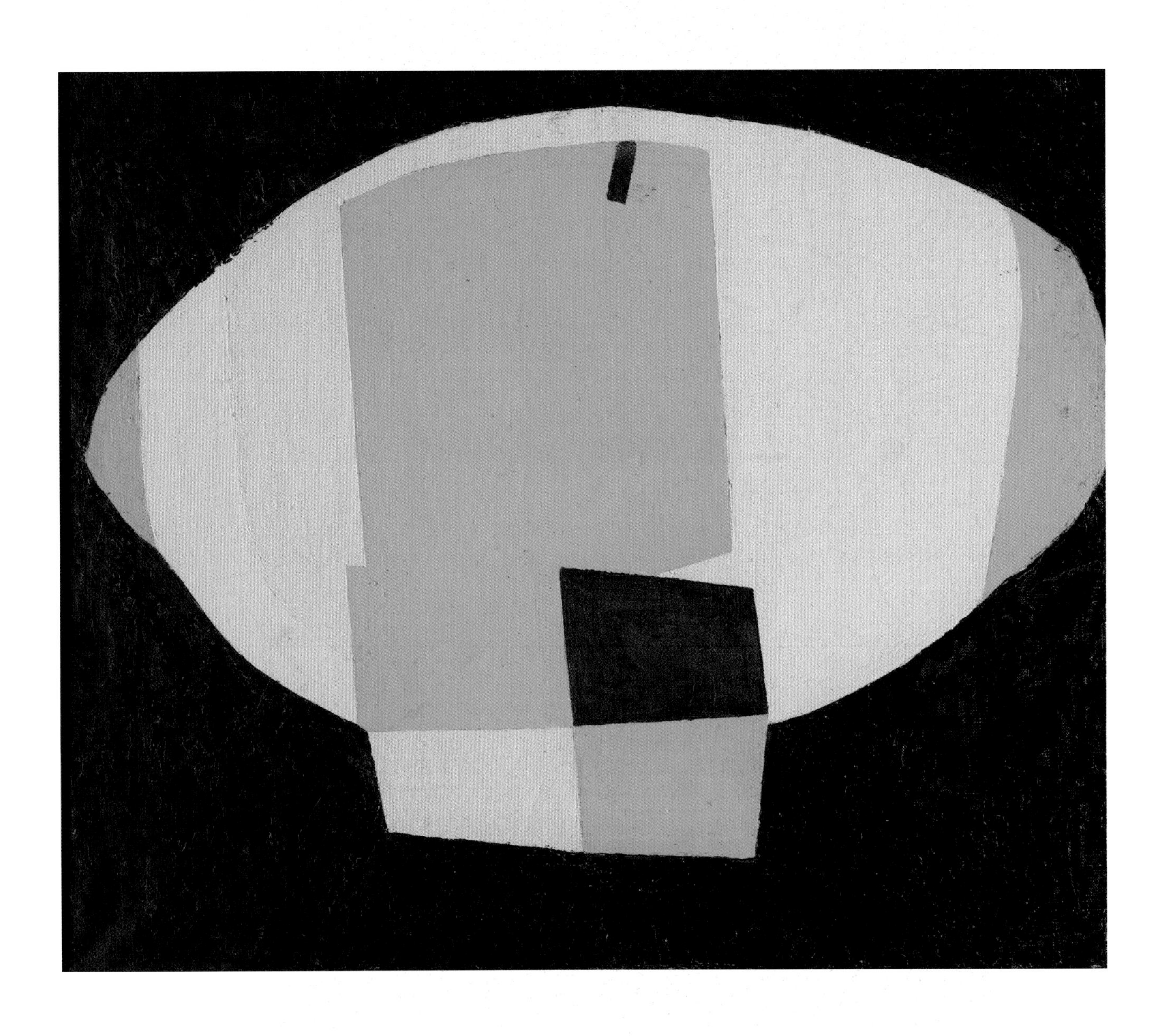

10-7
1940, 캔버스에 유채 Oil on canvas, 38×45cm

작품 *Work*
1940, 캔버스에 유채 Oil on canvas, 45×37.7cm

전위사진과 유영국

권행가

덕성여자대학교 인문과학연구소 연구교수

* 이 글은 2014년 정부재원(교육부)으로 한국연구재단의 지원을 받아 연구한 논문의 일부임(NRF-2014S1A5BA02016367)

고전과 전위의 병존: 유영국의 사진 읽기

유영국은 1930년대 후반 일본 전위미술 운동의 한가운데에서 그의 화업을 시작했다. 1937년부터 1942년까지 독립미술협회, 자유미술가협회, N.B.G. 양화동인전에 출품한 작품들은 당시 일본 전위미술을 대표한 두 양식인 구성주의와 초현실주의를 실험해 본 학습기의 산물이라 할 수 있다. 해방 후 자연에 근거를 둔 추상작업들이 모두 회화에 집중되어 있던 반면 이 시기의 작품들은 릴리프나 사진 같은 탈회화적 매체에 집중되어 있었다. 이러한 매체의 확대는 같은 시기 유학한 김환기나 이중섭 같은 작가들에게서는 볼 수 없는 유영국만의 특징이라 할 수 있다. 가령 자유미술가협회 출신의 작가들 중 주현(周現, 본명 이범승)이나 조우식(趙宇植)도 전위사진작업을 했지만 릴리프와 회화, 사진 세 매체를 횡단하며 작업을 하지는 않았다. 문화학원 시절부터 사진에 관심을 가지고 있었던 유영국은 1939년 부친으로부터 카메라를 선물 받자 오리엔탈사진학교(オリエンタル写真学校)에 들어가 정식으로 사진을 배웠다. 1938년부터 4년 동안 주로 재현성이 배제된 추상 릴리프 작업을 하던 유영국은 1942년 미술창작가협회에 사진 작품을 7점 출품하였다. 이때 그가 출품한 사진 중 5점은 경주를 소재로 한 사진이다. 절대적 기하추상에서 경주라는 고전적 장소성으로, 또는 포토몽타주라는 실험적 사진 작업과 경주라는 소재의 이질적 병존, 즉 전위와 고전 이 두 가지의 낯선 병존이 어떻게 가능했을까? 이를 이해하기 위해서는 당시 자유미술가협회전과 전위사진의 문맥을 들여다 볼 필요가 있다.

현재 유영국문화재단에 소장된 사진 중 유학기 사진 작업과 관련된 사진들은 28종이 남아있다. 이 중 1942년 미술창작가협회에 출품한 사진 작품으로 확인되는 것은 비록 사진엽서로만 남아있지만 〈사진 No.3〉 포토몽타주(photomontage) 한 점이다(p. 51). 이 작품 외에는 총 23종이 대부분 경주 남산과 석굴암 등을 촬영한 스트레이트 사진들이다.[1] 이

사진들 중 미술창작가협회 출품작이 포함되어 있는지는 확실치 않다. 사진의 뒷면에 "불국사 대웅전-불 18" "석굴암 내부불상-석 10" 식의 제목과 일련번호가 기록되어 있고, 일부를 확대해서 〈사진 No.3〉 에 사용한 것으로 보아 이 사진들은 출품용 작품을 위한 자료 사진으로 촬영되었을 것으로 보인다. 사진사학자 최인진은 이 일련번호들을 통해 대략 77점 정도의 경주 사진이 촬영되었을 것으로 보았다.[2] 일제강점기에 경주는 이미 관광지로 개발이 되어있긴 했지만 석굴암, 분황사, 경주박물관을 거쳐서 경주 남산의 동쪽과 서쪽 전역의 바위벽들을 오르내리며 사진을 촬영하는 것은 쉬운 일이 아니었다. 유영국의 경주 사진은 지금처럼 쉽게 촬영되는 관광지 사진이 아니라 답사를 통해 발견되고 사진이라는 미디어를 통해 재현된 또 다른 조형적 오브제로서의 공간이다. 그의 사진은 흔한 명소 사진의 문법을 따르기보다는 부분을 클로즈업하여 피사체의 조형적 구조나 재질을 드러내는 등 그의 추상 릴리프 작업과도 연관되는 부분이 많다. 현존 사진의 상황이 유영국 사진 작업의 전모를 파악하기에는 부족하지만 이 사진 자료들은 그가 이 시기동안 포토그램, 포토몽타주, 앙각 촬영, 부감 촬영, 클로즈업, 이중영상촬영 등 당시 일본의 전위미술계에서 사진이 지닌 조형성을 발견해가는 과정을 경험하고 있었다는 것을 보여준다.

사진을 배우다

유영국이 유학했던 1930년대 일본은 도시를 중심으로 모더니즘 문화가 절정에 달했던 시기이다. 라디오, 전화, 영화, 인쇄 및 사진복제기술의 발달 등 기계문명을 기초로 한 미디어의 보급이 활발하게 이루어지면서 복제기술시대를 맞이하였다. 독일에서 들어온 그래픽잡지의 영향으로 그래픽저널리즘이 비약적으로 발전했으며 소형카메라의 보급으로 아마추어 사진가 인구도 증가했다. 이러한 수요에 맞추어 1920년대 말부터 전쟁 전까지 일본 내에 오리엔탈사진학교를 시작으로 20여 개의 사진학교가 신규로 설립되었다. 1929년 개교한 오리엔탈사진학교는 감광재료를 생산하던 오리엔탈사진공업사가 설립한 학교이다. 처음 개교했을 때는 수업기간 3개월에 수업료 60엔으로 정원 50명을 모집했다. 입학자격은 심상소학교 또는 그에 준하는 학력을 소지한 자 중에 사진관을 운영하거나, 학교가 인정할만한 사진 기술을 가진 자, 또는 보통사진학교 졸업자라 하여 대체로 이미 사진 기술을 어느 정도 습득하고 있는 사진가들을 대상으로 한 영업사진교육을 목적으로 했다.[3] 이후 유영국 유학기인 30년대 후반에는 예과라 하여 년 1회(1-3월) 실시되는

초보자를 위한 실기연구강습회를 수료하면 사진학교에 입학자격을 주어 초보자들도 입학이 가능해졌다. 본과에 해당하는 사진학교는 매년 4-7월, 9-12월 3개월씩 2회 운영했으며 본격적인 촬영 및 수정 등 영업사진사나 신문사 카메라맨 양성을 위한 기초교육을 실시했다.[4]

이 같은 입학의 용이성, 짧은 교육기간, 직업교육의 실용성으로 인해 일제강점기에 오리엔탈사진학교는 한국인이 가장 많이 유학을 했다. 사진가로는 현일영, 김규혁, 임정식, 박천도, 조배현, 주운학 등이 배출되었으며 미술가로는 주현과 유영국이 있다.[5] 유영국은 1940년 3월 오리엔탈사진실기연구강습회를 수료하자마자 바로 본과로 들어가 7월에 졸업했다. 예과 3개월, 본과 3개월하여 총 6개월에 걸친 사진교육을 받은 것이며 영업사진가나 신문사 사진가 양성을 위한 재현적, 기록적 성격의 사진교육이 주가 되었을 것으로 보인다. 실제 그는 사진을 배운 이유가 일본에서의 체제기간이 길어지면서 생계수단으로 사진을 배웠고 공장직원 증명서 사진 같은 것으로 용돈을 벌었다고 했다.[6]

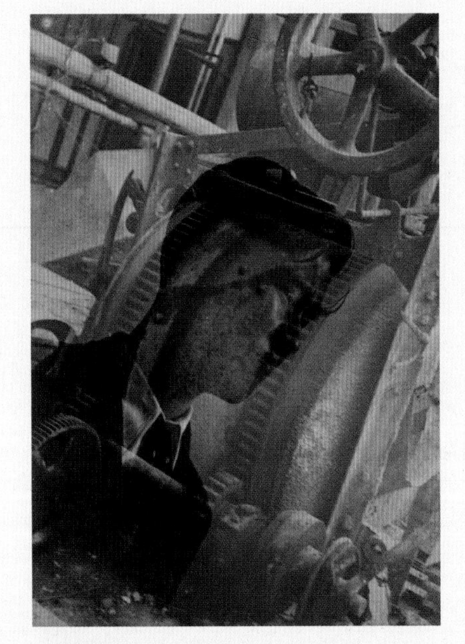

참고도판 1
츠카모토 시젠, 유영국의 모습을 이중촬영영상 기법으로 제작, 1940년대, 유영국미술문화재단 소장

그러나 그가 사진에 관심을 가진 것이 단순히 실용적 목적에서였다고만 볼 수는 없다. 오리엔탈사진공업사가 발행한 잡지 『フォトタイムズ(포토타임즈)』가 1928년부터 독일 즉물주의, 만 레이(Man Ray), 라즐로 모홀리 나기(László Moholy Nagy) 등을 비롯한 해외 최신 사진동향을 소개하면서 신흥사진운동의 거점 역할을 하고 있었고, 이 학교 출신이자 자유미술가협회의 창립회원인 에이큐(瑛九, 1911-60, 본명 스기타 히데오(杉田秀夫))가 1930년 오리엔탈사진학교를 나온 후 『포토타임즈』에 사진평론을 내기도 하고 포토그램을 발표하는 등으로 전위사진가이자 전위미술가로 주목받고 있었다. 그와 절친했던 주현이 《자유미술가협회전》에 처음부터 포토그램을 출품하고 있었으며 문화학원 동급생 츠카모토 시젠(塚本自然)이 그의 상반신을 이중촬영영상기법으로 제작한 것 등에서도 알 수 있듯이 (참고도판 1), 유영국은 사진이 단순히 기록적 재현도구로서의 기능을 넘어 새로운 시각미디어로 미술의 영역 속에서 주목받던 시기를 이미 경험하고 있었다.

《자유미술협회전》의 전위사진들

일본의 사진사의 문맥에서 보면 유영국이 유학했던 시기는 전위사진이 짧은 기간 융성했던 시기이다. 1930년대 후반 일본의 전위미술이 주로 초현실주의와 추상미술을 지칭하듯이, 전위사진도 구성주의와 초현실주의의 영향을 받은 추상사진, 포토몽타주, 초현실적사진 등을 이르는 말이다. 포토몽타주나 포토그램은 이미

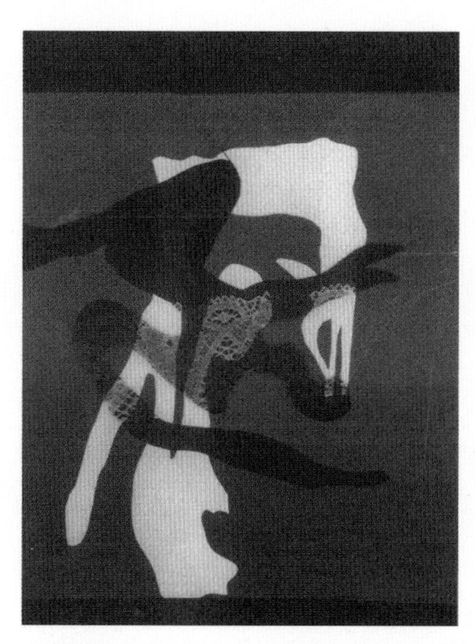

참고도판 2
에이큐, 『수면의 이유』에 실린 포토데생, 1936

1920년대 후반부터 신흥사진운동을 통해 알려져 있었다. 그러나 이러한 기법들이 미술계에서 새로운 조형실험으로 받아들여지고 전위사진협회(1938), 아방가르드 조형집단(1937), 나고야 포토아방가르드(1939) 등 전국적으로 전위를 표방한 사진단체들이 등장한 것은 1930년대 후반 초현실주의의 등장 이후부터이다.[7]

당시 자유미술가협회, 미술문화협회, 구실회 같은 전위미술단체에는 사진 작품이 적지 않게 발표되었다. 그중 유영국이 활동한 자유미술가협회는 특히 사진에 관심이 많아 전위사진의 발표의 장 역할을 하고 있었다. 1937년 2월 "예술의 자유로운 발전과 시대의 예술정신의 진흥을 기한다"라는 목적하에 창립된 이 협회는 공모전의 형식으로 운영이 되었는데 출품 부문을 보면 회화나 조각, 판화, 소묘, 콜라주, 오브제 외에 포토플라스틱(photoplastics)이 포함되어 있었다.[8] 이 때문에 1회전부터 포토플라스틱 부문에 전위사진가들이 출품을 했으며 한국인 중에도 주현, 조우식이 추상사진을 출품했다.[9] 주현은 유영국과 가까이 지내며 사진을 촬영해주기도 하고 경주 남산 촬영을 갈 때도 같이 가는 등 친밀한 관계를 유지하고 있었다.

자유미술가협회 작가 중 에이큐, 무라이 마사나리, 하세가와 사부로는 유영국과 친밀한 관계를 가졌거나 작품 사진엽서를 소장하고 있을 정도로 관심을 가졌던 작가였다는 점에서 주목된다. 에이큐는 1930년 오리엔탈사진학교를 나온 후 사진가로 활동하다가 포토그램 작품집 『眠りの理由(수면의 이유)』를 간행한 것이 계기가 되어 전위미술가로 데뷔한 작가이다(참고도판 2).[10] 당시 유영국과 문화학원을 같이 다녔던 김병기(金秉騏)는 에이큐가 전혀 나타나지 않다가 전시회에만 나타나던 작가로 만 레이의 영향을 받아 나사못 같은 것들을 암실의 인화지에 놓고 촬영하여 영상을 만들어내던 괴짜작가였다고 기억했다.[11] 에이큐의 포토그램 작품은 모양대로 자른 종이를 이용한 인형형상이나 레이스, 금속망 등의 물체를 인화지에 정착시키거나 펜라이트를 움직여 얻어진 빛의 궤적을 감광면에 정착시키는 방식으로 사진평면에 추상과 구상이 공존하는 형태이다. 그는 이러한 작업을 인화지를 사용한 데생이라 하여 포토데생(ポトデッサン)이라 했다. 원근법적 공간성에서 해방되어 인화지의 표면에 부유하는 듯한 그의 이미지는 기존의 재현적 회화의 한계를 넘어 기계적 시각미디어에 의한 새로운 표현방식을 제시한 예에 해당한다.[12]

에이큐처럼 직접적인 사진 작품은 아니지만 사진을 작업에 활용하는 것은 유영국과 친밀한 관계를 가졌던 무라이 마사나리의 작품들에서도 찾아볼 수 있다. 그가 《자유미술가협회전》에 지속적으로 출품했던 〈도시(Urbain)〉 시리즈 (1936-42년까지 지속)가 신문에 난 중국마을의 항공사진을 보고 그린 작품이라는 것은 잘

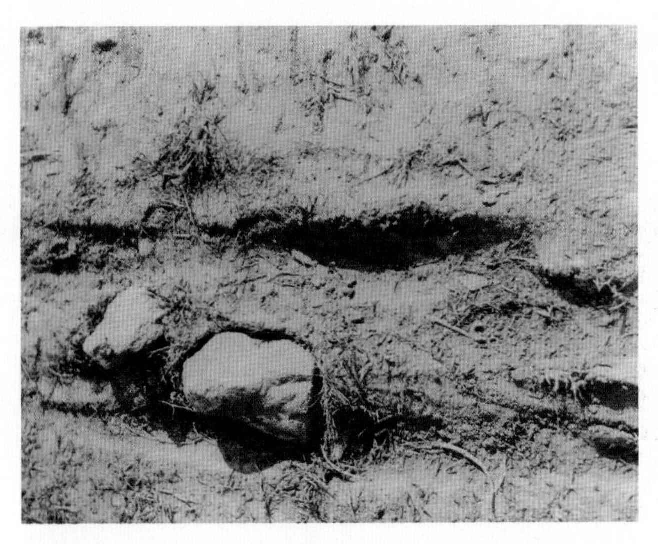

참고도판 3
하세가와 사부로, 〈향토지-길〉, 1939, 제3회 《자유미술가협회전》 출품작

알려져 있다. 김환기의 〈항공표지〉(1937)에서도 볼 수 있듯이 자유미술가 작가들 사이에서는 항공사진 뿐 아니라 과학사진, 의학사진 등 사진이라는 기계적 미디어가 만들어내는 새로운 시각에 관심을 보이는 경우가 많았다.

그러나 유영국과 관련하여 이 시기 자유미술가협회의 사진 작업 중 가장 주목되는 것은 협회를 이끈 대표적 작가이자 비평가이기도 했던 하세가와 사부로의 사진 작업이다. 하세가와가 사진을 출품한 것은 1939년 3회전부터로, 그해에 〈향토지(郷土誌)〉 시리즈를, 1940년 4회전에는 〈실내(室内)〉 시리즈를 출품하였다. 유영국의 소장품에도 이 시리즈의 사진엽서가 2점 들어있다. 〈향토지〉 시리즈는 주로 자연의 나무, 모래, 길, 그물망, 바위, 미닫이, 옷 등을 촬영한 스트레이트 사진으로 트리밍이나 클로즈업에 의해 대상의 기하학적 구조나 표면의 재질감 같은 조형성을 드러내는 데 초점을 두었다(참고도판 3). 〈실내〉(p. 52)는 하세가와가 직접 촬영한 것이 아니라 그의 지시대로 사카타 미노루(坂田稔, 1902-1974)가 촬영한 사진이다. 사카타는 나고야 전위사진그룹의 대표적 사진가로 《자유미술가협회전》에도 사진을 출품하고 있었다. 사진은 둥글게 말려진 신문지가 다다미 위로 떨어지는 장면을 포착한 것으로 초현실적 분위기를 자아낸다.[13] 여기서도 다다미방은 수직수평의 그리드 구조로 제시되고 있다.

이러한 특징은 유영국의 경주 사진들에서도 잘 보여진다. 가령 〈경주 오릉묘〉(p. 92)의 경우를 보면 다섯 개의 능이 있는 공간을 압축적으로 클로즈업하여 묘의 둥근 능선과 사각형으로 된 제석만을 정면에서 포착함으로써 단순하고 명쾌한 기하학적 구조를 추출해내고 있다. 이러한 시각은 불국사 대중전, 분황사탑, 남산 삼층석탑 같은 작품에서도 마찬가지로 드러난다. 반면 남산의 마애석불군들을 촬영한 사진들은 클로즈업을 통해 오랜 시간 속에서 마모되고 퇴화된 화강암의 재질과 선각의 조형성, 그리고 불상의 양감미와 곡선미 자체에 초점을 맞추고 있다. 이 점은 정영목이 지적했듯이 유영국이 경주를 촬영하는 방식과 시각이 릴리프 작업의 구성주의적 접근방식과 다르지 않다는 것을 보여준다.[14]

〈사진 No.3〉과 경주 남산 사진

1942년《미술창작가협회전》때 유영국은 총 7점의 사진작품을 출품했다. 〈사진 No.1〉부터 〈사진 No.5〉까지 5점은 경주 관련 사진이며 〈보도사진 6〉, 〈보도사진 7〉은 일본인의 반공훈련을 촬영한 사진일 것으로 추정된다.[15] 경주 사진 중 현재 확인되는 유일한 작품인 〈사진 No.3〉(p. 51)은 비록 사진엽서지만 이 시기 사진 작업의 성격을 파악하는 데 중요한 자료이다. 사진은 상단의 세 사각형과 하단의 사각형 총 네개의 흑백의 이미지가 포함된 사각형과 백색의 여백으로 구성되어 있다. 유영국에 의하면 경주 남산에서 촬영한 사진을 확대해서 베니어판에 흰 종이를 대고 붙여서 만든 포토몽타주이다.[16] 이 작품의 자료가 된 사진은 경주 남산의 탑곡 마애불상군(塔谷 磨崖佛像群) 중 동쪽 면에 새겨진 마애불상이다(참고도판 4). 현재 유영국의 경주 사진 23종 속에는 탑곡 마애불상이 서남산 탑골 석불이라 하여 2종 있으나 이 사진은 없어 어느 시점엔가 소실된 것으로 보인다. 경주시 배반동 산 69번지에 위치한 탑곡 마애불상군은 높이 10m의 거대한 암벽에 조성된 마애조각군으로 전체에 불상, 보살, 비천, 승려, 탑, 각종 동식물이 함께 조각되어 장엄한 불국토를 표현한 매우 이례적인 조각군이다. 이 중에서 유영국이 포토몽타주로 사용한 것은 동쪽 바위 벽면의 불조각이다. 높은 담벽 면에 본존을 중심으로 좌측에 합장공양하는 보살 1구와 비천상 7구가 본존을 향해 둥글게 배치되어 있는 구성인데, 일곱 비천이 단축법으로 표현되어 마치 하늘에서 내려오는 듯한 생생함을 주어 남산 불상군 전체에서 가장 자유분방하고 회화적인 조각군으로 유명했다.

〈사진 No.3〉을 보면 본존이 아니라 좌측의 협시보살의 두상 부분이 화면의 중앙 사각형 안에 배치되어 있으며 화면 상단에는 중앙과 우측의 비천상의 상체만 확대되어 놓여져 있다. 본존이 아니라 협시보살을 사용한 것은 협시보살이 측면상이기 때문에 윤곽선이 보다 두드러지기 때문이었을 것으로 보인다. 소재가 하늘에서 내려오는 비천상과 협시보살로 이루어진 불국토라는 의미이다. 그런데 경주 남산의 마애불상은 모두 경도가 강해서 조각을 하기 힘든 화강암에 조각된 불상이기 때문에, 단순한 선각을 사용한 회화적 표현이 발달되어 있었다. 따라서 불상들을 클로즈업할 경우 형상보다는 화강암의 마모된 암석 재질과 거친 선각이 두드러지게 된다. 유영국은 그 이미지를 다시 확대하여 부분적으로 잘

참고도판 4
경주 남산 탑곡 마애불상군 동면

참고도판 4-1
비천상 부분

라 몽타주를 하되 수직수평의 사각형의 반복 패턴으로 재구성했기 때문에 결과적으로 보여지는 이미지는 종교적 도상이 지니는 서술성과 내용성이 탈각되는 대신 시간의 흔적에 대한 흑백의 추상 같은 회화적 이미지가 되었다. 기본적으로 이 작품도 앞서 예로 든 경주 사진에서 보이는 구성주의적 시각의 연장선상에 있다고 할 수 있다.

그렇다면 이처럼 사진에서 구성주의의 문법을 포기하지 않았던 유영국이 왜 사진의 소재를 경주 남산에서 찾았을까? 일제강점기 경주는 신라불교문화의 보고이자 고전주의의 절정을 이룬 대표적 조선문화로 일본인과 조선인들에게 잘 알려져 있었다.[17] 경주 남산이 처음 조사 발굴된 것은 1902년 세키노 타다시(關野貞, 1868-1935)에 의해서이다. 이후 20년대 중반부터 조선총독부의 조사가 이루어져 1940년 『조선보물고적도록 2: 경주 남산의 불적』이 발간되었다.[18] 이 과정에서 1939년까지 남산에 보물로 지정된 불상군은 9군데이다. 이 중 배리 석불입상, 용장사 삼층석탑, 탑곡 마애조각상, 칠불암, 신선암, 불곡 석불좌상은 유영국이 촬영한 남산 지역과 일치해 유영국이 보물로 지정된 중요 문화재를 중심으로 촬영을 했다는 것을 알 수 있다.

총독부 조사 보고서에 의하면 경주 남산의 고적들은 신라 특유의 독특한 양식을 창안한 신라불교예술의 보고(寶庫)라고 평가되었다. 그중에서도 탑곡 불상군은 남산 불상군 중에서도 가장 회화적인 특징이 강한 불상군으로 "여래, 보살, 비천, 승려 등을 모두 한곳에 조성한 장관은 남산 전체에 걸쳐 유래가 없으며, … 한 폭의 그림처럼 융화되어 마치 정토 만다라의 도상을 예배하는 것 같다. … 그리고 비천상은 마치 일본 나라(奈良) 약시지(藥師寺)의 동탑 비천, 화염문을 보는 것 같은 느낌이다"라고 하여 일본 나라시대 문화와의 유사성이 지적되기도 했다.[19] 경주는 일본인들에게 이처럼 고대 일본이 신라와 삼한을 지배했다는 신공황후(神功皇后) 신화를 가시적으로 증명해주는 장소였다. 유영국이 이러한 총독부의 조사 보고서를 알고 있지는 않았을 것이다. 그러나 1902년부터 1940년까지 40여 년에 걸쳐 경주 석굴암 일대와 남산 일대가 발견되는 과정에서 조선인들에게도 신라예술의 보고로 내면화되고 있던 것은 사실이다.

1940년대 초 유영국이 경주를 찾을 무렵 일본의 전위미술과 전위사진계에서 전위라는 말은 불온하다는 이유로 모두 개칭되고 있는 상황이었다. 자유미술가협회도 1940년 미술창작가협회로 개칭 후 전위적 성격을 표방하기는 어려웠다. 전시체제 속에서 협회 내부에는 후생미술제작단이 조직되었으며, "유럽에서 이식된 회

참고도판 5
하세가와 사부로, 〈향토지-미닫이〉, 1939, 제3회 《자유미술가협회전》 출품작

화정신을 일본의 것으로 소화해 일본 민족의 전통적 정신을 수립하고 신세대예술을 창조하자"라는 결의하에 일본 민족의 전통 정신 수립이 요청되고 있었다.[20] 앞서 말했듯이 유영국은 전시 체제기에 추상을 하기 어려워 사진을 출품했다고 했다. 이 말은 더 정확히 말하면 비대상에서 대상으로, 또는 전통과의 관련성을 가져야했다는 말이 된다.

그러나 이러한 고전, 전통에 대한 관심이 단순히 전시 체제기의 국가주의적 요청에 대한 현실적 대응이라고만 볼 수는 없다. 이미 전위미술계 내부에서도 고전과 전위의 문제에 대해 지속적인 논의가 이루어지고 있었기 때문이다. 하세가와 사부로는 그 논의를 이끈 중심인물이었다. 그는 르 코르뷔지에(Le Corbusier)나 부르노 타우트(Bruno Taut) 같은 서구의 모더니스트 건축가들이 일본의 전통 즈키야(數奇屋), 일본의 전통 다실(茶室))에서 합리성과 예술성을 찾는 것을 지적하면서 다도(茶道), 이케바나(生け花), 다실 건축 같은 일본의 고전에는 이미 합리적 추상성과 초현실주의적 오브제로서의 성격이 들어 있음을 주장했다. 그리고 진정한 전위예술이란 가장 새로운 정신에 의해 고전을 철저하게 재검토한 위에 세워져야만 일본적으로도 세계적으로도 완전한 개화결실을 맺을 수 있음을 역설했다.[21] 그러나 "최근 유행을 무비판적으로 수입하는 것도 안 되지만 편협한 국수주의자도, 세태에 아부하는 반동적 일본주의자가 되어서도 안 된다. 각자의 새로운 방식으로 열심히 고전으로부터 배워야한다"[22] 라고 하여 편협한 국수주의와도 거리를 두었다. 다시 하세가와 사부로의 사진 〈향토지-미닫이〉(참고도판 5)로 돌아가 보면 직선, 격자 패턴의 단순, 명쾌, 간결함은 그가 일본건축에서 찾은 합리성임을 가시화한 것임을 알 수 있다.[23]

1940년 경성에서 《미술창작가협회전》을 개최했을 때 김환기는 유영국의 릴리프에 대해 "신흥 끽다점의 실내장식과 같은 극히 유행적인 무내용한 것 외에 아무런 느낌도 얻을 수 없었다. 2-3년이면 더러워지는 신흥 다방식 건물에 비하면 백년, 이백 년을 생활해온 우리들의 건물이 오히려 더러워질 줄을 모른다"[24] 라고 다소 신랄한 비평을 했다. 김환기의 이 같은 비평은 당시 하세가와의 논의의 연장선상에서 한국작가들이 한국의 전통건축에로 관심을 돌리고 있었던 것으로 보아진다. 이 비판이 있은 다음 해에도 유영국은 여전히 추상작업을 출품했지만 다른 한편에서는 경주를 카메라에 담기 시작했다.

1963년 제7회 《상파울로비엔날레》에 유영국이 참가했을 때 커미셔너를 맡았던 김병기는 전시 서문에서 유영국의 회화가 "견고한 광물적 지각과 물과 대기, 이

를 내리쪼이는 뜨거운 태양이 이루고 있는 풍토의 반영"이라고 하여 그의 작품에서 토착적 요소를 찾았다. 실제 해방 이후 《신사실파전》부터 유영국의 작품은 산, 산맥, 나무, 해변 등을 모티브로 한 추상화로 전환했으며, 이러한 특징은 1980년대 이후 말기에 더욱 두드러진다. 이런 점에서 본다면 유영국에 있어 사진은 비재현적 기하추상작업으로부터 나와 이처럼 한국의 산, 자연을 기반으로 한 특유의 '자연 추상' 또는 '자연주의적 추상화'로 진행하는 전환의 계기가 되었다고 할 수 있다. 그리고 그 전환의 동인은 전쟁기 식민지 출신의 작가와 일본 국내의 작가 모두를 포섭했던 여러 겹의 내셔널리즘이었다고 할 수 있다. 물론 해방 이후 유영국의 작업은 국제화와 한국적 정체성에의 요구가 동전의 양면처럼 얽혔던 현대 한국미술계의 판도 속에서 일제 강점기와는 다르게 읽어져야 하는 부분이다. 유영국의 포토몽타주 작업은 해방 이후 더 이상 지속되지 않았다. 여러 이유가 있겠지만 사진계에서도 생활주의 사진이 주류가 되고 국전에 사진부가 1964년에야 신설될 정도로 사진이 미술계에 진입하기 어려웠던 상황을 생각해보면 미술로서의 사진 작업을 발전시키기는 쉽지 않았을 것이다.

1 나머지 4종은 다른 사람의 작품이거나 유영국이 제작한 것인지 불확실한 사진들이다.

2 최인진, 「미술사진의 선구자, 유영국 선생」, 『유영국저널』, 유영국미술문화재단, 창간호, 2004, pp. 97-98.

3 武野谷武夫, 「日本寫眞敎育史編年資料集成(1927-30)」, 『日本大學藝術學部紀要』, 2000, p. 12.

4 『フォトタイムズ』, 1938년 12월 광고: 武野谷 武夫, 「日本寫眞敎育史編年資料集成(1935-38)」, 『日本大學藝術學部紀要』, 2001, p. 20 재인용.

5 이경민, 「한국근대사진사연구-사진제도의 형성과 전개」, 중앙대학교 박사 논문, 2011, pp. 146-149.

6 김철효, 유영국 구술, 「해방이전 일본에 유학한 미술인들」, 「한국기록보존소자료집」 제6호, 리움, 2006, p. 167.

7 西村智弘, 『日本藝術寫眞史』, 美術出版, 2008 , pp. 262-273.

8 포토플라스틱은 원래 모홀리 나기(L.Moholy-Nagy)가 포토몽타주를 발전시킨 조형적 사진을 지칭하는 개념으로 사용한 용어이다. 자유미술가협회는 유럽 구성주의, 바우하우스의 영향으로 재현적 회화를 넘어 재료가 지닌 물질적 속성, 구조, 본질에 천착하고 있었다.

9 《자유미술가협회전》의 한국인 출품목록은 김영나, 「1930년대 전위그룹전 연구」, 『20세기의 한국미술』, 도서출판 예경, 1998, pp. 63-142 참고.

10 이 작품집은 하세가와 사부로(長谷川三郞, 1906-57)와 평론가이자 시인인 도야마 우사부로(外山卯三郞, 1903-80)의 협력으로 1936년 4월 예술학연구회에서 간행되었다.

11 「도쿄 분카학원: 김병기 구술」, 『한국미술기록보존소 자료집』, 2004, p. 36.

12 谷田英理, 「前衛繪畵と機械的 視覺メディア」, 『近代畵說』 15, 2006, pp. 88-94.

13 이 작품들은 현재 고베시 코난학원 하세가와사부로 기념갤러리에 소장되어 있다. 사진의 이미지와 관련 자료를 흔쾌히 제공해준 기념관의 모리타 케이코(森田啓子)께 감사를 드린다.

14 유영국 사진과 구성주의와의 관계에 대해서는 정영목, 「유영국의 초기 추상, 1937-49」, 『미술이론과 현장』 제3호, 2005; 유영아, 「유영국의 초기추상: 일본 유학기 구성주의의 영향을 중심으로」, 서울대학교 석사 논문, 2010.

15 유영국은 구술에서 일본인 반공훈련장면을 촬영했지만 전시회에 보도사진을 출품하지는 않았다고 했다. 그러나 《자유미술가협회전》 출품목록에 기록되어 있고 당시의 평론 속에도 유영국의 보도사진이 언급되어 보도사진 출품은 사실로 보인다. 「美術創作家協會展」, 『旬刊 美術申報』, 1942. 4. 20.(22호)

16 김철효, 유영국 구술, 앞의 책, p. 167.

17 일제강점기 경주를 둘러싼 담론에 대해서 김현숙, 「근대시각문화속의 경우-석굴암을 중심으로」, 『한국근현대미술사학』, 17집(2006, 하반기), pp. 173-205 참조.

18 경주 남산은 초기에는 주로 고분이나 사찰 위주로 발굴이 되었는데 점차 불상군들도 발굴되기 시작하여 1915년 시정 5주년 조선물산공진회에 석조약사여래좌상이 출품될 정도로 일반에게까지 알려지기 시작했다. 이후 1925년부터 조선총독부 박물관에서 전면적인 조사를 실시하여 유적배치도가 만들어졌으며 32년에는 경성제국대학교 사진부의 협조를 받아 10일간 천막생활을 하면서 사진촬영을 하였다. 小場恒吉, 「慶州南山の佛跡」, 『朝鮮寶物古蹟圖錄 第二: 慶州南山の佛跡』, 조선총독부, 1940; 국립경주문화재연구소, 『세계문화유산 경주 남산』(민족문화, 2002)에 재수록.

19 국립경주문화재연구소, 위의 책, pp. 270-272.

20 難波田龍起, 「美術創作家協會 六回展を前に」, 『旬刊 美術申報』, 1942. 4. 1.(20호)

21 長谷川三郞, 「前衛美術と東洋の古典」, 『みづゑ』, 1937. 12. pp. 146-157. 하세가와 사부로의 전위미술론과 고전, 동양주의와의 관련성에 대해서는 김현숙, 「김환기의 도자기 그림을 통해 본 동양주의」, 『한국근현대미술사학』, 제9집, 2001, pp. 7-40 참조.

22 『論_長谷川三朗 SABURO HASEGAWA TREATISE』, 三彩社, 1977, p. 26.

23 하세가와 사부로는 1940년 사진작업 이후 전쟁이 끝날 때까지 소품을 제외한 일체의 작품 활동을 하지 않았다. 대신 다도, 하이쿠 등의 일본전통문화에 깊이 심취했다. 1948년 이후부터는 서예, 탁본 등을 활용한 수묵추상, 서예추상 같은 동서양의 접목을 시도했다.

24 김환기, 「구하던 일 년-화단」, 『문장』, 1940. 12.

경주 불국사 대웅전 불상 ***Gyeongju Bulguksa Daewungjeon Buddha***
1941–1942년경, 젤라틴 실버 프린트 Gelatin silver print, 10.6×15.6cm

경주 탑골 석불 동면 불상 ***Gyeongju Nsmsan Tapgok Buddhist Sculpture***
1941-1942년경, 젤라틴 실버 프린트 Gelatin silver print, 10.8×15.1cm

경주 동남산 계곡 마애삼존불 ***Gyeongju Eastnamsan Maaeseokbul***
1941-1942년경, 젤라틴 실버 프린트 Gelatin silver print, 15×10.6cm

경주 산신암(産神庵) 대마애불 ***Gyeongju Westnamsan Sanshinam Daemaaebul***
1941–1942년경, 젤라틴 실버 프린트 Gelatin silver print, 15.1×10.7cm

경주 서남산 마애삼존불 ***Gyeongju Westnamsan Maaebul***
1941–1942년경, 젤라틴 실버 프린트 Gelatin silver print, 15.1×10.8cm

경주 석굴암 내부 불상 ***Gyeongju Seokguram Buddhist Sculpture***
1941–1942년경, 젤라틴 실버 프린트 Gelatin silver print, 10.7×15.2cm

경주 오릉묘(五陵墓) ***Gyeongju Oreung***
1941-1942년경, 젤라틴 실버 프린트 Gelatin silver print, 10.2×15.2cm

경주 불국사 대웅전 *Gyeongju Bulguksa Daewungjeon*
1941–1942년경, 젤라틴 실버 프린트 Gelatin silver print, 10.6×15cm

경주 분황사탑 ***Gyeongju Bunhwangsa Pagoda***
1941–1942년경, 젤라틴 실버 프린트 Gelatin silver print, 15.3×10.6cm

경주 서남산석탑 ***Gyeongju Westnamsan Pagoda***
1941–1942년경, 젤라틴 실버 프린트 Gelatin silver print, 15.3×10.6cm

경주박물관 내 귀부(龜趺) ***Turtle-Shape Base in Gyeongju Museum***
1941–1942년경, 젤라틴 실버 프린트 Gelatin silver print, 10.5×15.5cm

경주 박물관 내 사초석(寺礎石) ***Foundation Stones in Gyeongju Museum***
1941–1942년경, 젤라틴 실버 프린트 Gelatin silver print, 15.4×10.7cm

유영국의 그룹활동

오광수
미술평론가

절대조형과 자유의지

유영국의 연대기는 일반적인 작품의 변화의 내용에 따라 이루어지기보다는 작가적 의지로 결정되고 있는 또 다른 측면을 엿보게 된다. 1964년 개인전을 기점으로 이전과 이후로 나누어지는 것은 객관적인 평가에 따른 변화를 좇아 이루어진 것이 아닌, 작가의 자유의지에 의한 것임에서 그러하다. 1964년 개인전에서 만난 필자에게 자신은 지금부터 이전의 그룹활동 중심에서 벗어나 개인전 중심으로 활동을 펼치겠다고 말한 바 있다. 개인전을 계기로 이전과 이후를 분명히 구획 짓겠다는 결연한 심경을 피력한 것이었다. 자신의 세계에 대한 진로를 이토록 분명하게 의식하고 그것을 자신의 자유의지에 따라 분명히 표명한다는 것은 놀라운 일이 아닐 수 없다. 이후 그의 활동은 자신이 밝힌 것처럼 개인전 중심으로 일관되었음은 말할 나위 없다. 여러 작가가 출품하고 있는 초대전 형식은 물론 그룹전은 아니다.

그룹이란 무엇인가. 여러 작가들이 모여서 활동하는 결속이 그룹이다. 이 그룹 속에는 대단위 그룹으로서 한국미술협회같은 결속체도 있고, 이와 유사한 미술인의 권익을 전제로 한 대(對)사회적인 결속체들을 흔히 만날 수 있다. 같은 지역 출신들끼리 모이는 일종의 친목단체도 그룹이며, 같은 캠퍼스에서 같은 스승 아래서 수학한 이들끼리 모이는 화수회적인 성격의 그룹도 있다. 그러나 유영국이 말하고 있는 그룹이란 조형 이념을 공유하는 단체, 이념을 공유하기 때문에 공동체로서의 활동을 스스로 설정해가는 단체를 이름이다. 유영국은 작가로서 데뷔할 무렵부터 이미 이념적 그룹에 속한 미술 운동의 전개를 체험한 바 있다. 《독립미술협회전》과 《자유미술가협회전》의 참여가 그것이다. 자유미술가협회는 1937년에 출범한 단체로 일본의 추상미술을 대표하는 그룹이기도 하다. 그러니까 유영국이 자유미술가협회에서 최고상을 수상하고 1943년 귀국하기까지 여기에 회우로서 참여하고 있었다는 것은 일본 최초의 추상미술운동의 중심에서

활동했음을 말해주는 것과 다름없다.

1910년대에서 30년대에 이른 기간은 일본화단이 그 어느 때보다도 그룹운동이 활발히 전개될 무렵이기도 하다. 이 시기의 활발한 문예부흥은 다이쇼 데모크라시라는 시기와 겹쳐지는데, 서구의 문물이 물밀듯 쏟아져 들어왔으며 서구화와 민주화가 소리 높게 추진되고 있음을 보여주었다. 유영국이 이 시대를 배경으로 작가로서 데뷔했다는 것은 그만큼 시대적 기운을 온몸으로 수용했음을 암시하는 것이기도 하다. 그가 애초에 절대조형과 이를 추진할 수 있는 자유의지도 이 같은 시대적 분위기에 크게 영향 받았음은 말할 나위도 없다.

일본미술에 나타나는 특징 가운데 그룹을 통한 화단 형성을 들 수 있다. 개인보다는 그룹이 우선시되고 그러한 그룹들이 난립하면서 거대한 조직체로 나타나는 것이 화단이란 것이다. 현대에 와선 이런 분위기가 많이 희석되긴 했지만 지금도 그들의 미술연감을 보면 소속란이 나오고 그룹에 속하지 않은 경우 무소속으로 기술되고 있는 것으로 보아 그룹 중심의 화단 형성이란 뿌리 깊은 전통이 아직도 명맥되고 있음을 보여주고 있다. 아마도 이 같은 현상은 비단 미술계에만 적용되는 것이 아니고 저들 특유의 민족적 성향이 아닌가 생각된다. 개별은 약하지만, 결집에 의한 힘은 어떤 민족보다도 강한 것으로 알려져 있다. 이 점은 우리와 퍽 대조적이지 않을 수 없다. 개인은 뛰어나지만, 단결은 제대로 되지 않는다는 것이 우리의 약점인 것을 감안하면 말이다.

10년대에서 30년대에 이르기까지 등장한 그룹운동은 일련의 모더니즘 운동이었다. 서구에서 일어난 새로운 이즘을 받아들이고 성숙시키기에는 이념 운동이 따르지 않으면 안 되었을 것이다. 이념의 지향에 있어선 이합집산의 진통이 따를 수밖에 없다. 그로 인해 결속체는 더욱 단단한 내연을 가질 수 있었으며 운동은 더욱 동력이 붙기 마련이다. 유영국 데뷔기의 그룹활동은 그 자신으로 하여금 투철한 이념형을 만든 것이었다고 해도 과언이 아니다. 그가 그토록 그룹운동에 집착한 것도 그만큼 변화의 촉진과 진행의 활기는 결속에 의해서 가능하다는 사실을 체험했기 때문이다. 물론 이 같은 자유로운 분위기가 급속한 모더니즘 운동을 지탱시켜준 것이 되었다. 40년대에 들어서면서 급속히 냉각되어지는 반전의 국면을 맞게 되기는 했으나 적어도 30년대 후반까지 지속되어 그 나름의 영향을 주었던 것은 사실이다. 유영국의 절대조형으로 향하는 대담한 도전과 이를 뒷받침하는 자유의지는 이 같은 시대적 분위기에 크게 영향을 받았음은 결코 간과할 수 없다.

유영국이 60년대 초까지 이 같은 그룹운동이 갖는 변화의 촉진을 확신하고 있

었다. 국전이란 보수적인 아성이 군림하고 있었던 시대, 이 성채를 무너뜨릴 수 있는 것은 모더니즘 운동의 추진이지 않으면 안 된다는 사실을 자각하고 있었기 때문이다. 이를 자각하고 있었다는 것 자체가 어쩌면 근대인으로서의 그의 면모를 조명케 하는 이유이기도 하다. 이인범은 이를 두고 다음과 같이 기술하고 있다,

"신분질서가 엄존하던 때에 화가, 어부, 교수, 양조업자 등 종횡으로 넘나들던 직업 편력이나 어떤 일에 종사하든 그가 이루고자 했던 세계를 향한 신념과 자율적이고 주체적인 태도에서 화가 유영국은 근대적 의미의 자유인 그 자체였다."

이인범은 폭넓은 의미에서 근대인으로 규정하지만 나는 조형세계란 좁은 영역에서 그가 보여주었던 자유의지에서 근대인으로서의 모습을 읽을 수 있었다.

신사실파의 결성: 해방공간 미술그룹

1943년에 귀국한 유영국은 1945년 해방과 미군정하의 해방공간에서는 아직 고향 울진에 머무르고 있었다. 앞선 이인범이 말한 것처럼 어부로서의 생활을 영위하고 있었다. 그가 김환기의 권유로 상경하기까지는 화가로서의 작업은 휴업상태였던 것이다. 그는 언젠가 이런 말을 하였다. 만약 일제가 망하지 않았더라면 자신은 영영 화가로의 길에 다시 들어설 수 없었을 것이라고. 이 같은 절박한 심정은 일본이나 한국을 통틀어 모더니즘 운동에 참여하였던 모든 미술가들에게 해당되는 것이었을 것이다. 일본의 대표적인 추상화가 사이토 요시시게(齋藤義重)가 붓을 꺾고 행상의 길에 들어서 종전을 맞은 것이나 유영국이 고깃배를 타면서 해방을 맞은 것은 서로 닮아 있다. 이들은 군국주의가 계속 득세하였다면 화가의 길로는 영영 돌아오지 못했을 것이다.

해방 후 유영국의 상경은 1947년 서울대학교 예술학부 미술과가 생기면서 교수로 초빙된 것이다. 서울에서의 생활이 시작되면서 동시에 작가 활동이 재개되었다. 그의 작가로서의 활동의 재개도 그룹활동으로 바로 이어진다. 신사실파 결성이 바로 그것이다. 그룹의 동인은 김환기, 이규상과 유영국 3인이었다. 이들은 1930년대 후반 일본에서의 자유미술가협회에 참여했던 작가들로, 추상을 지향한 우리나라 최초의 모더니스트들이었다. 1947년에 결성되고 이듬해인 1948년에 1회전이 열렸으니까 유영국의 상경과 더불어 그룹이 출범한 셈이다. 그런데 창립 당시에도 그 명칭에 대한 논란이 없지 않았으나 이후 미술사 논의에 있어 빈번히 문제가 제기되고 있는 편이다. 신사실이란 명칭은 김환기의 제안이었다는 설은 전해지고 있으나 정작 왜 신사실인지에 대해서는 그 언급을 찾을 수 없다. 1회전을 리뷰한 김용

준에 의하면, "신사실파는 동인 삼인 중 이규상, 유영국 양씨는 순수미술의 종기(말기)를 답습하는 정도로 사실주의에서 찾는 객관성이 전혀 결여되어 신사실과는 너무 유리되었으며, 김환기 씨만 새로운 시야에서 대상의 미를 감각하려는 노력이 엿보였다"[1] 라고 언급하고 있다. 여기에 따르면 3인 중 김환기만이 신사실에 해당되는 대상의 새로운 탐구를 보일 뿐 이규상과 유영국은 30년대 후반에 추구하였던 추상주의 영역에서 벗어나지 못하고 있다는 지적이다. 대체로 새로운 그룹의 결성에 있어선 나름의 이념표방으로서 매니페스토(Manifesto)가 있기 마련인데 전혀 그런 것이 없다는 점으로 미루어 본다면, 3인이 동의하는 이념적 체계가 미처 마련되지 못한 상황에서 출범부터 서두른 것은 아닌지 하는 의문이 제기된다. 삼인의 처지는 다르지만 해방 전후의 상황으로 보아선 제대로 작업을 할 수 없는 처지였음은 부정할 수 없다. 다만 김환기만 다소 여유가 있었지 않았나 싶다. 1회전의 작품은 김환기의 몇 작품 외에는 전하고 있지 않다. 작가의 이름과 작품의 명제만이 가까스로 기재된 리플릿에 의하면 유영국과 이규상의 작품은 〈회화〉 아니면 〈작품〉으로 일관되고 있다. 김환기의 명제가 구체적인 대상을 지니고 있는 것과는 대조를 이루고 있다.

주의 주장에 의한 언술이 없다고 하더라도 작품으로서 충분히 표명할 수 있다. 그러나 작품이 없고 보니 김용준이 지적한 바에 따르지 않을 수 없다. 신사실에 대한 개념은 김환기의 작품에서만 엿볼 수 있을 뿐 이규상이나 유영국은 여전히 자유전의 연장에서 벗어나지 못한다는 것으로서 말이다. 그러나 김용준의 사실에 대한 이해도 다분히 고식적인 일면이 없지 않다. 사실을 자연주의적 입장에서만 가능한 것으로 보는 고정관념 말이다. 우리가 받아들이고 있는 서구의 새로운 사조에 대한 해석은 때로 지나치게 외피적인 것에 머물고 있는 경우가 있는데, 사실이란 개념도 그중의 하나로 볼 수 있다. 19세기 쿠르베가 주창한 리얼리즘은 자연 대상보다는 오히려 당대적 진실이란 상황에 그 무게가 주어지고 있다는 사실에서 말이다. 그러니까 좀 더 사안에 밀접한 번역이란 사실주의라기보다는 현실주의라 했어야 하지 않았을까. 또한 신사실파란 명칭도 신현실파라고 해야 정확하지 않을까.

이 점에 대해서 나는 유영국을 논하는 자리에서 이렇게 피력한 바 있다. 다소 장황하지만 여기에 인용해본다.

"세 사람의 동인 가운데 이규상, 유영국이 〈회화〉와 〈작품〉으로 일관하고 있는 점에 대조적으로 김환기는 〈꽃가게〉, 〈실과 장수〉, 〈달밤〉과 같은 구체적인 자연 모티브를 보이고 있다. 이규상, 유영국이 동경시대의 작품의 맥락에 그대로 연계되

는 반면, 김환기는 전전의 추상경향과는 완전히 동떨어진 자연 모티브를 지향한 것이다. 김용준의 비평의 요지는 신사실이라 표명된 이념에 두 사람은 전혀 상응되고 있지 못한 만큼 김환기는 새로운 시야에서 대상의 미를 추구하고 있어 이념표방에 가장 밀착되고 있다는 것이다. (중략) 김환기의 명제들로 미루어본다면 김용준의 지적처럼 새로운 시야에서 대상을 바라보는 리얼리즘에 연계되어 있음이 분명하다. 그런데 일반적 리얼리즘 즉 자연주의는 아님이 그의 일부 작품을 통해서 확인된다. 대상은 엄연히 자연에서 취재된 것임이 분명함에도 일반적 리얼리즘의 방법과는 일정한 거리를 두고 있다. 여기에 그의 신사실의 개념의 요체를 어느 정도 파악할 수 있을 듯하다. 현실적 모티브이기는 하지만 그것이 객관적 표출에 기반한 자연주의는 아닌, 당면한 시대정신에 부응한 현실감각으로서의 자연의 회기라고 할 수 있는 것이다. 당연히 시대정신이란 조선미술건설본부에서 이미 천명한 바 있으며 해방공간을 통해 줄곧 논의의 중심을 이끌어왔던 왜색탈피와 민족미술의 건설임에 다름이 없다. 구태를 벗어나 새로운 시대에 부응하는 민족미술의 확립이란 새나라 건설과 연결되는 것이었다."[2]

신사실에 대한 논의는 3인의 추상미술가들이 참여하고 있다는 사실의 중대성에 힘입어 아직도 심심찮게 이어지고 있는 편이다. 70년대에 이일이 밝힌 견해도 논의 가운데 하나로 볼 수 있다. 그는 이렇게 기술하고 있다.

"요즈음 나로서는 뉴 리얼리즘 또는 누보 레알리즘(모두 신사실주의 내지는 신현실주의를 의미한다)이라는 것과 전혀 별개의 것이라는 것만은 틀림이 없을 것 같다. 오히려 그것은 자연에 대한 새로운 비전의 제시, 새로운 방법론의 제시를 뜻하는 것이 아니었나 추측된다."[3]

뉴 리얼리즘이나 누보 레알리즘이란 경향이 60년대에 들어와 등장하고 있음을 고려할 때 이 명칭 개념과 신사실파를 직접 연계시킨다는 것은 무리이나, 자연주의를 내포한 사실은 아니란 점에선 또 하나의 해석임이 분명하다. 어쨌거나 신사실파와 해방공간이란 시대적 현장과는 떼어놓을 수 없는 관계라는 점에서 더욱 주도한 추구가 요청된다.

50년미술협회: 실현되지 못한 도전

삼인에 의한 공통된 신사실의 개념을 추출해 내기는 어려웠을 것이다. 통념적인 자연으로서의 사실이란 개념을 넘어선, 새로운 현실 상황에 바탕을 둔 진실의 추구란 자칫 관념으로 빠질 수 있다. 이들은 무언가 시대가 요구하는 진실을 어떻

게 조형을 통해 구현해낼 수 있을까를 나름으로 고민했을 것이 분명하다. 이규상, 유영국이 절대한 조형의 방법 속에서 시대의 진실을 어떻게 구현해낼까를 고민한 반면, 김환기는 구체적인 현실 속에서 당대의 진실, 그리고 민족미술의 유형을 어떻게 모색할 것인가를 고민한 흔적이 역력하다. 이인범의 다음 언급에서도 이 점을 엿볼 수 있다.

"김환기가 대상적인 회화와 비대상적인 회화를 오가며 조형주의적이고 구성주의적인 태도를 드러내는 반면, 유영국의 경우는 오히려 해체적이며 구축적인 성격을 여러 작품에서 보여주고 있다."[4]

두 작가의 시도는 그들이 출발에서 시도했던 방법의 연장임을 헤아려보게 한다. 김환기가 비구상(자연에서 출발하면서 점진적으로 추상에 이르는)의 경향인 반면 유영국은 추상(이미 완성된 절대추상에서 출발하는)의 경향이었다는 점에서 이후의 방법적 전개를 유추해보게 한다. 김환기가 비교적 자연스럽게 자연적 이미지를 원용할 수 있었던 것은 그가 애초에 자연에서 출발하면서 형태를 요약해가는 추상의 길을 걸었기 때문에 가능한 것이었다면, 유영국은 도형중심의 구성주의에서 출발하기 때문에 자연을 끌어들인다는 것이 그만큼 어려운 일이었다는 점이다. 이인범이 지적하고 있듯이 그가 자연적 이미지를 원용하기 위해선 형태의 해체와 이를 다시금 종합하는 방법에 의하지 않을 수 없었을 것이다. 부산 피난시절에 열렸던 제3회《신사실파 부산전》에 출품된 것으로 유추되는 몇 작품 속에서 이 같은 단면을 확인할 수 있다. 그리고 신사실파가 자동 해체된 이후 50년대 후반의 작품 속에서 두 작가의 대비적인 경향이 두드러지게 나타나고 있다. 김환기는 극도로 제약된 형태 속에 그가 추구하려고 하는 한국적인 정서의 세계를 양식화할 수 있었다면, 유영국은 형태의 환원 속에서 자연의 본질을 찾으려고 한 흔적이 극명하게 드러나고 있기 때문이다. 그러니까 김환기가 자연 속에서 요약된 형태를 만들어간 반면, 유영국은 구성적인 도형 속에서 자연의 원형을 발견하려고 한 것이다. 그러니까 도형으로서의 삼각형은 절대적인 형태이자 동시에 산의 원형이 되는 것이다.

유영국은 신사실파에 속해 있으면서도 1950년에 결성된 50년미술협회에 가담하고 있다. 이는 본격적인 미술운동으로서 그룹활동이 절실했기 때문으로 본다. 50년미술협회는 해방공간을 통해 노정되었던 정치적 이데올로기에 편승된 미술가들의 이합집산에 환멸을 느낀 일부 중견작가들이 참다운 창작활동을 펼칠 것을 다짐하면서 출범한 순수한 조형단체였다. 여기에 참여하고 있는 작가는 김환기, 최재덕, 이쾌대, 장욱진, 유영국, 남관, 김만형, 김병기, 진환, 김영주, 이봉상, 류경채, 김

종하, 이건영, 박고석, 윤자선, 박상옥, 문신, 이세득이었으며 최고위원은 남관이, 협회 준비위원으로는 김환기, 유영국, 장욱진, 남관, 김병기, 김영주, 이봉상이 추대되고 있다. 면면들을 보면 당대 우리나라 미술을 대표하는 중견작가들의 결성체임이 분명하다.

그런데 당시 서울대 미대 학장이었던 장발로부터 협회 탈퇴의 종용을 받고 유영국은 서울대 미대 교수직을 그만 두게 된다. "그때 50년미술협회란 걸 했어요. 좌익, 우익 할 것 없이 우리 모두 같은 세대로 한국 화단의 중심이 되자는 취지에서 만들어진 건데, 장발 씨는 좌익에 노이로제가 걸린 사람이었어요. 언젠가 이 전시를 경복궁에서 하기로 했는데 그 전에 서울대 미대 교내전이 있었어요, 이 전시 때문에 문제가 생겨서 사표를 쓰고 나왔습니다"라고 유영국은 당시를 회고한 적이 있다. 50년미술협회의 구성을 보니까 상당수가 좌익활동을 했던 작가들로 서울대 교수가 이들과 행동을 같이 한다는 것이 바람직하지 않다는 장발의 견해였다.

그러나 의욕적으로 출범한 50년미술협회은 그해 일어난 동란으로 인해 자동 해체되는 운명을 맞는다. 여기에 가담하였던 작가들이 먼 후일에까지 아쉬움을 말하는 것을 보아 당시 이 그룹에 거는 미술계의 기대가 어떠했는가를 헤아려보게 한다.

모던 아트협회와 현대작가초대전: 현대미술운동의 정점

유영국의 그룹활동은 1957년에 와서 재개된다. 1957년에 출범한 모던 아트협회에 가담한 것이다. 신사실파의 동인이었던 유영국과 이규상을 비롯해 박고석, 한묵, 황염수가 1956년경부터 모이기 시작하면서 1957년에 결실을 본 것이다. 1957년은 모던 아트협회 외에도 신조형파, 창작미술가협회, 백양회, 현대미술가협회 등 다섯 개의 단체가 출범한 해였다. 한 시기에 이렇듯 많은 그룹이 출범했다는 사실 자체도 주목을 끌기에 충분한 것이었지만 각기 조형이념을 표방했다는 점에서 비로소 이념에 의한 화단형성이 이루어질 수 있다는 기대도 만만치 않았다. 흔히 1957년을 우리미술의 현대적 기점으로 설정하려는 논의도 이에 기인한 것이다. "이념의 빈곤과 일부의 몰지각한 세력다툼 및 섹트주의로 말미암아 부조리의 현실을 구축"하려는 현상에 다름 없었기 때문이다. 김영주는 당시 그룹운동의 절실함을 다음과 같이 간명하게 기술하고 있다.

"그룹운동이란 첫째로는 화단이란 막연한 광장에 사조를 이룩할 수 있는 과제를, 둘째로는 미술문화의 경향과 작가 자신의 방법을 반성, 혁신시킬 수 있는 과제를, 셋째로는 조형예술의 영역과 시대사회의 관계를 분명히 마련할 수 있는 과제를

안고 있다"[5]라고 전제하고 모던 아트협회는 이 과제를 저항의 자세에서, 현대미술가협회는 비합리의 정열의 자세에서 밝혀 나가야 한다고 주문하고 있다. 김영주는 기성의 중견작가 그룹으로서 모던 아트협회와 신진작가 그룹으로서 현대미술가협회에 그룹운동의 과제를 실현시킬 수 있는 책무를 부과한 셈이다.

그럼에도 불구하고 이들 그룹이 당대의 절실한 과제를 실천하기엔 그 나름의 문제가 있다는 것도 직시하고 있다. 모던 아트협회의 구성요건이 그룹운동의 주자로서의 역할에는 다소의 의문점을 갖지 않을 수 없다는 것이다.

"모던 아트는 이름 그대로 전위적인 미술형식과 조형의 영역이다. 현대라는 막연한 언어보다도 금일이라는 절실한 시추에이션과 인간의 조건을 반영하며 분석하고 표현해야 하는 것이 모던 아트의 본질인 것이다. 그렇다면 이번 제1회전에 출품한 작품의 일부까지도 전위적인 미술형식과 조형의 영역인 모던 아트로서 규정할 수 있겠는가 하는 문제가 대두하게 된다. 유영국, 이규상 씨의 추상적이며 비구상적인 회화의 장르와 한묵 씨의 반추상적인 레알리자숑을 빼놓고는 박고석, 황염수 씨의 경향은 낡은 형식에 속하는 방법이다."[6]

모던 아트란 개념을 어느 선까지로 볼 것이냐는 관점에 따라 후기인상파 이후 추상미술에 이르는 과정 전체를 모던 아트로 포괄할 것인가 아니면 전후 추상미술로 국한한 전위적 경향만으로 제한할 것인가가 논의될 수 있겠는데, 김영주는 전후 추상으로 모던 아트를 제한하고 있다. 모던 아트 그룹의 개개인을 본다면 개성이 뚜렷한 작가들임엔 이의가 없다. 그러나 그룹운동으로서의 결속의 조건엔 맞지 않는다는 것이 김영주의 주장이다. 다음과 같은 주문에 전혀 상응하지 못하고 있음을 보여주고 있는 것이다. "그룹은 서로서로 그 행동이념에 책임을 져야하며 … 화단의 올바른 형성의 계기가 될 수 있는 역량을 갖추지 않으면 안된다"[7]라는 것이 김영주의 그룹운동의 조건이다. 몇 차례의 전시를 거친 후 1959년에 그룹을 정비해보면 이규상, 유영국이 탈퇴하고 새롭게 김경, 정점식, 정규, 문신, 천경자가 가담하고 있다. 이왕의 황염수, 한묵, 박고석과 더불어 회원은 증가하였으나 여전히 이념표방에 있어선 확고한 태도를 보이고 있지 않은 편이다. 이렇게 되면 그룹운동으로선 명분을 갖추지 못하고 단순한 친목단체로 명맥될 뿐이다.

그룹의 진로가 불분명한 상태에서도《모던 아트협회전》에서 가장 주목을 받은 것은 유영국이었다. 아마도 모던 아트협회 시절과 이어지는《현대작가초대전》시절, 그러니까 1957년에서 1962년에 이른 시기야말로 유영국의 작가로서의 면모는 어느 절정에 이른 인상을 준다. 그룹운동에 대한 열정도 놓지 않는 가운데 자신

에로 향한 탐구의 열정은 그 비유를 찾을 수 없게 하고 있다. 이봉상은 제1회《모던아트협회전》에 출품된 유영국의 작품을 두고 다음과 같이 피력해주었는데 이 같은 평가는 한 작가로서의 견고한 자기세계를 이룩한 결실에 대한 감동으로 읽혀지게 하고 있다.

"타협 없는 전진을 꾀하는 작가로서 인상 깊은 유영국 씨의 작품을 대하였을 때 그의 일관된 표현의식에 부러움을 금치 못하였고, 그중에서도 특히 필자에게 충동을 준 것은 〈산맥〉, 〈호수〉, 〈새〉, 〈생선〉을 들 수 있다. 여기서는 구상을 재인식함으로써 이루어지는 조심스러운 순결화한 형태미를 가져와 씨의 과거에서의 한 개의 점화를 보여주는 것 같다."[8]

여기에서 초기의 절대추상에서 벗어나 보다 자유스러운 형태의 본질을 천착하려는 의도를 지적하고 있으며 여러 평자들 역시 이 점을 지적하고 있다. 〈계곡〉, 〈노을〉, 〈산〉, 〈해변〉 등의 명제만 보아도 자연 이미지를 충분히 환기시킨다. 그렇다고 그의 작업이 구체적인 산이나 명시적인 해안으로 나타난 것은 아니다. 그는 결코 초기의 절대적 조형에 대한 신념을 포기하지 않았다. 변화라면 이 절대한 조형 속에 자연적 이미지를 굴절시켰을 뿐이다. 그래서 그것은 단순한 도형의 삼각형이 되기도 하고 산으로 유추되는 환원의 형상이 되기도 한다. 추상적 도형으로서 삼각형이라고 하면 삼각형이고 산의 이미지를 함축한 삼각형이라고 하면 산을 연상시키는 삼각형이 될 뿐이다. 자연을 연상시키면서도 결코 자연에 예속될 수 없는 것은 조형의 진실 속에서만 자신을 가누기 때문이다. 이를 두고 이일은 다음과 같이 말하고 있다,

"그 단순하면서도 긴장감이 감도는 구성, 일체의 너스레한 시각적 효과를 거부한 밀도 짙은 면과 면의 대비 … 이른바 순수 조형적 시도에서 우리는 유영국의 놀라운 선각적인 조형의식을 목격하게 되는 것이다."[9]

그룹은 아니지만 그가 참여하였던《현대작가초대전》(그가 김영주와 더불어 이 전시를 이끌어 나갔다)은 현대미술운동에 핵심적 역할을 했다는 점에서 평가되고 있다. 어쩌면 그는 이를 정점으로 자신의 그룹운동을 정리한 것인지도 모른다. 1962년도의 신상회 창립에 가담하고 있으나 이 땅에서의 그룹활동은 사실상 마감되었다고 스스로 확인했음이 분명하다. 1964년 개인전을 열면서 지금부터는 개인전에 의한 자기세계의 모색기가 될 것이라고 분명히 밝힌 내면에는 이 같은 배경이 있음을 간과할 수 없다.

1 김용준 , 「신 경향의 정신」, 「서울신문」,1948. 12. 29.
2 오광수, 『유영국, 삶과 창조의 지평』, 마로니에북스, 2012, p. 75.
3 이일, 「조형과 자연의 변증법 - 유영국」, 『계간미술』, 1978. 겨울
4 이인범, 「자유정신과 자연을 향한 '랩소디'」, 『유영국 1916-2002』, 마로니에북스, 2012, p. 274
5 김영주, 「신감각의 집단」, 「조선일보」,1957. 5. 31.
6 김영주, 위의 글
7 김영주, 「반발과 저항의 자세」, 「평화신문」, 1957. 4. 16.
8 이봉상, 「하나의 방향설정」, 「조선일보」, 1957. 4. 13.
9 이일, 위의 글

인간은 과거에는 자연의 아름다움만을 그리고 묘사했던 반면,
이제 새로운 정신을 통해 스스로 아름다움을 창조한다.
이러한 새로운 아름다움은 새로운 인간에게는 필수불가결하며,
그 안에서 인간은 자연과의 등가적인 대립으로써 자신의 이미지를
표현한다. 새로운 예술이 탄생한 것이다.

- 몬드리안, 「신조형주의: 조형적 등가가치의 일반이론」 중에서, 1920

직선이 있는 구도 *Composition*
1949, 캔버스에 유채 Oil on canvas, 53×45.5cm

작품 *Work*
1953, 캔버스에 유채 Oil on canvas, 65×50cm

작품 *Work*
1953, 캔버스에 유채 Oil on canvas, 65×52cm

바다에서 *On the Sea*
1957, 캔버스에 유채 Oil on canvas, 130×97cm

작품 *Work*
1957, 캔버스에 유채 Oil on canvas, 101×101cm

산 *Mountain*
1957, 캔버스에 유채 Oil on canvas, 100×81cm

사람 *A Man*
1957, 캔버스에 유채 Oil on canvas, 59×48cm

바다에서 *On the Sea*
1957, 캔버스에 유채 Oil on canvas, 61×53cm

작품 *Work*
1957, 캔버스에 유채 Oil on canvas, 100×100cm

산 *Mountain*
1957, 캔버스에 유채 Oil on canvas, 97×130cm

작품 *Work*
1957, 캔버스에 유채 Oil on canvas, 73×100cm

작품 *Work*
1958, 캔버스에 유채 Oil on canvas, 102×130cm

작품 *Work*
1958, 캔버스에 유채 Oil on canvas, 102×102cm

새 *Bird*

1958, 캔버스에 유채 Oil on canvas, 100×73cm

아침 *Morning*
1958, 캔버스에 유채 Oil on canvas, 100×73cm

계곡 *Valley*
1958, 캔버스에 유채 Oil on canvas, 162×130cm

바다풀 *Sea Plant*
1959, 캔버스에 유채 Oil on canvas, 130.2×96.1cm

산(흙) ***Mountain****(Soil)*
1959, 캔버스에 유채 Oil on canvas, 130.6×194cm

산(지형) ***Mountain****(Topography)*
1959, 캔버스에 유채, Oil on canvas, 130.8×193cm

작품 *Work*

1959, 캔버스에 유채 Oil on canvas, 130×102cm

작품 *Work*
1960, 캔버스에 유채 Oil on canvas, 162×130cm

산 *Mountain*
1960, 캔버스에 유채 Oil on canvas, 100×100cm

작품 *Work*
1961-2, 캔버스에 유채 Oil on canvas, 161×129cm

산 *Mountain*

1960, 캔버스에 유채 Oil on canvas, 136×211cm

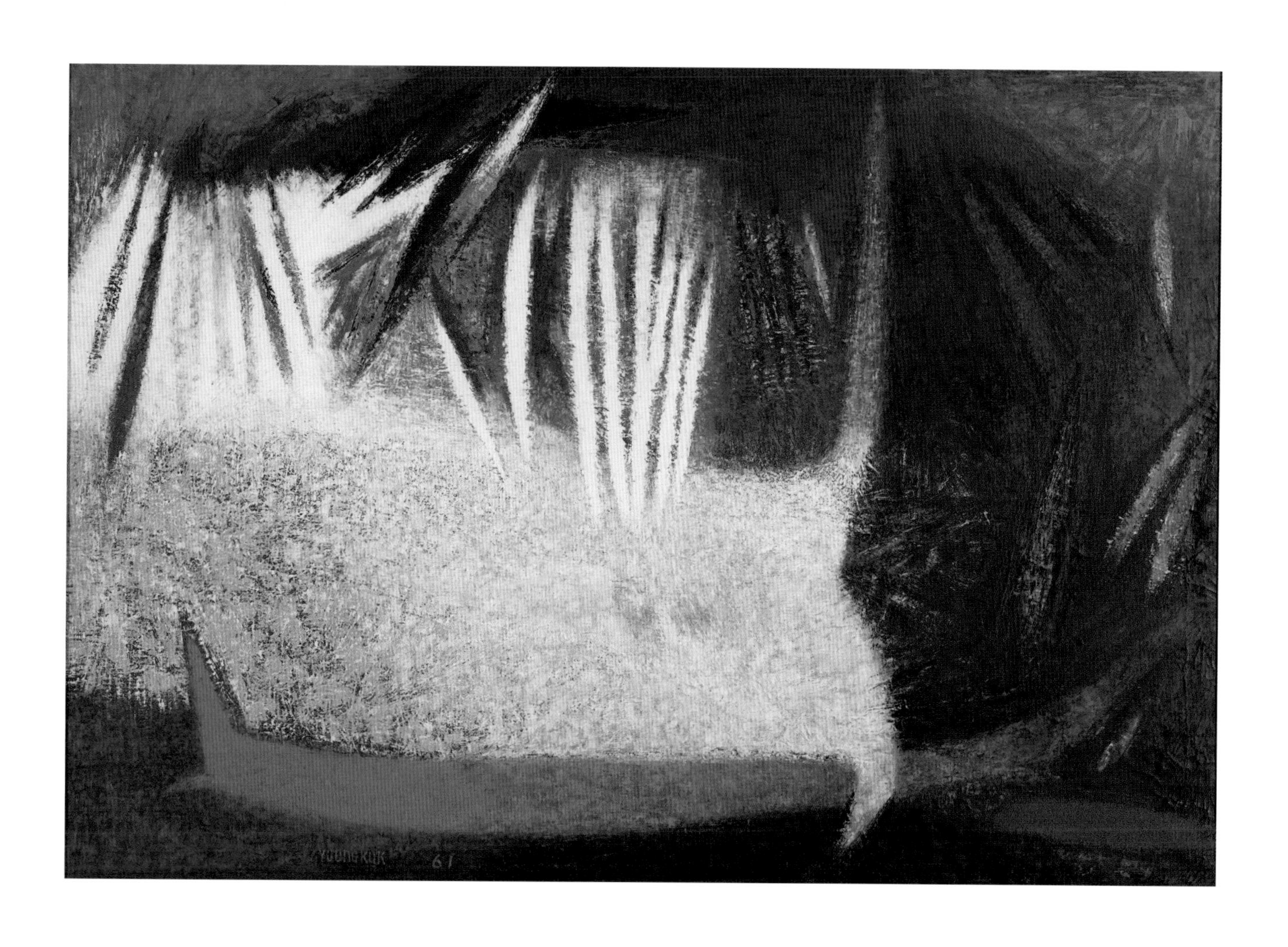

산 *Mountain*
1961, 캔버스에 유채 Oil on canvas, 136×194cm

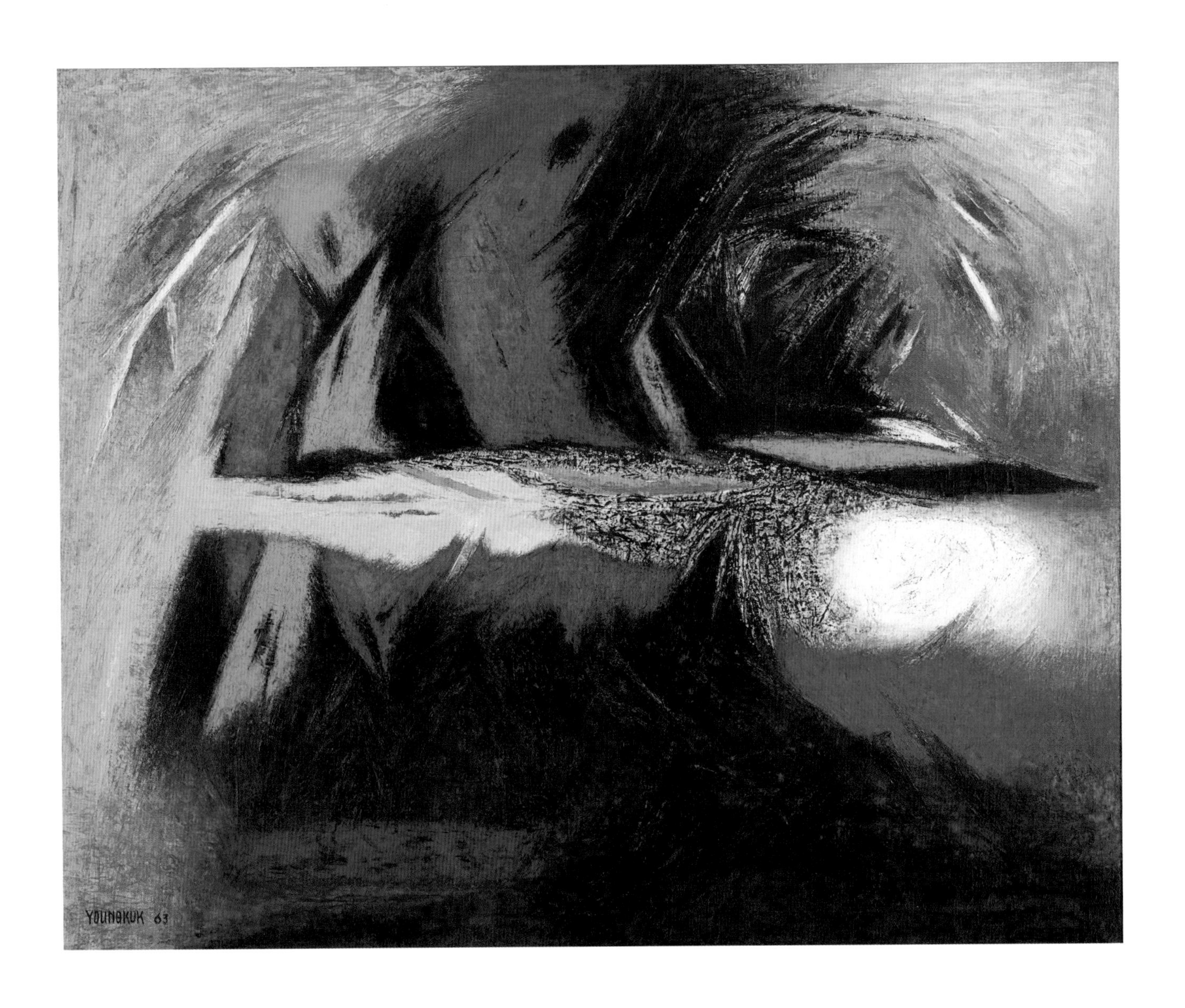

작품 *Work*
1963, 캔버스에 유채 Oil on canvas, 130×162cm

산 ***Mountain***
1962, 캔버스에 유채 Oil on canvas, 130×194cm

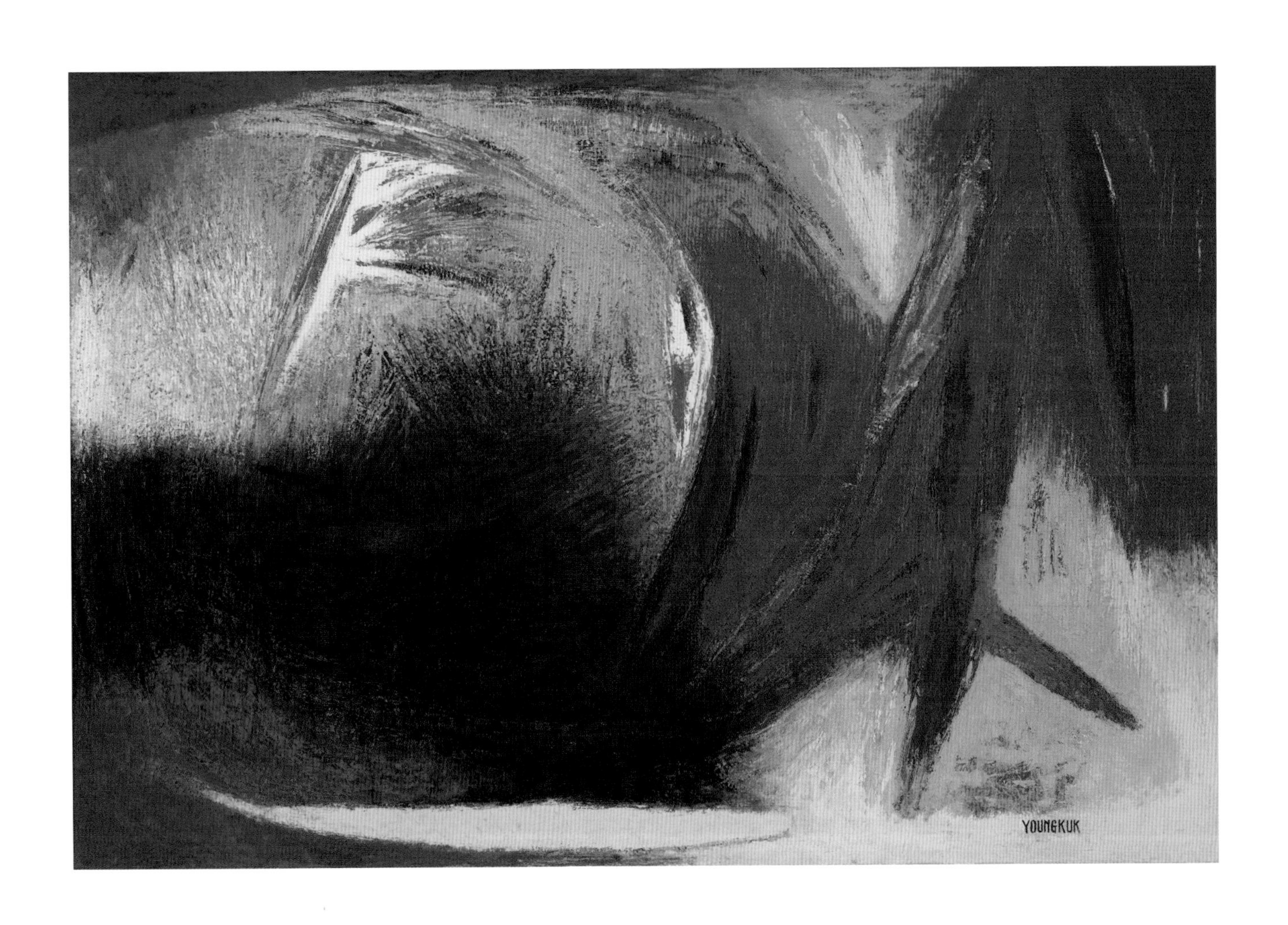

작품 *Work*
1962, 캔버스에 유채 Oil on canvas, 130×194cm

해토(解土) ***Thawing of the Ground***
1961, 캔버스에 유채 Oil on canvas, 130×162cm

추상과 황홀: 유영국의 1964년 이후

이인범

상명대학교 교수

'한국 추상미술의 거목', 유영국(劉永國, 1916-2002). 그는 1916년 강원도 울진에서 태어나 2002년 87세 되던 해 11월 11일에 서울대병원에서 지병인 심장병으로 세상을 떠났다. 유영국이 예술의 경이로움에 눈을 뜨기 시작한 것은 경성제2고보(현 경복고교) 재학시절 자유주의자인 미술교사 사토 쿠니오를 만나 미술부에 드나들면서이다. 그리고 본격적으로 예술세계에 발을 들인 것은 제2고보를 도중에 자퇴하고 도쿄 문화학원(文化學院) 유화과에 입학하는 1935년 봄이다. 그로부터 2년이 경과한 1937년 초봄, 제7회《독립미술협회전》[1](3. 13–4. 4, 도쿄부립미술관)에 초현실주의적이면서도 구축주의적인 경향의 유화 작품 〈랩소디〉[2](p. 37, 엽서)와 곧 이어 제1회《자유미술가협회전》(7. 10–19, 도쿄 우에노·일본미술협회)에 초현실주의적인 경향의 〈작품 B〉(p. 49)를 출품하여 입선하면서 화단에 데뷔하고 있다. 그리고 1999년 제21회《예술원미술전》(10. 11-31, 서울·예술원미술관)에 출품한 〈작품〉(p. 209, 1999, 캔버스에 유채, 105×105cm)를 끝으로 활동을 마감하고 있다.

유영국의 생애를 가로지르는 화두는 한 마디로 추상(抽象, abstraction)이다. 군국주의로 치닫던 1930년대 후반, 예술에 입문하며 그가 지향점으로 삼은 것은 절대적이고도 구축주의적인 추상이다. 눈에 보이는 그 어느 것에도 마음을 실을 수 없던 암울했던 일제 강점기에 그가 새로운 세계를 꿈꾸는 방식은 구축이다. 그런데 해방 후 그는 자신이 몸담고 있는 자연과 삶의 세계에 감정을 이입하며 이 땅과 대지를 노래하는 일에 착수하고 있다. 그런 점에서 억압으로부터의 해방을 국가공동체 구성원의 한 사람으로서 그가 얼마나 환희에 차 있는지, 그에 따라 예술 의욕이 어떻게 꿈틀거렸을지 짐작하게 한다. 이후 그의 회화적 관심은 한반도의 자연을 벗어난 적이 없다. 그것도 겉모습의 재현이 아니라 줄곧 그 근원적 추상을 향하면서 말이다.

20세기 서구 조형 혁명의 총아로 일컬어지는 추상미술

은 어느덧 이질적인 문화적 기억을 지닌 대한민국의 한 시대를 대표하는 고유한 예술양식으로 자리 잡게 되는데, 그것은 누가 뭐래도 그에게 크게 신세지고 있다. 지난 세기의 온갖 격동을 거스르며 전개된 유영국의 활동 편력은 크게 3시기로 나눌 수 있다. 첫 번째 시기는 1935년부터 1943년까지로 일본에 유학하던 청년기이다. 이 시기에 그는 전위적이고 실험적으로 자신의 예술관을 모색하며 구축주의적인 릴리프, 회화, 사진 작업을 실천하고 있다. 태평양 전쟁 발발로 고향 울진으로 돌아온 후 약 5년 동안 어업 등 생업에 종사하는데, 두 번째 시기는 그로부터 상경하여 1948년 신사실파 창립부터 그룹을 중심으로 모던아트 운동을 전개한 1964년까지의 시기이다. 이 기간 동안 그는 식민지 시대에 틀 지워진 대한민국 미술계의 구조를 혁신하는 일과 더불어 식민 서사에 찌든 재현 미학에 대항하며 자신의 추상 이념을 실천하고 있다. 마지막은 1964년 말 첫 개인전을 기점으로 작고할 때까지 원숙기로 그동안의 그룹전들을 접고 개인전을 통해 작품세계에 두께와 깊이를 천착하고 있다.

이 글은 유영국 생애의 마지막 시기, 즉 후기에 관한 에세이이다. 특히 1960년대 중반 지천명의 나이에 일어난 입장 전환, 즉 그룹운동을 접고 개인전을 통해 노년에 펼친 그의 삶과 작품세계를 조명한다.

해방 후 펼쳐진 유영국의 작품 활동에서 중대한 전환은 1960년대 중반 무렵에 일어나고 있다. 그는 신사실파를 시작으로 그때까지 작품 활동의 거점으로 삼던 일련의 동인 그룹이나 공적영역에서의 집단 활동들로부터 선을 그으며, 1964년 초겨울에 연 첫 개인전(1964. 11. 14 – 19, 신문회관)을 기점으로 자신의 작업 방법을 바꾸고 있다. 어느덧 나이 50세를 눈앞에 두고 있었으며, 화단 데뷔로부터는 27년째 되던 해의 일이다. 태평양전쟁, 한국전쟁 같은 전쟁들로 화가로서 '잃어버린 10년'[3]을 보내고 난 뒤 서울로 돌아와 다시 작품 활동을 재개한 1955년 늦봄으로부터는 10년째 되던 해이기도 하다. 그러니까 도쿄에서 8년 남짓 예술 이념을 정립하고 난 뒤 그가 공백을 딛고 다시 화가로서 한국 미술계에서 재기하여 모던 아트운동을 추동시킨 핵심적인 인물로 우뚝 서게 된 시점이었다. 함께 활동하던 대부분의 동료 작가들이 너나 할 것 없이 도불전이니 귀국전이니 하는 이름으로 개인전들을 여러 차례 개최하고 났던 터이니, 누구보다도 왕성하게 활동했던 화가로서 연 개인전 치고는 꽤나게 늦은 일이었다.

그런데 이후 작고할 때까지 유영국은 무려 15차례에 이르는 개인전을 스스로 개최하거나 초대받으며 자신의 작품이 안고 있는 과제들에 비로소 정면으로 마주

하고 있다. 그런 점에서 늦깎이로 연 유영국의 첫 개인전은 작가 자신에게나 한국 현대미술사의 전개에서 매우 각별한 의미를 지닌다. 어떠한 운동적 성격의 예술공동체로부터도 홀연히 떠나며 열고 있다는 점에서 이 첫 개인전은 화가 유영국에겐 그 자체가 전향 선언에 가까운 일이지만, 동시에 현대 한국미술 운동사에서 국면이 새롭게 전환되는 하나의 사건으로 볼 만하다.

모던아트운동에서 예술 내부로

유영국이 그룹 활동을 떠나는 배경은 어떤 것일까? 그것은 그의 예술이나 우리 미술사의 전개에서 어떤 의미를 지니는 것일까? 그리고 이를 통해 어떠한 변화가 일어나고 있을까?

유영국의 후기 예술세계에 들어가는 문 앞에서 먼저 당시까지 유영국의 예술 활동에서 그룹이 얼마나 절실한 핵심적 거점 노릇을 했는지 살펴보도록 하자. 데뷔 이래 그가 가지고 있던 비전이나 문제의식은 그룹운동과 떼려야 뗄 수 없으니 말이다. 파시즘의 광기로 넘치는 나찌의《퇴폐미술전》(1937)이나《독일미술대전》의 분위기를 반영이라도 하듯이 그대로 전이되는 가운데 일제가 군국주의로 치닫던 1930년대 후반에서 1940년대 초반에 유영국이 도쿄에서 펼쳤던 추상예술은 그가 둥지를 쳤던《자유미술가협회전》(1937-43)이나《N.B.G.양화전》(1937-39)을 빼놓고는 상상조차 할 수 없는 일이다. 당시 미술계의 구조를 결정짓다시피 했던《조선미술전람회》나《문부성미술전람회》같은 관전들의 국수적이고 전체주의적인 미학을 등지고, 피식민지인으로서 구축주의적으로 새로운 유토피즘을 기도하거나, 서구의《추상-창조전》(1931-36)이나《큐비즘과 추상미술전》(1936)같은 동시대 국제주의 미술의 흐름과 어깨를 나란히 하며 아방가르드적이고 실험적인 작업들에 나설 수 있었던 것은 그 개인의 기질과 의욕만큼이나 동인 그룹 구성원들의 자유를 향한 동지적 열망에 기초하고 있다.

그 양상이 해방 이후라고 조금도 다를 것이 없다. 나라를 되찾았다고는 하나, 제도적 측면에서나 미학적 측면에서 신-식민주의적인 혼돈으로부터 자유롭지 못했던 한국 미술계에서, 유영국 개인이 작품 활동, 게다가 당시에는 예술로 평가받지도 못했던 추상미술에 가담하는 것은 만만한 일은 아니었다. 그래서 주도적으로 그룹을 결성하는 일이란, 현대미술 운동을 위한 기지를 확보하는 일과 다르지 않았으며, 비켜갈 수 없는 과제였다.《신사실파전》(1948-53),《50년미술가협회전》(1950),《모던 아트협회전》(1957-58), 현대미술가연합(1960-61),《신상회전》

(1962-64), 하다못해 고보시절에 만난 한 자유로운 일본인 미술 교사에 대한 존경심에서 비롯된《2·9 동인전》(1961-64)까지도 어느 하나 예외가 될 것이 없다. 그 각각은 때로는 좌우 이데올로기에 함몰되어 정치판에 휩쓸리며 진정한 예술의 구원적 힘을 망각하던 시절엔 조형이념으로 대응하고자, 때로는 시대착오적인 국전 제도를 극복하고 예술의 본질과는 아무 관련도 없이 국전 권력을 둘러싸고 펼쳐지던 미술계 분규를 함께 넘어서고자, 아니면 새로운 시대에 걸 맞는 미술제도나 미학적 규범을 정립하는 동력을 확보하기 위하여 그때그때마다의 시대정신을 구현해내려는 절박한 시도의 산물이었다.

그렇다면 왜 그는 1960년대 중엽에 이르러 그룹 활동을 그만두고 있을까?

당시에 어느 정도는 젊은 미술인들에게 제도적으로 활동 공간이 열리고 있었다. 예컨대, 1957년 그가 주도한 모던 아트협회로 그룹전 시대가 열리며 현대미술운동이 싹텄는가 하면, 그렇게 창립한 모던 아트협회를 탈퇴하면서까지 그가 적극 지지에 나선「조선일보」주최의《현대작가초대전》은 회를 거듭하는 가운데 국전의 대안적 활동공간으로 터를 잡았다. 4·19 혁명기엔 현대미술가연합의 대표위원으로 그 개혁을 앞에서 지휘하는 가운데 이를 바탕으로 일찍이 여러 차례에 걸쳐 출품 거부라는 소극적 태도로 대응할 수밖에 없던 입장에서 벗어나 일시적이긴 하지만 1961년 제10회《국전》을 이른바 '개혁 국전'으로 이끌어내기도 했다. 그리고 그 이듬해엔 다시 복고적으로 되돌아간 제11회《국전》에 맞서 신상회를 조직하여 미술인들에 의한 자율적인 신인 공모전 형식도 실험했던 터였다. 한편, 1963년엔 한국 최초의 본격적인 국제전 진출로 기록되는 제7회《상파울로비엔날레》에 출품했다. 이러한 일련의 미술계 풍경이나 지형도로 보건대 이미 적지 않게 과거의 그것과는 판이하게 바뀌었음을 알 수 있다.

그런데 유영국에게 제도적 틀이나 토대의 변화가 전부일 수는 없다. 공적인 제도적 장치는 단지 예술의 조건일 뿐 자신이 지향하는 예술적 가치 자체가 될 수는 없으며, 미술인들이 안고 있던 과제나 모순은 스스로 풀지 않을 수 없는 일이니 말이다. 게다가 한때 현대미술을 추진하는 동력이다시피 했던 앵포르멜 미학은 이미 기력을 잃은 상태였으며, 한편으로는 4·19 혁명으로 민족 문화의 정체성에 대한 자각이 일어나는 가운데 다른 한편으로는 미술계가 국제화단에 노출되면서, 그나마 형성되어 온 기존의 예술 정의마저도 크게 흔들리고 있었다.

한국의 모던 아트를 앞서 이끌어 왔으면서도 유영국이 그룹운동으로부터 철수한 것은 이러한 전후사정과 무관하지 않다. 과제들에 당면하여 이전과 달리 그는

철저하리만치 공적 영역으로부터 물러나 자기 자신을 예술의 내부에 가두는 것으로 대응하고 있다. 그리고 과제를 자신 안으로 내면화하는 일로 경계 짓고 있다. 역동적이었던 그때까지의 젊은 시절의 그룹운동들과 비교하여 보건대, 이렇듯 스스로를 마주하며 펼치는 노년에 들어서의 활동은 겉으로 보기에는 적막하기 그지없다. 그런데 그 깊이와 두께는 겉보기와 크게 다르다. 그의 예술여정은 마치 면벽수도하는 고승의 그것과 다를 바 없이 전개되고 있으니 말이다.

몇 가지 이슈들

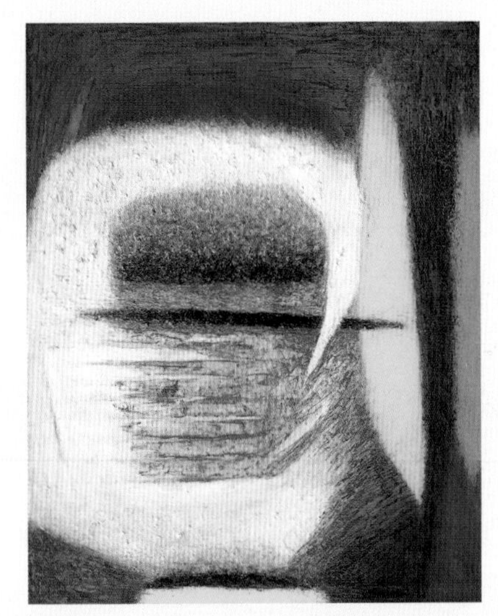

참고도판 1
유영국, 〈작품2〉, 1964, 캔버스에 유채, 162×130cm

참고도판 2
유영국, 〈작품3〉, 1964, 캔버스에 유채, 162×130cm

유영국의 첫 번째 개인전은 몇 가지 점에서 문제적이다. 〈작품〉이라는 제목 아래 일련번호가 붙여진 100호가 넘는 15점의 대작들로 구성된 이 전시에서 그가 던지는 화두가 어떤 것인지 살펴보자. 가깝게는 얼마 전까지 발을 적셨던 비정형적인 앵포르멜 미학의 한계를 어떻게 타개하여 새로운 비전을 열 것인가 하는 문제는 그 자신을 포함한 당시 한국 현대미술이 안고 있는 과제였다. 다른 하나는 스스로에게는 훨씬 더 근본적인데, 청년기에 몰입했던 절대적 추상에서 벗어나 신사실파에 가담한 이래 자신이 설정했던 예술적 과제 즉, 추상 이념을 통해 어떻게 이 땅의 자연과 삶의 전망을 열 것인가 하는 것이었다.

출품작들 가운데 〈작품 2〉(참고도판 1, 1964, 캔버스에 유채, 162×130cm)나 〈작품 3〉(참고도판 2, 1964, 캔버스에 유채, 162×130cm)은 좋은 사례이다. 이 작품들은 여러 사람들의 눈길을 끌었는데, 그 까닭은, 50년대 말 이래 광물질과 같은 질감으로 표출되던 무정형의 물질적 카오스 상태나 색면이나 필획의 유동성 때문이 아니었다. 오히려 화면을 구성하는 요소로 새롭게 떠오른 광휘에 찬 빛이나 색채들과 관련된다. 녹(綠), 황(黃), 적(赤), 청(青) 같은 원색들이 때로는 속도감 넘치는 필획으로 때로는 일정한 면적을 지닌 색면들로 화면을 구성하는 새로운 질서로 자리 잡고 있다. 이러한 시도들을 두고, 당시 여러 일간지에 실린 비평가들의 리뷰는 다음과 같다.

"색감엔 생생한 감동이 가득"(김영주), "원색의 구사와 다이내믹한 구성에서 하나의 바이탈리티(생동감, vitality)를 형성"(오광수), "시원스럽고 널찍한 그리고 한가롭게 전개되는 포름과 예리한 속력과 방향을 갖는 갈댓잎 모양의 맵시 있는 원색기호로 어떤 생생한 이야기를 부동"(이구열), "면의 획선 분할 속에 덤덤하고 큼직한 공간표정이 울려나오는 청(青)의 기조. 그 위를 덮어씌운 황(黃)과 주(朱)의 강렬한 대조에 우리는 씨의 전반세계를 파괴 부정하려는 의욕을 보는 것"(방근택).

그리고 한 해를 마감하는 가운데 유영국을 "탐구적인 '색채의 마술사'"[4]로 일컫는 일마저 주저하지 않는다.

시대의 한복판에 섰던 화가 유영국을 둘러싼 평자들의 위와 같은 언급들, 그리고 그들 사이사이에서 어렵지 않게 미묘한 미끄러짐 현상들이 읽혀진다. 예컨대, 김영주는 "'정신적인 유체(流體)'를 고정시킬 수 있는 특이한 존재 이유를 지니고 오늘날 그는 완성의 시대로 도달했다"고 하는 반면, 방근택은 "정체된 그 답답한 화풍에 1930년대 초창기 '모던 아트'의 융통성 없는 한계를"언급하며 갈라서고 있다. 그 차이는 실은 바로 한 해 전인 1963년 유영국이 제7회《상파울로비엔날레》에 출품했던 작품들인 〈숲〉(참고도판 3)과 〈산〉(참고도판 4) 두 작품 사이에서 작가 스스로 드러냈던 딜레마를 반영해 주는 것이기도 하다. 〈숲〉은 1950년대 말 이래 지속되었던 물질감과 두터운 텍스처로 인해 몰 형식적인 느낌을 준다. 반면, 〈산〉은 기하학적이고 구성주의적인 질서에의 동경으로 읽혀진다. 그런 점에서 유영국 개인이든 화단이든 이 무렵 당면한 과제는 '모던 아트'의 외부 환경을 어떻게 혁신해 낼 것인가 하는 문제가 아니라 예술적 문제 자체에 어떻게 접근해야 할지 결단하는 일이었다. 그러니 다만 그에 대해 묻고 답하며 집중할 장소가 절실히 요구되는 상황이었다.

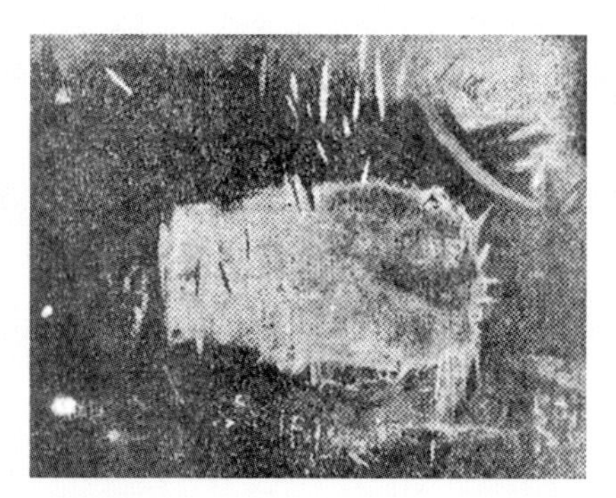

참고도판 3
유영국, 〈숲〉, 1963, 캔버스에 유채, 크기 미상

참고도판 4
유영국, 〈산〉, 1963년, 캔버스에 유채, 크기 미상

한동안, 적어도 1972년까지 유영국은 격동하는 세계나 자연을 기하학적 구조와 질서로 환원시키는 일을 주요 이슈로 삼는다. 그 단면은 식민지 조선과 식민 모국 일본의 관계가 아니라 1965년 한일협정으로 국가 대 국가의 관계에서 일본의 국립뮤지엄이 처음 개최한《한국현대회화전》(1968. 7. 19 - 9. 1, 일본·도쿄국립근대미술관)에 출품한 5작품 가운데 하나인 〈원(円)-C〉(p.172, 1968, 캔버스에 유채, 135×135cm)에서 잘 드러난다. 정사각형의 캔버스 구조와 엄정하게 중첩된 기하학적인 원들이 빚어내는 구성이나 주황색이라는 순도 높은 색으로 덮힌 화면에서 물질성이나 드라마틱한 역동성을 드러내던 표출적인 흔적은 찾아보기 어렵다. 그 대신 극도로 절제되고 단순화된 구조와 광휘에 찬 색면들이 거대한 자연의 산과 대지 너머의 근원적 형상이나 에이도스(eidos)에 도달하고 있는 듯하다.

이러한 양상들은 청년기의 구축적인 절대 추상작업들, 예컨대 〈작품 1(L24-39.5)〉(p. 70, 1939, 유리지 재제작 1979, 혼합재료, 70×90cm)나 〈작품 404-D〉(p. 73, 1940, 유리지 재제작 2002, 혼합재료, 90×74cm)같은 작품들을 환기시키기에 충분하다. 그런데 그것이 결코 단순한 과거에로의 회귀는 아니다. 1930년대의 구축적 작업들은 백색 모노크롬 릴리프로 나라 잃은 유민으로서 새로운 유토피즘을

꿈꾸는 아방가르드적인 실험들이었던 반면, 이즈음에 광휘에 찬 색면을 통해 구축해 가는 작업들은 새로운 이상 국가를 꿈꾸는 시대를 살아가는 국가공동체 구성원의 한 사람으로서 작가가 모색하는 체계와 질서를 향한 비전과 열락으로 보기에 어려움이 없으니 말이다. 물론 여기에서 여태까지 그가 보여 주었던 아방가르드적인 전투성은 눈에 띄지 않는다. 오히려 그보다는 미학적 완결성을 향한 작가의 의지가 두드러져 보인다.

그렇다면, "단지 모던 아트풍의 초기 추상의 해석상의 새로움이 상황적으로 맞아진 데서 이 작가의 조형의 특이한 의미가 부여될 뿐"이라며, 이 시기의 유영국의 작품세계를 "명확한 선과 면의 구조적 편집에 골몰"[5]한 것이라는 평론가 오광수의 언급은 다만 형식적인 전위미술운동사를 세대론적 관점으로만 바라본 일면적인 코멘트는 아닐까? 그런 점에서 당시 유영국과 동반했던 동 세대 화가이자 비평가 김영주의 다음과 같은 첫 개인전 평도 되돌아 볼만하다. "그것은 순수한 힘의 꿈을 실현한 세계요, '자기를 극복한 예술이다.'" "전위는 항상 불안 속에서 방황하라는 법은 없다. (중략) 우리 시대의 찬란한 금자탑을 느낄 수 있는" "유영국은 오늘날 태양을 바라보고 있다. 삶의 절실함을, 낡은 철학의 생리에 스스로 굴레를 벗기고 그 조화는 실존의 인간과 인간 사이에 엮는 자전의 시대를 맞이하고 있다."[6]

추상과 황홀

일제 강점기에 태어나 여러 개의 컴컴한 역사의 터널을 통과하고 난 뒤 새로운 국민국가를 디자인하던 시대를 살며, 한 예술가로서 이 시기에 유영국이 모색하는 미학의 새로움은 마치 난세에 플라톤이 꿈꾸던 이상 국가를 환기시키기라도 하는 것 같다.[7] 국가의 상실, 두 차례에 걸친 참담한 전쟁, 남북분단과 이데올로기 갈등, 여러 차례의 혁명적 격동, 분열, 혼돈, 암흑 등. 20세기 한국사를 짓눌러 왔던 공동체의 불행한 역사적 현실과 그 어둠을 헤치며 유영국이 1960년대 중엽 이후 그려가는 그림들에서 우리는 온갖 국민 국가 담론들이 무성하게 교차되는 가운데 한 화가가 꿈꾸던 것이 어떤 것인지를 적어도 징후적으로 읽어낼 수는 있으니 말이다. 어떻든 노년에 펼쳐지는 이러한 유영국의 작품세계에서 무규정적인 마티에르와 질료들로 뒤엉켰던 50년대 말 60년대 초의 실존적 흔적들은 이제 적극적이고 긍정적인 비전으로 눈부신 빛, 순도 높은 색채로 질서 잡힌 기하학적인 추상에 자리를 내 주는 듯하다.

당시 주디 노스(Judy North)가 『코리아 타임즈(Korea Times)』에서 지적하는

것도 다르지 않다.

물론 삼각형은 산이고, 원은 빛을 나타낸다. 하나의 자연 사물은 다양한 층위의 빛을 방사하고 그림들은 산 형태의 안에서 그것을 관통하며 그 주위에 그리고 그 위에서 지속되는 유희하는 빛의 직접적인 결과이다.
때로는 산 형태는 빛을 거슬러 날카롭게 초점이 맞춰지고 어둡게 덩어리로 모습을 나타나고 때로는 삼각형들은 다른 삼각형들 속으로 그리고 밑으로 겹쳐진다. 여기서 우리는 밤낮으로 늘, 감각의 기분과, 그리고 빛과 어슴푸레함 속에서 늘 체득되는 산들을 마주할 수 있다.[8]

이렇듯 유영국의 후기 작품세계에서는 서구의 절대 추상을 하나의 보편적인 이념으로 받아들이면서도 집요하게 그것을 이 땅의 대지와 자연, 그리고 삶에 한층 밀착되고 있다. 그리고 현란한 빛과 색채를 동반하는 가운데 그 기하학적 근원 구조를 찾는 구도 정진이 지속되고 있다. 1968년에 세 번째로 열린 개인전(11. 11 - 11. 24, 서울·신세계화랑)에 〈원(円)〉이라는 제목 4점과 더불어 〈산(山)〉(p. 180, 1968, 캔버스에 유채, 135×135cm)이라는 제목의 작품 14점이 출품되었는데, 그 가운데 하나인 〈산〉(p. 181, 1968, 캔버스에 유채, 136×136cm) 같은 연작들에서 우리는 유영국이 어떻게 산이라는 눈앞에 현전하는 자연을 엄정한 정사각형이라는 캔버스 구조 속에 기하학적 대각선 구조로 거듭하여 환원시켜 구축해가고 있는지를 알 수 있다. 이러한 시도들을 평론가 이일(李逸, 1932-97)의 지적대로 단지 '개념적인 도식'에 함몰되었다거나 서구의 차가운 기하학적 추상에 무리지어 일컫는 것만으로 다가서기에는 적지 않은 거리가 있다. 그 밖의 다양한 양태의 풍경화들뿐만 아니라 동아시아 전통에서 만나게 되는 그 어떤 산수화들 이상으로, 거기에서 '자연의 입김'을 살갗으로 호흡하거나 우주적 깊이를 간과할 수 없으니 말이다.

그렇다면 금강석같이 단단하면서 광휘를 내뿜는 유영국의 이 시기 작품들의 미학적 에너지의 근원은 무엇일까? 이 〈산〉과 〈원〉 연작들이 발산하는 에너지들을 단지 면 구성이나 색채라는 조형요소들이나 양식적 동서 비교만으로 설명하기란 그리 여의치 않다. 1948년 신사실파 출품작부터 치며 자연을 그린 지 20년이 경과하던 시점에서 열린 세 번째 개인전을 개최하며 한 신문과의 인터뷰에서, 왜 하필 산만 그리느냐는 물음에 그는 다음과 같이 대답한다. "떠난 지 오래된 고향 울진에 대한 사랑 때문이다. 그리고 산에는 뭐든지 있다. 봉우리의 삼각형, 능선의 곡선,

원근의 면, 다채로운 색."[9] 이 작품들의 동인 가운데 하나가 그림공부를 하고 돌아와 '잃어버린 10년'동안 새로운 감각과 몸으로 마주했던 첩첩이 에두르고 있는 울진의 산과 계곡, 바다의 살아있는 자연체험이라는 사실을 그는 그렇게 고백하고 있다. '잃어버린 10년'동안 마주할 수밖에 없었던 대지! 한반도를 달리다가 백두대간이 멈추는 곳, 고향 울진의 대지 체험이 화가로서 '잃어버린 10년'에 일어나는 사건이라는 사실은 꽤 역설적이다.

그의 그림은 단순한 캔버스 위에 유채화가 아니다. 그 작품들이 발산하는 에너지는 형식적으로는 겹겹이 쌓인 그동안의 작업의 기억들과도 깊게 연관되어 있다. 1930년대의 릴리프 작업에서 축적된 구축적 경험, 50년대 말 60년대 초 앵포르멜 미학에 발을 적시며 수행했던 산(山)을 비롯한 자연 탐구 경험들이 고스란히 투영되고 있으니 말이다. 목공소에 버려진 나뭇조각이나 베니어판 같은 미술의 외부를 덧붙여 새로운 세계를 추구하던 30년대 경험들은 이제 바로 나이프로 층층이 색을 쌓고 다시 뜯어내며 기운생동하는 자연의 두께와 깊이를 구축해 가는 그만의 구도자적 수행의 흔적으로 드러난다. 지금 이곳에서 유영국이 실천하는 색면들은 50년대 말 60년대 초 표현적인 앵포르멜의 양상을 드러내면서도 동북아시아 전통의 기운생동하는 거벽산수에 겹겹이 포개진 문화적 기억들을 다시 불러내며 빛을 발산하고 있다. 이렇듯 "1950년대 말 두터운 마티에르와 무정형의 세계에 몰입하며 무규정적인 현상으로부터 1960년대를 거치며 앵포르멜에서 기하학적인 순수 형상으로 환원해 가는 과정은 그 과정에서 자신이 마주하던 존재들과 더불어 그것을 가능하게 해 주는 빛, 태양으로 귀환해가고 있다."[10] 〈산〉과 〈원〉 연작들의 감동이나 울림은 현상세계의 카오스로부터 존재의 근원을 찾고, 몸으로 체험한 대지와 자연의 숨결들을 파고들며 그 질서를 탐색하며 그가 도달한 곳에서 흘러나오는 바로 그 무엇이다. 유영국은 기하학적 질서와 광휘에 찬 색면을 통해 대지와의 대화에 나서고 있다.

개최하는 매번의 개인전들 마다 변주를 거듭한다. 그 변곡점은 대략 1972년과 1977년 두 차례로 보인다. 1972년을 기점으로 1977년까지 약 5년 동안 자연을 향해 있던 그의 시선은 이제 그 대지에 누적되어 온 인공의 영역으로도 넓혀진다. 예컨대, 〈작품〉(1973, 캔버스에 유채, 134×134cm) 같이 깊은 산 속에 오랜 세월 동안 계곡과 더불어 또 하나의 자연이 되다시피 한 옛 사찰 건축물들이나 문화인류학적인 기억이 드리워진 해(日)와 달(月) 같은 자연을 유기적 곡면들로 구축하기도 한다.

어느덧 70년대에 들어설 무렵엔 옵아트, 해프닝, 팝아트, 미니멀리즘, 개념미술, 모노하 같이 서구로부터 밀려드는 새로운 물결 속에 AG협회나 ST그룹 구성원들에 의해 새로운 실험들이 감행되고 있다. 그리고 이어 한국적 모더니즘 미술이라는 이름 아래 백색모노크롬 회화가 그리고 80년대에 들어서는 민중적 민주주의라는 정치적 이슈 아래 민중미술이 집단적 영향력을 발휘하는 가운데 전개되고 있다. 그렇지만 한국의 모더니즘을 진두지휘하다시피 했던 유영국은 이제 노경에 접어들어 오로지 예술이란 무엇인지 묻고 답하며 말없이 어딘가를 향해 가고 있다.

1977년부터는 한 걸음 더 나아간다. 추상을 향한 탐색 이전에 생활 주변의 자연 사물들에 귀의라도 하듯이 그의 태도는 관조적이 된다. 〈작품(Work)〉(1980, 106×106cm, pp.151-157 참조) 같은 작품은 좋은 사례이다. 이즈음에 이르면 그는 어떠한 조형 이념으로부터도 자유로워진 듯하다. 산, 나무, 동산, 펼쳐진 들판도 댐, 길 같은 주변의 인위적인 흔적들마저도 그저 친밀한 대화 상대일 따름이다. 다사다난했던 시간의 흐름 끝에 도달한 노년에, 그는 자신이 그동안 치열하게 실천하려 했던 예술적 비전들을 다시 불러내어 반복적으로 곱씹으며 음미하기도 한다.

모던 아트를 싹 틔워 간과할 수 없는 새로운 삶의 영역으로 일궈낸 유영국에게 세간의 평가가 주어지기 시작한 것은 아이러니컬하게도 그가 홀로 자신의 내부를 향해 있을 때이다. 화가로 살며 작품 한 점을 가까스로 판 것도 환갑의 나이에 이른 1975년 현대화랑의 다섯 번째 개인전에서다. 그럼에도 불구하고 1979년, 뮤지엄 시스템이 제대로 갖춰지지도 못했던 시절 국립현대미술관은《유영국초대전》(6. 4-6. 17, 서울·덕수궁국립현대미술관)을 개최하여 대중으로부터 거리를 두며 고된 화가 노동자이기를 자처했던 유영국의 화업을 기리며 스스로를 뮤지엄다운 뮤지엄으로 일으켜 세우는 방편으로 삼고 있다. 이 전시는 공예가인 장녀 유리지에 의해 사진 이미지에 기초해 재제작된 1930년대 후반 초기 릴리프 작품을 포함하여, 1957년부터 1977년도 사이에 제작된 100여 점의 대표작들로 구성되어, 작가 자신은 물론 한국현대미술사를 증거해 준 매우 기념비적인 전시로 기록되고 있으며 이와 더불어 간행된 화집『YOO YOUNG-KUK』(대영문화사)은 우리나라 카탈로그 발간사에 뚜렷한 족적을 남기고 있다.

〈작품(Work)〉(p. 209, 1999, 캔버스에 유채, 105×105cm)을 끝으로 화가로서 유영국의 노동은 마침표를 찍고 있다. 이 작품에서 정사각형의 캔버스를 좌우대칭으로 나누는 수직선 위에 색가를 달리하는 붉은 색면의 몇 개의 삼각형의 꼭짓점들이 정렬되고 있다. 근대화 과정에서 격동하며 뒤흔들리지 않을 수 없었던 이

대지와 자연에서 유영국은 짙푸른 깊이의 녹색을 위로하는 주황의 광휘로 빛나는 삼각형들을 그 근원적 형상으로 삼아 그자신이 걸어온 추상예술의 세계가 어떤 것인지를 총 정리하는 듯하다. 여기서 대지와 자연은 단지 공간적 구조로서만이 아니라 시간의 랩소디로 되살아나고 있다. 지금까지 그랬듯이 그 화면엔 도도하게 시간의 강물, 생명의 강물이 흐르는 듯하다. 유독 이 절필작에서 이 세상의 무게를 훌훌 털어내고 난 뒤에나 가능한 상승 운동이 느껴지는 것은 근거 없는 것이 아니다. 산산이 부서져 흩어지고 만 세상에서 그는 덧없는 문학적 위로 대신에 추상을 통해 인간의 존엄성과 자유의 가능성을 평생에 걸쳐 일으켜 세우고 있다. 그래서 화가 유영국은 이 대지와 자연, 그 첩첩의 산들과 함께 황홀한 법열, 절대적 자유와 추상의 왕국으로 비상하는 듯하다.

1 독립미술가협회는 1930년 가을, 이과회(二科會) 소속 화가들 가운데 하야시 타케시(林武), 니기시 코타로(三岸好太郎) 등 야수파와 표현주의 계열 화가들이 중심이 되어 결성한 전위적 경향의 재야미술단체로서 한국인으로는 유영국 외에 구본웅, 김만형 등이 참가했다.

2 제7회 《독립미술가협회전》에 출품했던 작품 〈랩소디〉는 현재 엽서본 이미지로만 남아 있다. 이 작품은 비사실주적인 연극과 아방가르드 연극이론으로 새로운 활력을 불러일으킨 러시아의 연극인 메이에르홀트(Vsevolod Yemilyevich Meyerhold)가 연출한 〈Le Cocu magnifique〉(크로멜링크(Fernand Crommelynck)의 희곡)를 위해 구축주의자 류보프 포포바(Lyubov Popova)가 1922년에 제작한 무대세트의 이미지에 영향받은 유화작품으로, 향후 화가로서 유영국이 평생에 걸쳐 지속했던 진취적이고 아방가르드적인 태도를 이미 앞서 예고하고 있다.

3 화가 유영국은 생전에 1940년대 초부터 태평양전쟁이 일어난 이래 한국전쟁까지 고기잡이, 농사, 양조업 등 고향 울진에서 생업에 종사하며 붓을 내려놓아야 했던 '잃어버린 10년'을 늘 직업화가로서 뼈아픈 회한으로 기억하곤 했다.

4 「〈64년의 얼굴〉 유영국 씨」, 「조선일보」, 1964. 12. 15.

5 오광수, 「미술 1968년 · 세 개의 유형 : 비평초 · 한국현대회화전」, 『공간』, 1968. 7.

6 김영주, 「찬란한 금자탑: 유영국 개인전을 보고」, 「조선일보」, 1964. 11. 17.

7 플라톤이 『국가』 제6장 '태양의 비유'와 제7장의 '동굴의 비유'에서 나눈 대화의 몇 구절을 인용해 보자. "누군가가 눈길을 그 대상들에 보낼 경우에, 이를 그것들의 빛깔(표면) 위로 낮의 빛이 퍼져 있는 동안에 하지 않고, 밤의 어두운 빛이 퍼져 있는 동안에 할 땐, 눈은, 마치 그 속에 맑은 시각이 없기라도 한 것처럼, 침침해서 거의 눈먼 거나 마찬가지인 것처럼 보인다는 사실을 자네는 알고 있겠지?" "그렇지만 태양이 대상들의 빛깔을 비출 때는, 눈이 또렷이 보게 되고, 또한 같은 이 눈 속에도 맑은 시각이 있는 것처럼 보일 것이라 나는 생각하네." "그러면, 여보게나 글라우콘! 이 전체 비유(eikōn)를 앞서 언급된 것들에다 적용시켜야만 하네. 시각을 통해서 드러나는 곳을 감옥의 거처에다 비유하는 한편으로 감옥 속의 불빛을 태양의 힘에다 비유함으로써 말일세. 그리고 위로 '오름(anabasis)'과 높은 것에 있는 것들의 구경(thea)을 자네가 '지성에 의해서[라야] 알 수 있는 영역'으로 향한 혼의 등정(登程 : anodos)으로 간주한다면, 자네는 내 기대에 적중한 셈이 될 걸세. (중략) 즉 인식할 수 있는 영역에 있어서 최종적으로 그리고 각고 끝에 보게 되는 것이 '좋음(善 : to agathon)의 이데아'이네. 그러나 일단 이를 본 다음에는, 이것이 모든 것에 있어서 모든 옳고 아름다운(훌륭한) 것의 원인(aitia)이라고, 또한 '가시적 영역'에 있어서는 빛과 이 빛의 주인을 낳고, '지성에 의해서[라야] 알 수 있는 영역'에서도 스스로 주인으로서 진리와 지성을 제공하는 것이라고, 그리고 또 장차 사적으로나 공적으로나 슬기롭게 행하고자(prattein)하는 자는 이 이데아를 보아야만(idein) 한다고 결론을 내려야만 하네."(517a-c)

8 Judy North, "〈Art Review〉 Exhibit 'Personal Statement'", *The Korea Times*, 1968. 11. 21.

9 「산(山)만 그리기 20년: 유영국 씨」, 「경향신문」, 1968. 11. 20.

10 이인범, 「1963-68년 유영국의 작품들」, 『유영국 저널』 제6집, 2009, pp. 24-25.

내 그림은 주로 '산'이라는 제목이 많은데, 그것은 산이 너무 많은 고장에서 자란 탓일 게다. 〈숲〉이라는 그림도 내가 어렸을 때 마을 앞에 놀러 다니던 숲이 생각나서 그린 것이다. 무성한 잎과 나뭇가지 사이로 잔디밭에 쏟아지는 광선은 참 깨끗하고 생기를 주는 듯 아름답다 … 항상 나는 내가 잘 알고, 또 언제든지 달려갈 수 있는 곳에서 느낀 것을 소재로 하여 즐겨 그림을 그린다.

- 유영국

작품 *Work*
1964, 캔버스에 유채 Oil on canvas, 130×194cm

작품 *Work*
1964, 캔버스에 유채 Oil on canvas, 129×161cm

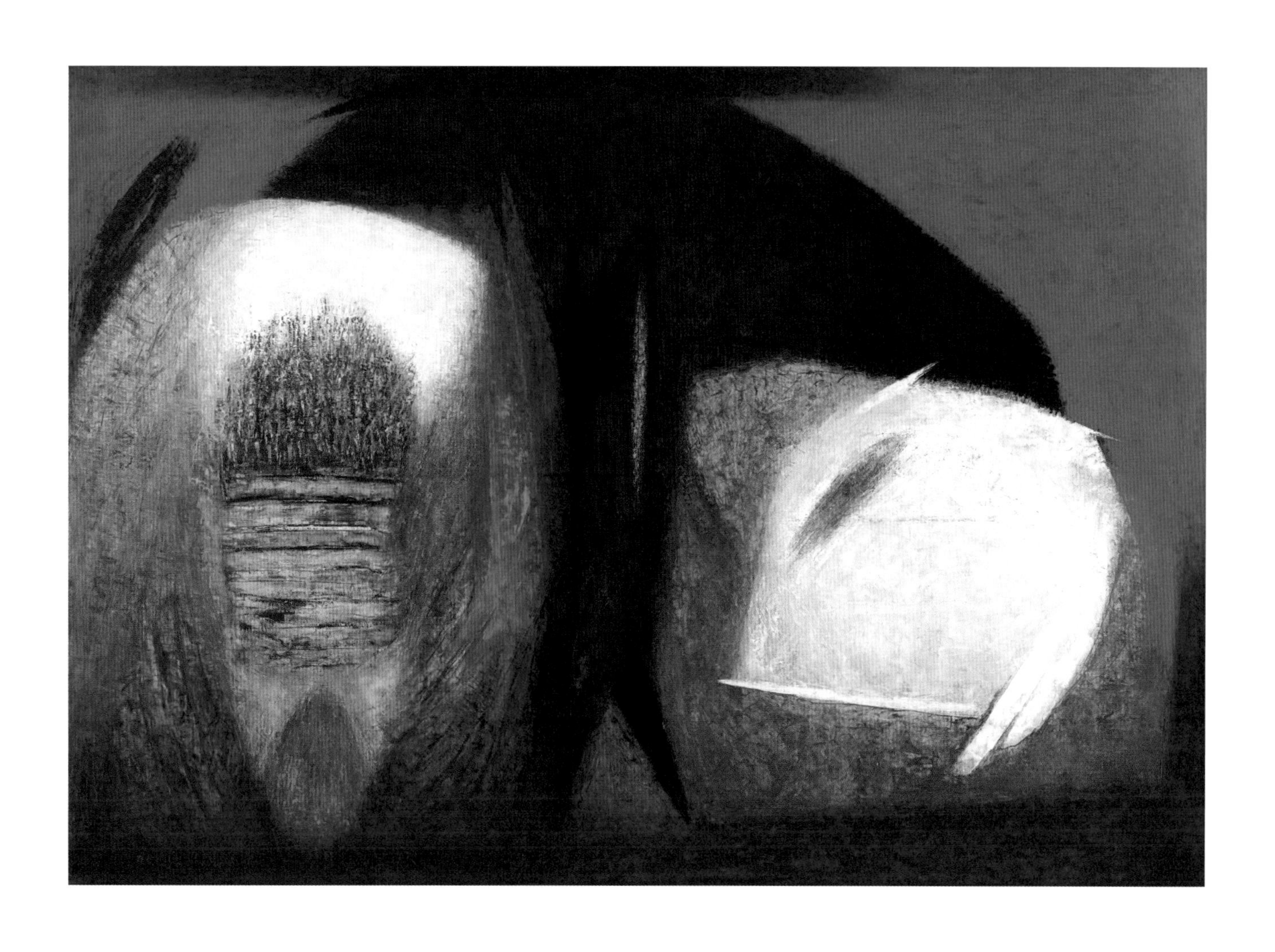

작품 *Work*
1964, 캔버스에 유채 Oil on canvas, 130×194cm

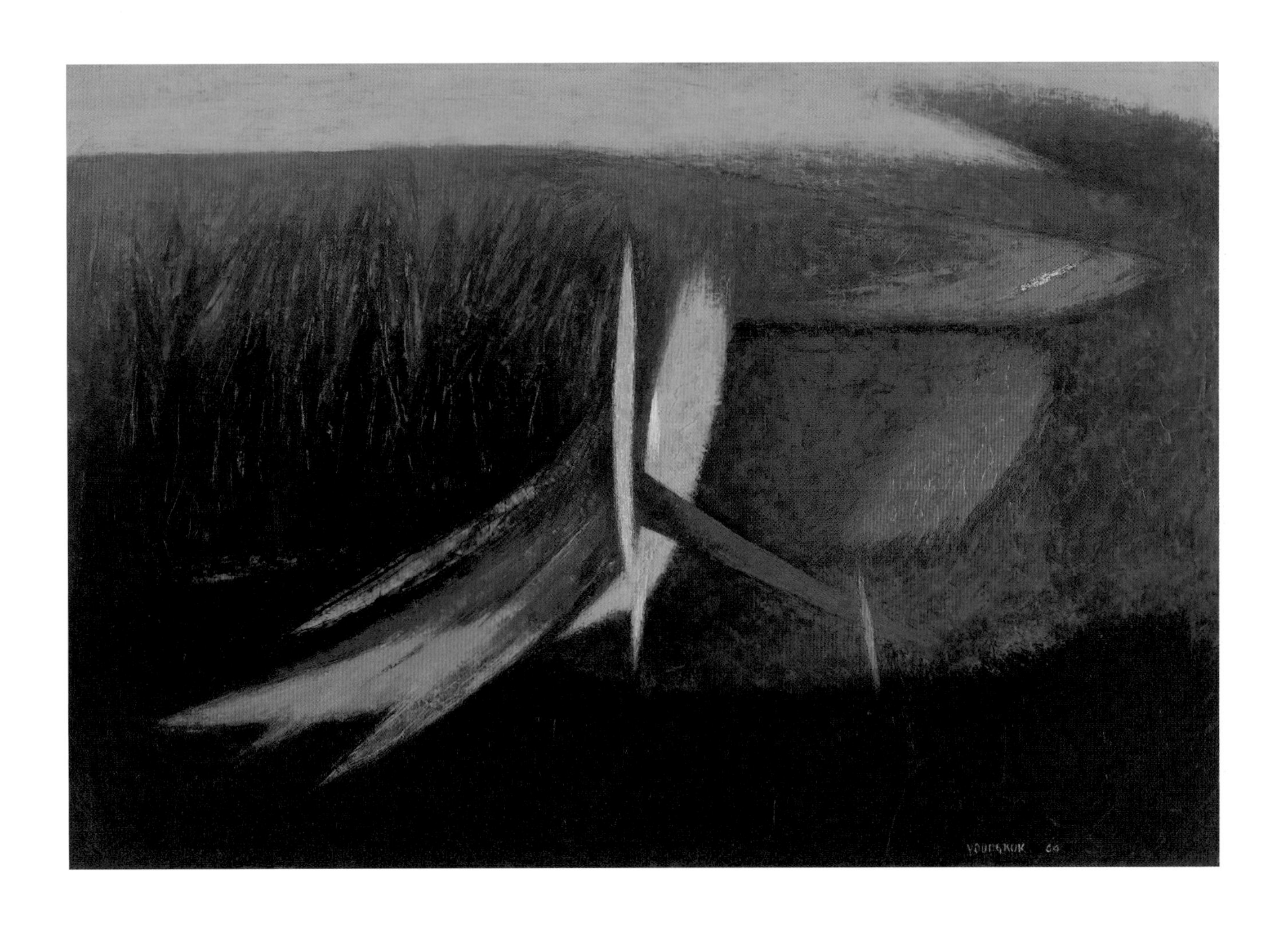

작품 *Work*
1964, 캔버스에 유채 Oil on canvas, 130×194cm

작품 *Work*
1964, 캔버스에 유채 Oil on canvas, 139×215cm

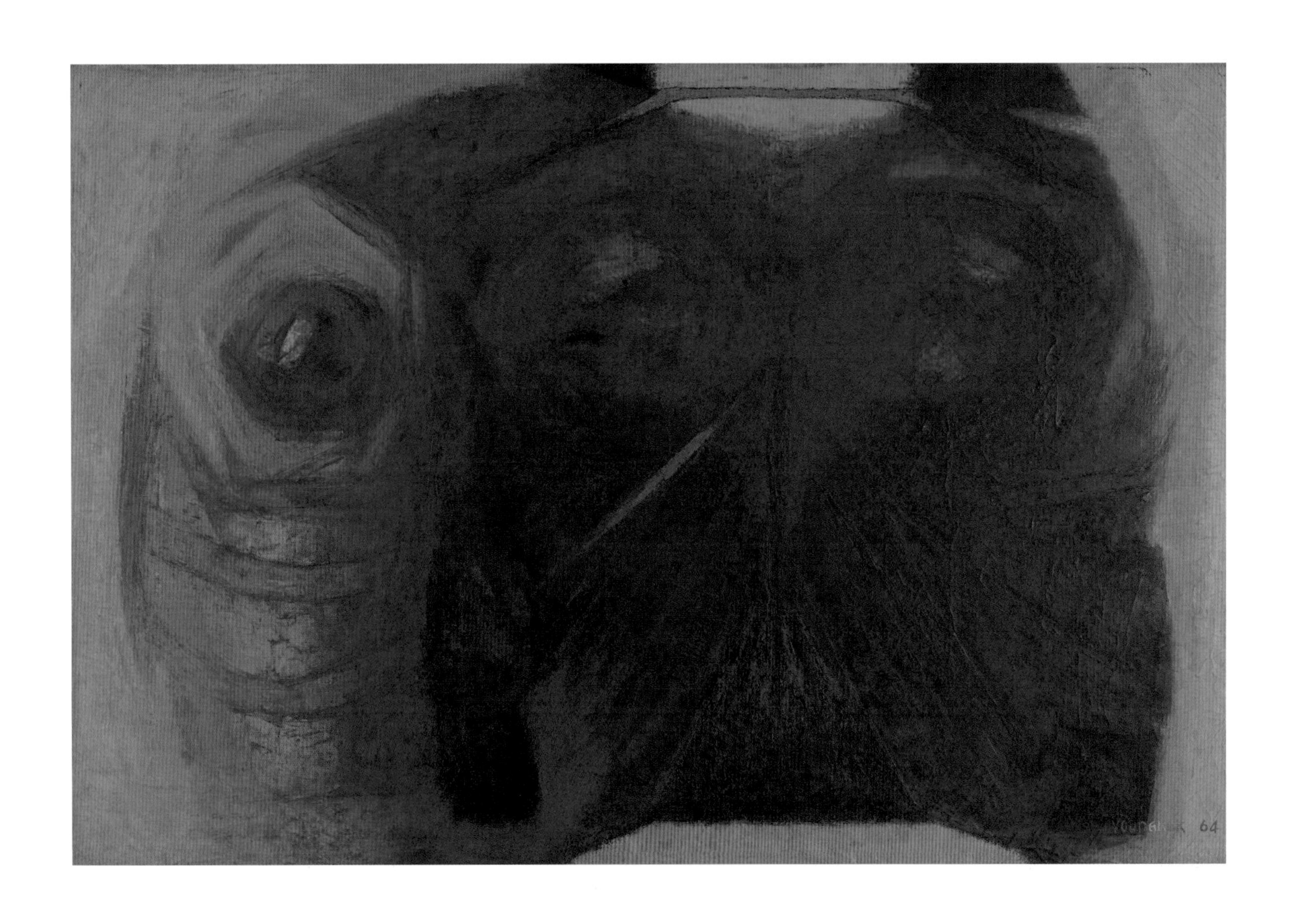

작품 *Work*
1964, 캔버스에 유채 Oil on canvas, 130×194cm

작품 ***Work***
1964, 캔버스에 유채 Oil on canvas, 130×195cm

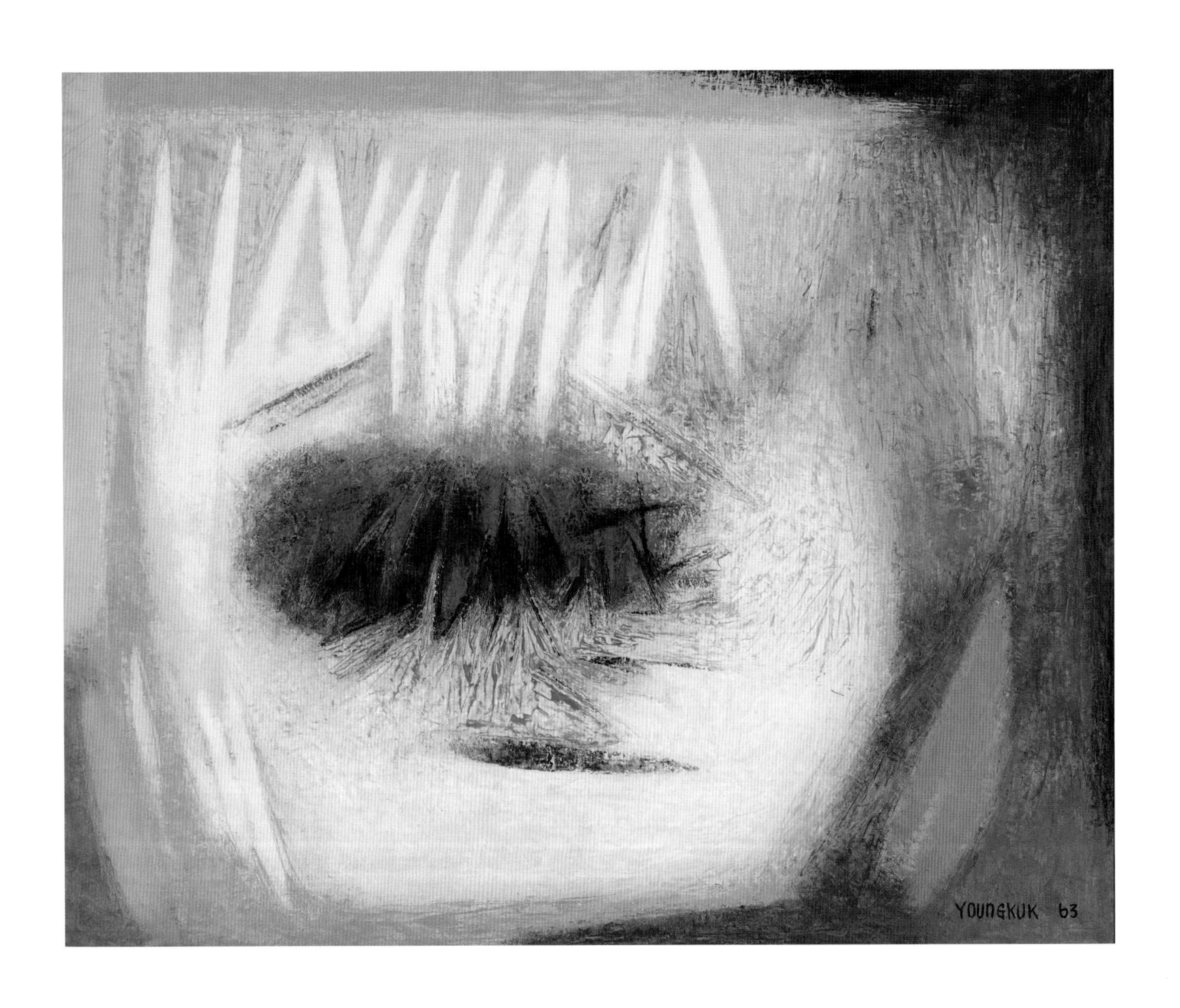

작품 *Work*
1963, 캔버스에 유채 Oil on canvas, 130×162cm

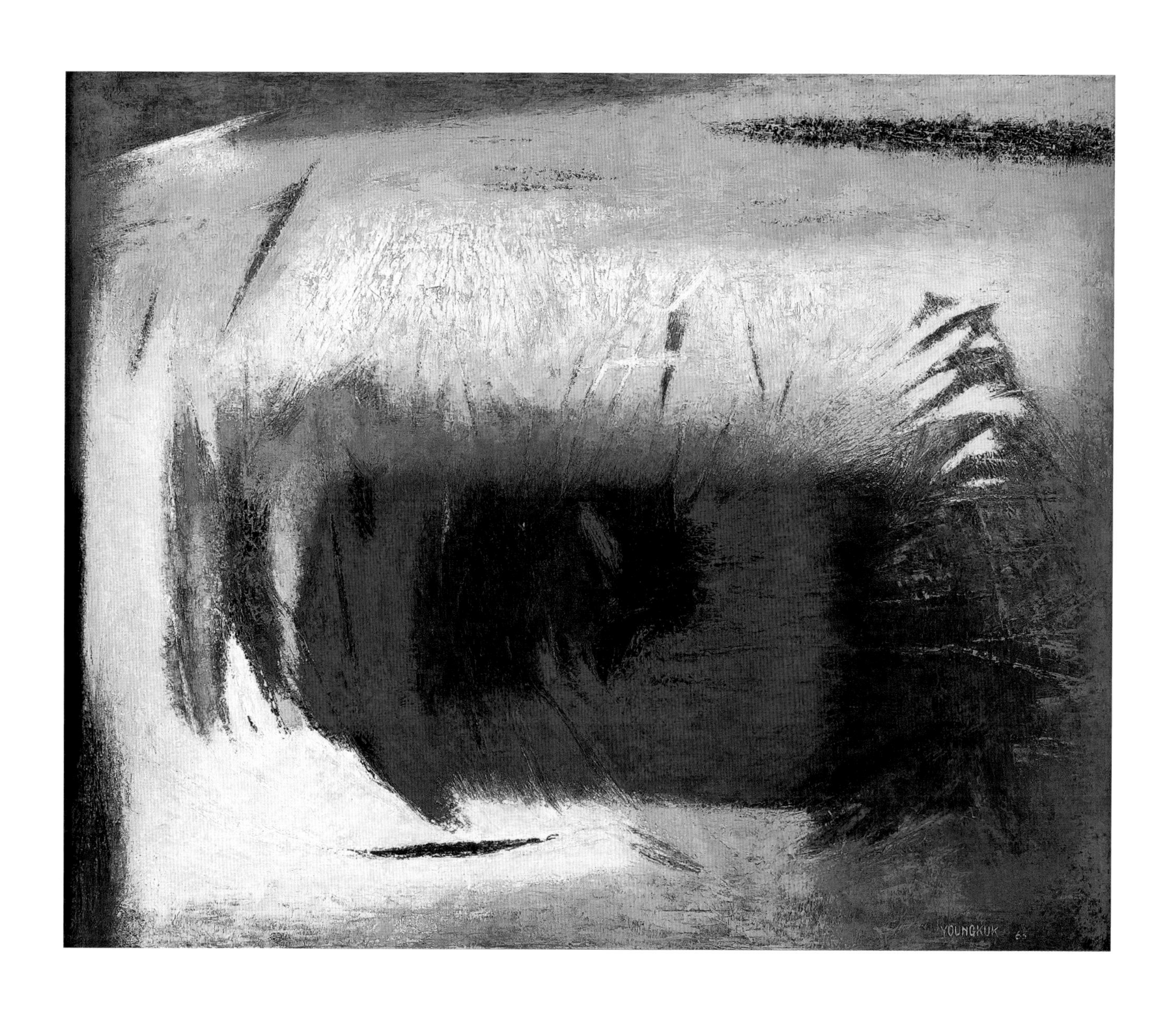

무제 *Untitled*
1965, 캔버스에 유채 Oil on canvas, 130×162cm

산은 내 앞에 있는 것이 아니라 내 안에 있다

-유영국

작품 *Work*
1967, 캔버스에 유채 Oil on canvas, 130×130cm

작품 *Work*
1966, 캔버스에 유채 Oil on canvas, 162.3×129.7cm

작품 *Work*
1968, 캔버스에 유채 Oil on canvas, 81×81cm

산 *Mountain*
1966, 캔버스에 유채 Oil on canvas, 162×130cm

무제 ***Untitled***
1965, 캔버스에 유채 Oil on canvas, 159.5×128.5cm

작품 *Work*
1965, 캔버스에 유채 Oil on canvas, 130×162cm

작품 *Work*
1967, 캔버스에 유채 Oil on canvas, 130×130cm

산 *Mountain*
1968, 캔버스에 유채 Oil on canvas, 129×129cm

산 *Mountain*
1968, 캔버스에 유채 Oil on canvas, 136×136cm

작품 *Work*
1968, 캔버스에 유채 Oil on canvas, 136×136cm

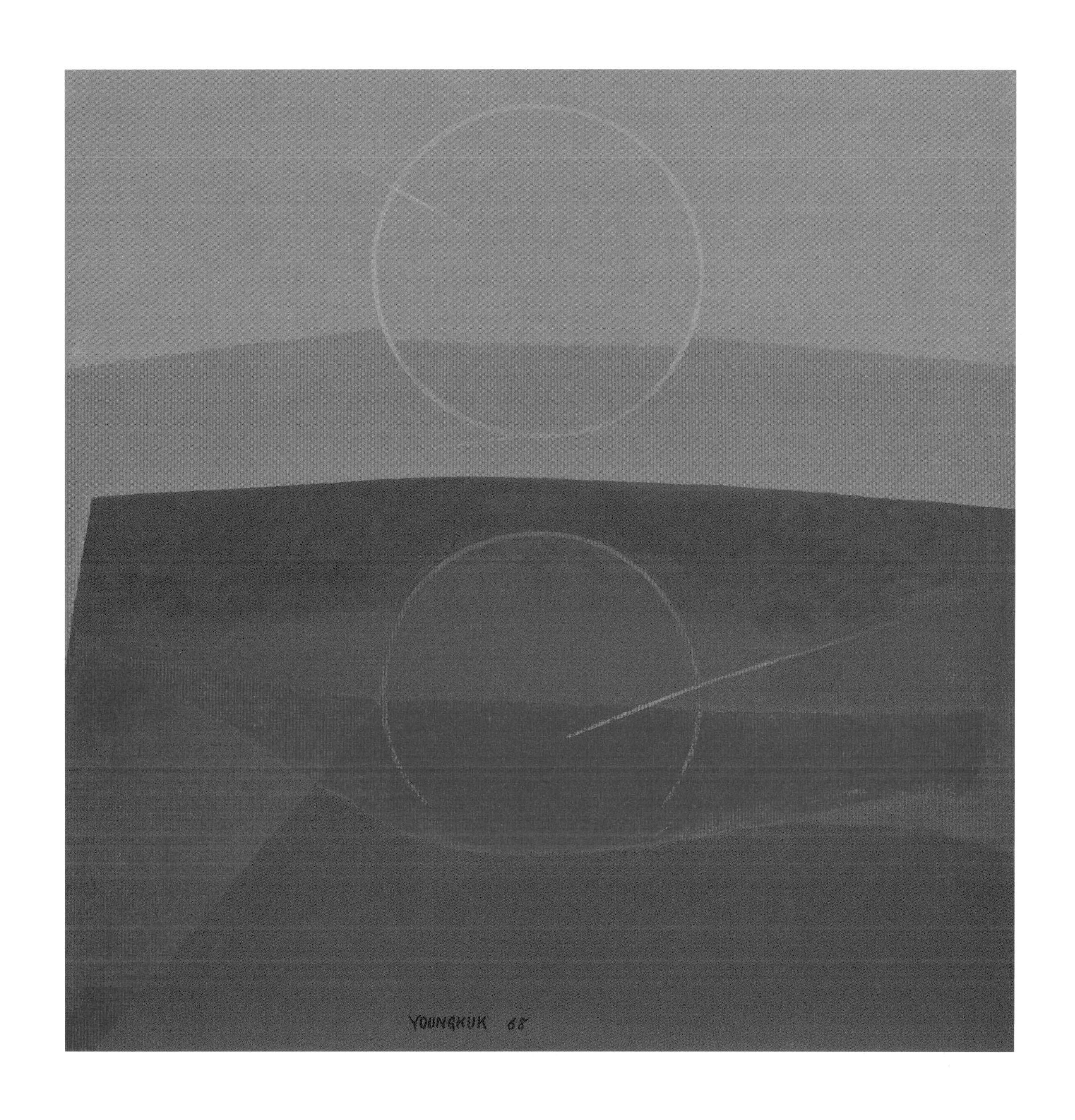

원(円)-A *Circle-A*
1968, 캔버스에 유채 Oil on canvas, 136×136cm

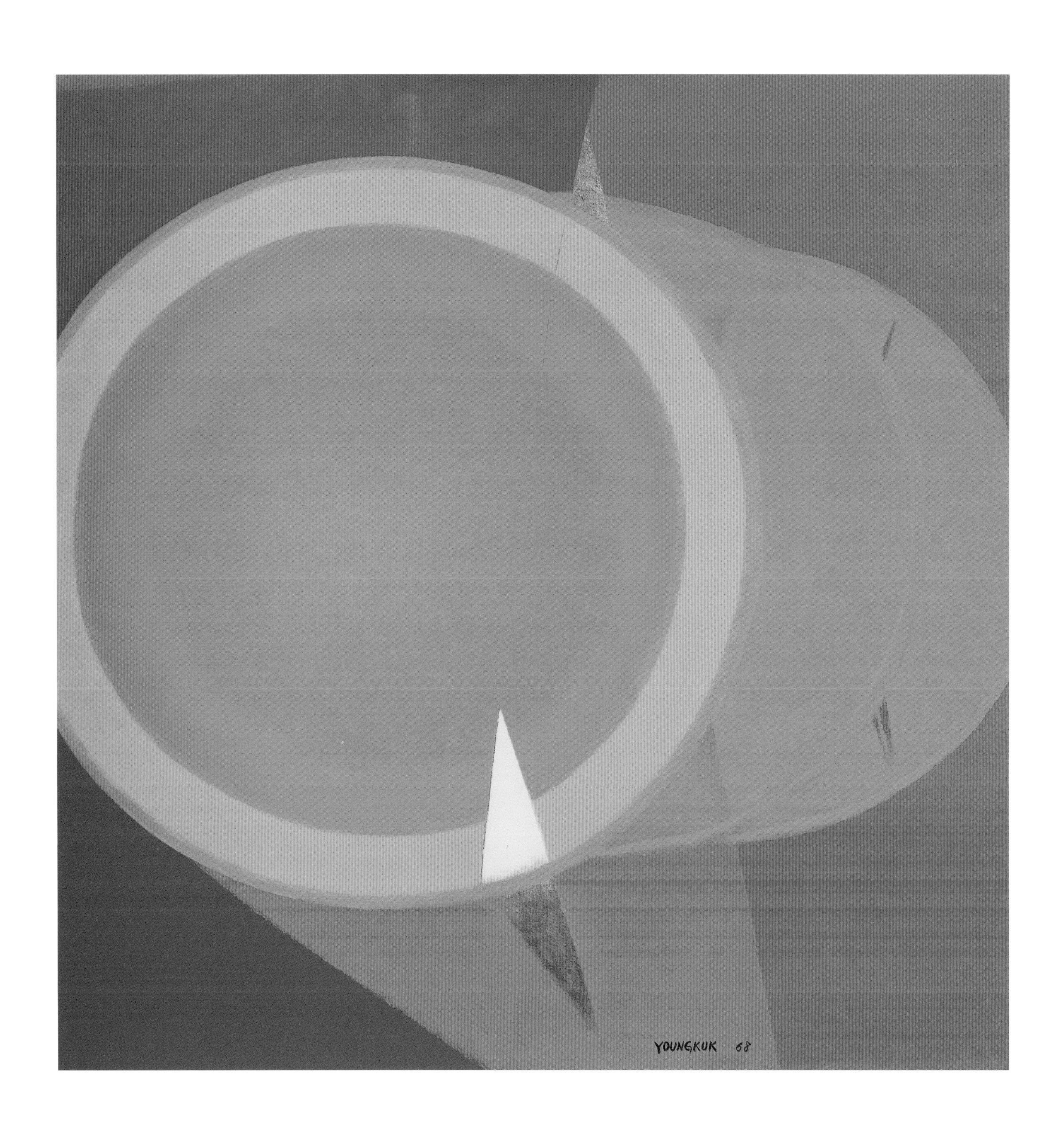

원(円)**-C *Circle-C***
1968, 캔버스에 유채 Oil on canvas, 135×135cm

작품 *Work*
1968, 캔버스에 유채 Oil on canvas, 136×136cm

산 *Mountain*
1974, 캔버스에 유채 Oil on canvas, 106×106cm

산 *Mountain*
1977, 캔버스에 유채 Oil on canvas, 130×130cm

작품 *Work*
1969, 캔버스에 유채 Oil on canvas, 136×136cm

산 *Mountain*
1968, 캔버스에 유채 Oil on canvas, 136×136cm

작품 *Work*

1969, 캔버스에 유채 Oil on canvas, 136×136cm

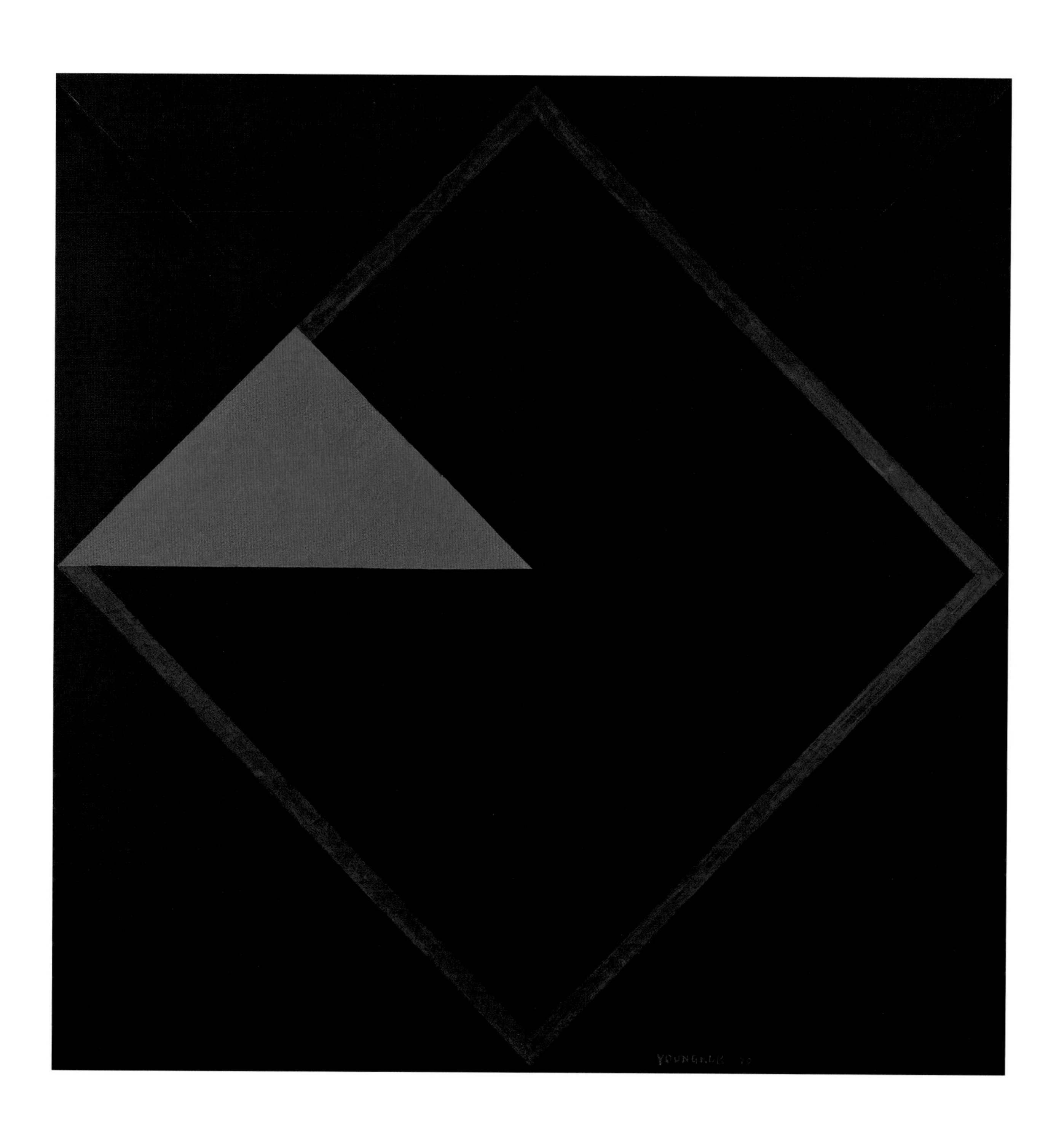

작품 *Work*
1970, 캔버스에 유채 Oil on canvas, 136×136cm

산 *Mountain*
1968, 캔버스에 유채 Oil on canvas, 135×135cm

산 *Mountain*
1968, 캔버스에 유채 Oil on canvas 136×136cm

창작과정에서 막다른 골목에 이르렀을 때에 나는 항상 뚫고 나갈 길이 있다고 생각한다. 그래서 한 작품은 다음 작품을 위한 과정이고, 계속적으로 작품을 해야 되는 근거가 된다.

- 유영국

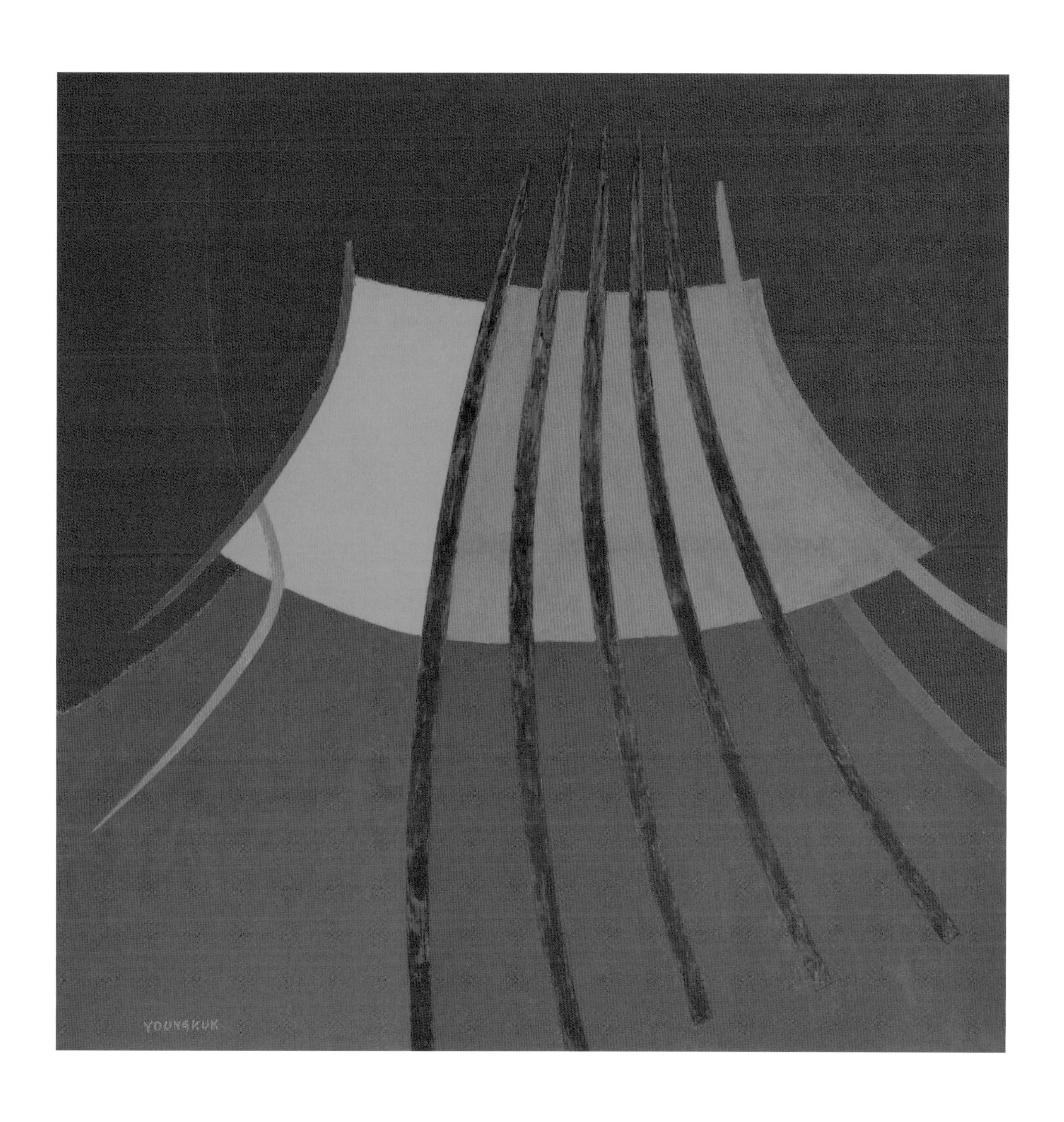

작품 ***Work***
1979, 캔버스에 유채 Oil on canvas, 135×135cm

작품 ***Work***
1979, 캔버스에 유채 Oil on canvas, 106×106cm

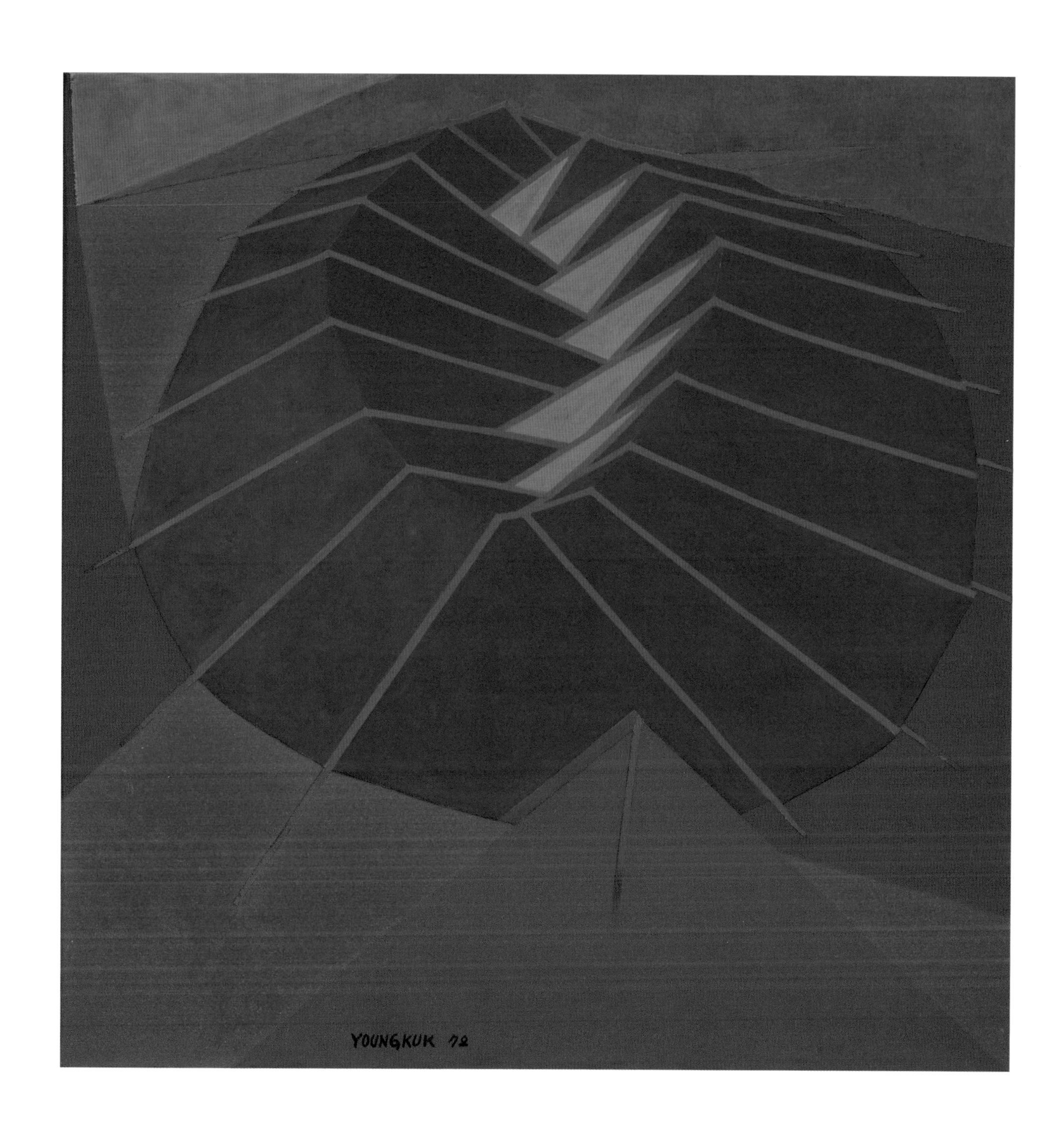

산 *Mountain*
1972, 캔버스에 유채 Oil on canvas, 133×133cm

작품 *Work*
1970, 캔버스에 유채 Oil on canvas, 136×136cm

작품 *Work*
1970, 캔버스에 유채 Oil on canvas, 136×136cm

산-Red *Mountain-Red*
1994, 캔버스에 유채 Oil on canvas, 126×96cm

산-Blue *Mountain-Blue*
1994, 캔버스에 유채 Oil on canvas, 126×96cm

나는 예순 살까지는 기초를 좀 해 보고, 이후 자연으로 더 부드럽게 돌아가 보자는 생각으로 그림을 그렸다... 그림 앞에서 느끼는 팽팽한 긴장감, 그 속에서 나는 다시 태어나고 새로운 각오와 열의를 배운다. 나는 죽을 때까지 이 긴장의 끈을 바싹 나의 내면에 동여매고 작업에 임할 것이다.

- 유영국

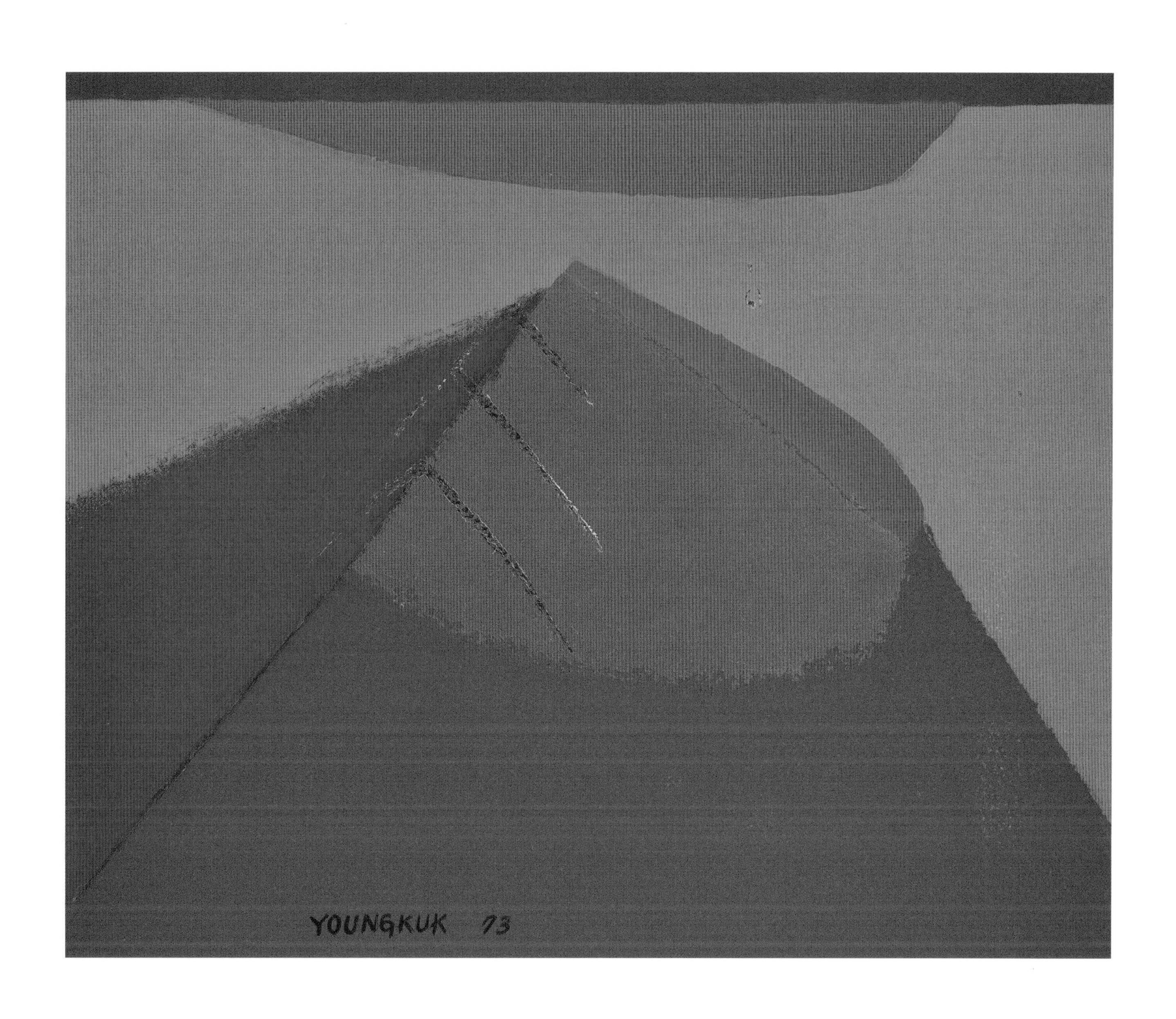

작품 *Work*
1973, 캔버스에 유채 Oil on canvas, 53×65cm

작품 *Work*
1980, 캔버스에 유채 Oil on canvas, 53×65 cm

작품 ***Work***

1979, 캔버스에 유채 Oil on canvas, 105×105cm

작품 *Work*
1989, 캔버스에 유채 Oil on canvas, 135×135cm

작품 ***Work***
1988, 캔버스에 유채 Oil on canvas, 130×194cm

작품 *Work*
1987, 캔버스에 유채 Oil on canvas, 135×135cm

무제 *Untitled*
1984, 캔버스에 유채 Oil on canvas, 130×162cm

작품 *Work*
1981, 캔버스에 유채 Oil on canvas, 91×73cm

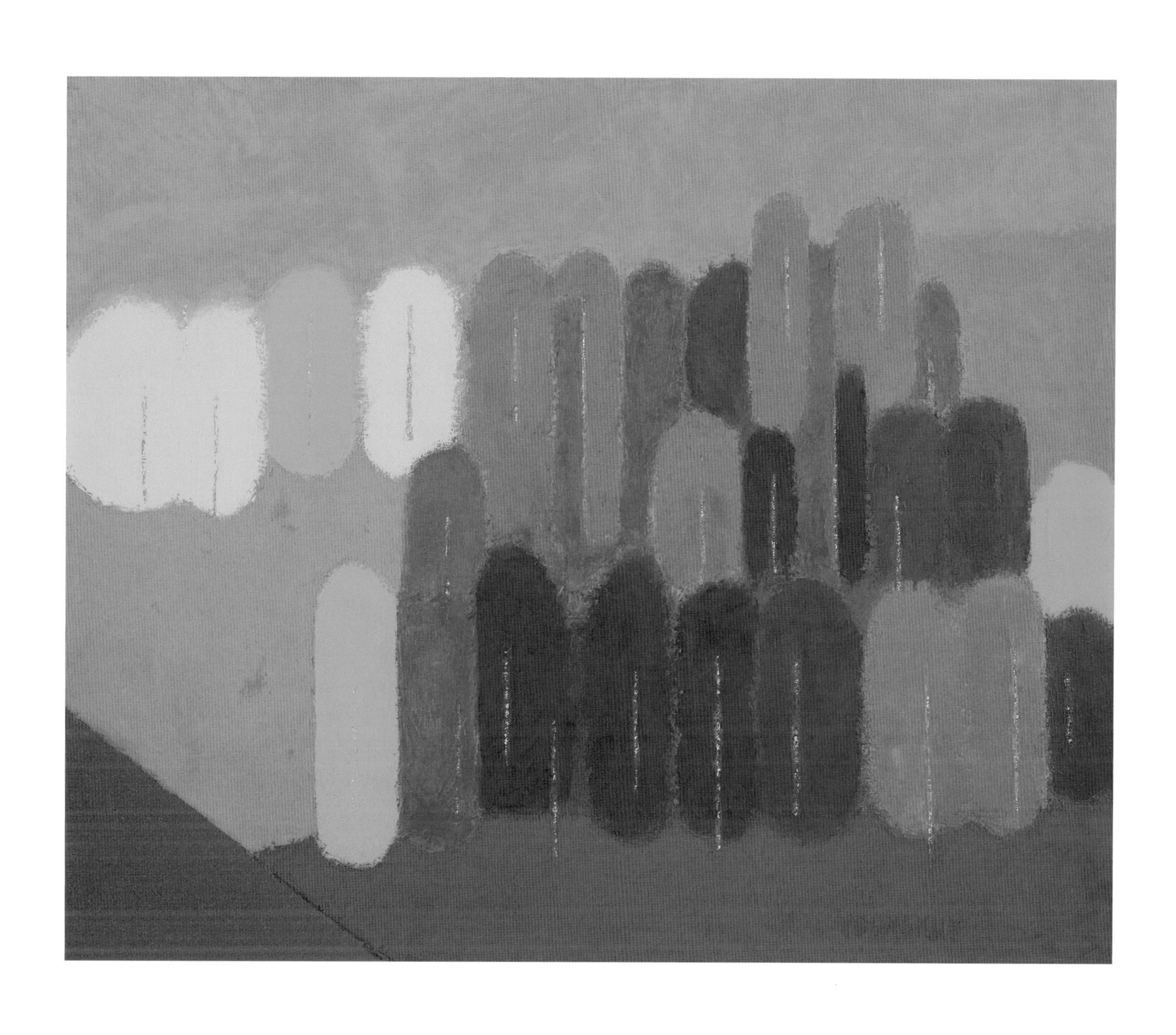

산과 호수 ***Mountain and Lake***
1979, 캔버스에 유채 Oil on canvas, 53×65cm

작품 *Work*
1989, 캔버스에 유채 Oil on canvas, 105×105cm

산 *Mountain*
1980, 캔버스에 유채 Oil on canvas, 106×106cm

작품 ***Work***
1982, 캔버스에 유채 Oil on canvas, 73×100cm

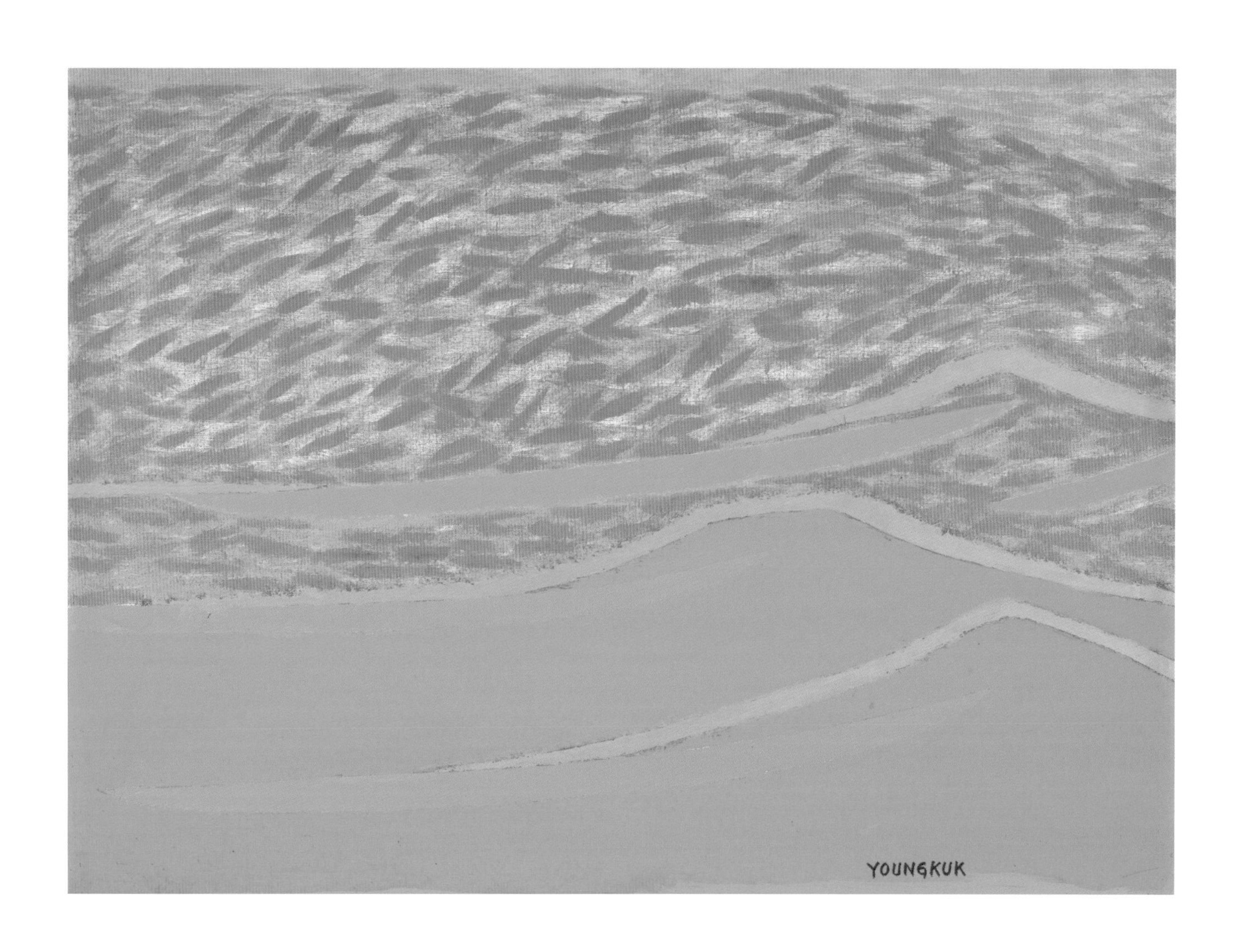

작품 *Work*
1981, 캔버스에 유채 Oil on canvas, 73×100cm

작품 *Work*
1989, 캔버스에 유채 Oil on canvas, 65.4×91cm

작품 ***Work***
1994, 캔버스에 유채 Oil on canvas, 66×91cm

산 *Mountain*
1970, 캔버스에 유채 Oil on canvas, 104×104cm

무제 *Untitled*
1993, 캔버스에 유채 Oil on canvas, 105×105cm

세월이란 참으로 묘한 것이어서 어떤 시대고 간에 꼭 있을만한 사람을
반드시 심어놓고 지나갑니다. 그 시대 그가 아니면 있을 수 없는 그런
일을 하는 사람들을 역사는 빠뜨리지 않는다는 것입니다 … 선생님의
빈소에서 그 분의 영정을 바라보는데, 문득 '아, 한 시대가 마감하는구나!'
하는 생각이 나는 것이었습니다.

- 최종태, 「고인에게 바치는 편지」 중에서, 2002

작품 *Work*
1999, 캔버스에 유채 Oil on canvas, 105×105cm

유영국과의 가상 대화

윤명로

작가, 유영국미술문화재단 이사장

* 이 글은 작가 유영국과 윤명로(1936-)의 가상 대화이다. 평소 말씀이 없으셨던 작가 유영국에게 후배 작가 윤명로가 여쭤보고 싶었던 질문과 이에 대한 답변으로 구성되어 있다. 유영국의 답변은 주로 『유영국 저널』(유영국미술문화재단 발행)에 실린 그의 아내 김기순 여사를 비롯한 가족 및 주변 인물들의 증언을 참고하되, 윤명로 작가의 상상이 가미된 것이다(편집자 주).

윤 선생님은 어디서 태어나셨는지요?

유 강원도 울진에서 태어났어요. 울진의 천석꾼이었던 유문종의 4남 4녀 중 여섯째로 태어났지요. 지금은 행정상 경상북도이지만 누가 고향이 어디냐고 물으면 나는 늘 강원도에서 태어났다고 해요. 조상들이 원주에서 울진으로 내려왔기 때문에, 누구보다도 내 고향 울진에 대한 애착이 강해요. 옛날부터 보부상들이 태백중령을 가로지르며 넘나들었다는 불영계곡과 나라에서 큰일이 있을 때마다 베어다 썼다는 금강송의 군락지가 바로 울진에 있어요. 또한 동해 쪽으로는 주변에 대나무가 많다고 해서 '죽변'이라고 부르는, 아름답기로 소문난 죽변항이 있고요. 죽변항은 한때 포경선이 드나들었던 곳으로, 울진 대게와 오징어, 정어리, 명태 잡이로 유명하지요. 바다 어디에서 고등어가 잡힌다고 하면 수백 척이 넘는 배들이 모여들었는데, 나도 이때가 되면 배 한 척을 몰고 어부와 함께 바다로 나가곤 했지요.

윤 어부로 고기잡이도 하셨나요?

유 조선업을 하시던 선친으로부터 배 한 척을 물려받아 멀리 남해 바다까지 내려가 만선이 될 때까지 고기를 잡기도 했지요.

윤 가족에 대해서도 한 말씀 해주시겠어요?

유 1944년 사리원여자고등학교를 졸업한 김기순과 결혼하고 슬하에 2남 2녀를 두었어요. 맏딸 리지는 타일러대학 대학원을 졸업하고 서울대학교 미술대학 교수가 되었고, 둘째 딸 자야는 프랑스 아르데코에서 섬유디자인을 전공했어요. 큰아들 진은 펜실베니아 대학에서 석박사학위를 받고 카이스트 교수가 되었고 둘째 아들 건은 버클리대학과 하버드대학에서 건축을 전공하고 귀국해서 설계사무소를 경영하고 있지요.

윤 참으로 다복한 가정이시네요.

유 어느 가정이나 다 그렇겠지만, 선친께서 어떤 일이 있어도 자식들만은 가르쳐야 한다고 늘 말씀하셨어요. 그때만 해도 경제 사정이 넉넉하지 않았지만, 다행히도 아이들이 스스로 학비를 벌거나 장학금을 받아 명문대학을 졸업했어요. 이후에도 전공을 살려 봉사하고 있는 것을 보면 참으로 흐뭇하지요.

윤 경성 제2고보를 다니셨지요? 그때는 일본제국주의의 식민통치를 받던 시대였는데, 학창시절을 어떻게 기억하고 계신지요.

유 나는 시골에서 초등학교를 다녔는데, 공부도 잘하고 그림도 곧잘 그린다고 칭찬을 받곤 했어요. 그러자 아버님과 형들이 가족회의까지 열어 영국이는 공부를 시켜야 한다면서 서울로 유학을 보냈어요. 그래서 입학한 곳이 경성 제2고보였지요. 둘째 형님이 이 학교 1회 졸업생이었기 때문에 자연스럽게 여기를 선택하게 되었어요. 그런데, 경성 제2고보 4학년 때였어요. 내가 키도 크고 공부도 열심히 하니까 담임이 급장(반장)을 시켰어요. 그러더니 뒷자리에 앉아 누가 잘못했는지 날마다 일러바치라는 거예요. 같은 반 친구들인데 도저히 그렇게 할 수가 없었지요. 그때부터 학교가 다니기 싫어졌어요. 고민 끝에 졸업을 1년 앞두고 학교를 그만두고 고향으로 내려갔지요.

윤 이후 바로 일본 유학을 떠나셔서 도쿄에 있는 문화학원에 입학하셨지요? 특별히 문화학원을 찾아가신 이유라도 있으셨나요?

유 평소 제2고보 미술교사였던 사토 쿠니오 선생을 존경했어요. 장욱진, 임완규, 김창억, 이대원, 권옥연도 사토 쿠니오 선생한테 배웠는데, 훗날 다들 한국 화단의 걸출한 화가들이 되었지요. 원래 나는 1등 항해사가 되어 오대양 육대주를 자유롭게 돌아다닐 생각을 한 적도 있었으나, 고보 졸업을 하지 못해 입학이 불가했지요. 항해사의 꿈에서 깨어나자 나는 문득 미술시간에 배웠던 폴 고갱이 생각났어요. 항로를 담당하며 견습 도선사로 선원 생활을 하다가 타히티에 정착했던 폴 고갱 말이에요. 왜 세무사를 하다가 화가가 된 앙리 루소나 목사가 되려다가 화가가 된 반 고흐도 있었고 … 훗날 쇼와(昭和) 몇 년이던가 가도가와쇼텐(角川書店)에서 발행한 『세계미술전집』을 본 적이 있었어요. 어쨌든 화가가 되는 것도 항해사만큼이나 간섭받지 않고 자유로울 수 있으리라는 생각을 했던 것 같아요. 결국 1935년 도쿄로 가서 문화학원 미술과에 입학하게 되었지요.

윤 문화학원에서 유학 시절을 어떻게 보내셨는지요?

유 상선의 꿈을 접고 문화학원을 선택한 것은 비교적 자유로운 학풍 때문이었어요. 광성 고보 출신의 김병기, 오산 고보 출신의 이중섭과 문학수를 만난 것도 문화학원에서였지요. 입학을 하고 나서 두어 해 지나서였던가. 처음으로 제1회《자유미술가협회전》에 김환기와 함께 작품을 출품했어요. 나보다 세 살 연상이었던 김환기를 만난 것도 이 무렵이었고요. 그리고 졸업을 하자마자 제2회《자유미술가협회전》에서 협회상을 받았어요. 막연하게 폴 고갱과 반 고흐를 생각하며 시작했던 화가로서의 꿈이 현실로 다가왔지요. 참으로 열심히 작업에 몰두했어요.

윤《독립미술협회전》에 출품하셨던 작품 〈랩소디〉를 기억하세요?

유 1937년 제7회《독립미술협회전》에 출품했던 작품이지요. 캔버스 위에 유채로 그린 그림인데, 지금은 겨우 엽서 한 장만 남아 있네요. 당시 내가 22살이었을 거예요. 이후에는 더욱 급진적으로 추상미술을 추구했는데, 화가가 그토록 중요시하는 '붓'을 던져 버리고, 베니어판과 골판지, 자와 컴퍼스 등을 사용하면서 구성적인 작업을 해나갔지요. 전시(戰時) 때인데도 당시 학원의 분위기는 상당히 자유로운 편이었어요. 아마 실험적인 모더니즘이 급진적으로 일본에 유입되던 때가 아니었나 생각되네요.

어떻든 내가 항해사의 꿈을 접고 화가의 길로 들어서리라고는 상상도 못했지요. 그런데도 한때 사무치는 외로움 때문에 금강송의 솔잎을 씹던 울진으로 돌아가 죽변항에 닻을 내리고 찬란하게 솟아오르는 태양을 향해 노를 젓고 싶은 생각에 빠져들었어요. 우키요에(浮世繪)의 후손들 속에서 자꾸만 잊혀져 가는 우리말을 곱씹으며, 참으로 말없이 그리고 묵묵히 외로움을 달래면서 열심히 그림을 그렸지요. 그러자 랩소디, 자유분방하면서도 민족적 색채가 짙은 보헤미안들의 한이 담긴 서사시가 생각이 났어요. 헝가리안 랩소디, 많이 들었던 곡이지요. 작곡가가 프란츠 리스트(Franz Liszt)였던가. 그때 내 생각으로는 위대한 작가는 폴 고갱도 아니고 앙리 루소나 반 고흐도 아니었어요. 형상성이 있는 사실적인 그림이나 구상적인 작업보다는 류보프 포포바 같은 러시아 작가, 혹은 말레비치의 기하학적 형태로 그려진 추상적인 작품들이 더 신선해 보였어요. 그림이란 일단 완성되고 나면 아무리 마음에 드는 작품일지라도 되돌아 갈 수 없다는 것을 깨닫게 된 것도 이 시기였지요.

윤 선생께서는 오리엔탈사진학교도 다니셨지요?

유 문화학원에는 프랑스 유학을 다녀온 선배들이 몇 분 있었는데, 그 가운데 문화학원 1회 졸업생으로 무척 추상적이고 모던했던 무라이 마사나리 선생이 있었어요. 워낙 유명한 작가여서 여간해서는 만나기가 어려웠던 분이지요. 니혼대학 출신의 김환기도 무척 좋아했고요. 그런데 어느 날이었던가. 김환기가 찾아와 함께 선생 댁을 찾아간 적이 있었어요. 매우 추상적이고 기하학적인 형태로 구성된 작품들이 작업실에 가득했어요. 그런데 그때 문득 알아볼 수도 없는 모던 아트만 가지고는 그림 한 점 팔 수 없겠구나 하는 생각이 들었어요. 매달 부친이 송금해주는 돈으로 생활하고 있었지만, 그림을 팔아서 살아간다는 것은 가능성이 없어 보였어요. 아마 김환기도 나와 똑같은 생각을 했을 거예요. 그래서 나이가 들어서도 부모님 도움 없이 그림을 그릴 수 있는 길이 무엇일까 생각하다가 시내 곳곳에 있던 사진관들이 생각났어요. 동경에서 DP점(사진현상소)이라도 열면 그림을 그리면서 굶지는 않겠구나 하는 생각도 들었어요. 그래서 먼저 오리엔탈사진실기강습회를 수료하고 오리엔탈사진학교를 들어갔지요. 지금도 어딘가에 졸업증서가 있을 거예요. 사진학교를 졸업하고 나자 신문사 보도사진 기자가 되고 싶었어요. 신문사 기자가 되면 이곳저곳을 돌아다니며 새로운 소식들을 카메라에 담아 내 사진들을 많은 독자들에게 알릴 수 있겠구나 하는 생각이 들었어요. 아마 태평양전쟁이 시작한 직후였던 것 같아요. 그 무렵에 찍었던 사진이 경주 남산이었어요. 아는 선배를 통해서 신문사 입사 통지서를 기다리고 있었는데, 곳곳에서 포성 소리가 들려 왔어요. 고국으로 돌아갈 생각은 전혀 없었는데, 고향에 계시는 부모님과 가족들이 걱정스러웠어요. 그러면서도 취직이 되면 동경에서 계속 그림을 그리면서 스스로 살아남아야겠다는 생각으로 밤잠을 이루지 못했던 때가 한두 번이 아니에요. 지금도 그때 사용했던 라이카 카메라가 어딘가에 있을 거예요. 그때 라이카는 웬만한 집 한 채 값이었지요. 당시에는 독일제 라이카가 최고였어요. 고향에 돌아와서도 필름이나 인화지, 현상액들은 대부분 일본을 다녀오는 사람들에게 부탁해서 썼던 때라 많은 사진을 찍지는 못했어요. 그렇지만 내가 사진기를 워낙 좋아하니까 아이들이 핫셀블라드를 사주어서 틈이 나면 고향을 찾아가 불영계곡과 죽변 주위를 사진에 담곤 했어요. 암실이나 현상시설이 여의치 않아서도 그랬지만 자꾸만 그림이 너무 그리고 싶었어요. 처음에는 돈벌이를 위해 배워둔 사진 기술이었지만, 나도 모르게 렌즈와의 교감을 통해서 얻은 사진의 기법들을 그림 속에 담아내고 싶었지요.

윤 사진계에서도 선생을 일컬어 "한국사진의 선구자"라고 하는데요.

유 과찬이에요. 돈벌이를 생각하여 시작했던 사진을 1942년이었던가, 《미술창작가협회전》에 회우 자격으로 보도사진들을 출품한 적이 있었어요. 그런데 태평양전쟁이 막판에 이르자 할 수 없이 8년여 간의 유학생활을 접고 귀국해야 했지요. 집으로 돌아와서도 사진 기법과 그림을 결합시켜 보고자 했던 생각을 지금도 지울 수가 없어요. 울진에서 서울로 이사 온 뒤에도 사진을 너무나 좋아해서 한 사람이 겨우 드나들 수 있는 공간에 사진 작업을 위한 암실을 꾸미고, 스스로 찍은 사진을 인화하기도 했지요. 그러자 얼마 후에 한국전쟁이 일어났어요.

윤 사진 이외에 다른 취미는 없으셨나요?

유 태평양전쟁과 한국전쟁을 겪으면서 뭐 특별한 취미를 가질 수 있었겠어요. 다만 나는 동경에 있을 때 탱고를 정말 좋아했고, 친구들과 함께 북해도까지 가서 스키를 탄 적도 있어요. 한국으로 돌아와서도 스키를 타고 싶어 어린애처럼 눈 오기만 기다린 적도 많았어요. 그리고 울진에 살았기 때문에 누구보다도 수영을 참 좋아해요. 그리고 휘파람도 잘 불지요. 동경에 있을 때 외로울 때면 혼자서 조용히 휘파람을 불곤 했지요. 피난살이 때는 아내가 기진맥진해서 집으로 돌아오면, 바닷가 모래밭에 앉아 휘파람을 불어주기도 했지요.

윤 귀국 후 해방, 전쟁 등의 상황을 겪으면서 선생께서는 '잃어버린 10년'을 아쉬워하셨는데요. 그때 얘기를 좀 들려주시죠.

유 귀국해서 고향 울진으로 돌아온 뒤에 형님이 경영하던 어업을 물려받았고, 뱃사람들과 함께 배를 타고 다니면서 두 해 가까이 고기를 잡으러 다녔지요. 그러면서도 생활이 안정되면 서울로 올라가 그림을 그려야 한다는 생각이 간절했어요. 그러던 중 1947년 무렵에 김환기로부터 연락이 왔어요. 서울대학교에 응용미술과가 생겼으니 서울로 오지 않겠냐는 것이었지요. 그래서 어업이고 뭐고 다 집어던지고 일본에서 그렸던 그림들을 가지고 이듬해 서울로 이사를 했어요. 당시 나는 일본사람들이 살던 적산 가옥에 살았지요. 그런데 얼마 있다가 한국전쟁이 일어나고 말았어요. 집을 구입하고 나서 얼마 안 되었던 때라 경제적으로 여유가 없었어요. 그래서 헌 리어카 하나를 사서 고향 친구들과 함께 동대문시장에서 숯 장사를 하기도 했지요. 집에 있었던 광목, 베, 명주들을 시골로 들고 다니면서 잡곡하고 바꿔 오기도 했고요. 그러던 어느 날 인민위원회에서 왔다는 붉은 완장을 찬 청년에게 끌려갔지

요. 아마 요즈음의 중앙시장 언저리가 아닌가 생각되네요. 이미 많은 청년들이 끌려와 있었지요. 그때는 그림이고 뭐고 앞날에 대한 희망이 전혀 보이지 않았어요. 며칠 후 새벽이 되자 완장을 찬 청년이 다시 나를 부르더니 집으로 돌아가라는 거예요. 왜 그랬는지는 모르겠지만 지금 생각으로는 키가 크고 비쩍 말라서 쓸모가 없어서였는지 모르겠으나, 어쨌든 며칠 저녁을 지옥에 있다가 되살아난 것 같은 기분이었어요. 돌아와 아내에게 지난 시간들을 이야기했더니, 내가 끌려간 날로부터 어머님이 새벽이 되면 하루도 빠지지 않고 장독대에 정화수를 올려놓고 지극정성으로 내가 무사하기를 빌었다는 거예요. 어머님의 기도 덕분에 살아 돌아왔는지도 모르지요.

그 일이 있은 후 1·4 후퇴 때 나는 다시 가족들을 데리고 울진 본가로 피난을 떠났어요. 그러나 동란에 가족들을 먹여 살리기에는 가장으로서 너무 힘겨웠고, 그래서 다시 아내와 상의를 해서 부친으로부터 받은 양조 면허를 가지고 옛날부터 양조장에 있었던 일꾼 한 사람을 불러, 떨어져 나간 문짝들을 다시 달고 술을 담그기 시작했어요. 동해안을 따라 내려온 피난민들로 술이 금방 모자랐지요. 전쟁 통에는 술 소비가 엄청나기 때문에 돈도 많이 벌었어요.

회고해보면 태평양전쟁과 한국전쟁이라는 전란 속에서 살아남은 것만으로도 기적 같아요. 가장으로서 어떻게 해서든지 가계를 꾸려 나가야겠다는 일념으로 나도 모르게 5년이라는 시간을 훌쩍 보냈지요. 해방 직전의 혼란기, 그리고 한국전쟁 피난 기간 동안 그림을 그릴 수 없었던 이 시기를 나는 스스로 '잃어버린 10년'이라고 해요. 그 후 나는 이 10년에 대한 보상을 위해서라도 더욱 열심히 그림을 그려야 한다고 스스로 마음을 동여매곤 했지요.

윤 (독백) 대화는 여기서 끝났다. 1960년대 이후 나는 유영국 선생과 같은 시대를 공유하며 함께 시간을 보내왔다. 선생의 행적은 늘 나의 관심사였으며, 언제나 나는 그 분을 존경 어린 시선으로 보아왔다. 불모지 같은 한국 화단에서, 선생이 좋아하셨던 '소나무'처럼 늘 당당하고 꿋꿋하게 '선구자'의 자리를 지켜 주셨다. 그 분이 살아계신다면 더 많은 것들을 여쭤보았을 텐데 … 어쩌면 이런 질문들을 그때 했었다 하더라도 그 분의 대답은 이처럼 구구절절하지 않았을 것이다. 유영국 선생은 이런 말을 툭 내뱉을 뿐이었다. "작가는 작품으로 말하는 거야."

YOO YOUNGKUK 1916-2002

The 100th Anniversary Exhibition of a Korean Modern Master

작가 연보

Artist Biography

작가 연보

이인범

상명대학교 교수, 『유영국저널』 편집인

유영국 생가 사진

1916 **4월 7일** 강원도(1963년 행정구역 개편으로 경상북도로 편입) 울진군 울진읍 읍남리 216번지(현 울진읍 말루길 118-21)에서 아버지 유문종(1876-1946)과 어머니 홍동호(1880-1963) 사이에서 4남 4녀 중 여섯째로 태어나다. 본관은 강릉이며, 시조는 문양공(文襄公) 유전(劉荃)이다.

증조 할아버지 유한열(1800-?)은 1840년대 생활 터전을 강원도 원주에서 울진으로 이주한 것으로 알려져 있다. 할아버지 유재업(1845-1913)은 풍수지리에 일가견이 있어 그의 조부의 묘를 강원도 울진군 대흥리 가시령 시싯골 산중에 쓰고, 울진과 부산 지역을 오가며 상업으로 성공, 약 2,000석 규모의 농지를 매입하며 지주가 되었다. 강릉에 있는 고가(古家)를 매입하여 울진으로 이축하기도 했다. 아버지 유문종은 전통적인 한학 교육을 받았으며, '태백산의 호랑이'라는 별명을 지닌 의병장 신돌석(申乭石, 1878-1908)에게 거액의 군자금을 제공하고, 1925년 제동초등학교를 설립하여 명문사학으로 발전시키는 등 사회교육사업에 기여하였다. 그는 아들 넷과 사위를 일본에 유학시켰으며, 유영국이 행하는 자율적 판단과 행동을 존중하여 화가로서 독자적 성격을 일구는 데 든든한 버팀목이 되었다고 전해진다.

1926 **5월** 울진공립보통학교(당시 5년제)에 입학하다. 유영국의 생가에서 약 1.5km 정도 떨어진 울진 읍내에 위치해 있던 이 학교는 1908년 명동학교로 개교하여 1912년 울진공립보통학교로 학제가 변경된 후 1924년부터는 9학급으로 편성되었다.

보통학교 시절, 유영국의 학과 성적은 매우 우수하였다. 유영국이 그린 그림이 교장실에 걸린 적이 있으며, 미술에 재능이 있었던 것으로 보인다.

卒業證書

劉永國

大正五年四月七日生

普通學校修業年限六年ノ全課

科ヲ卒業セシコトヲ證ス

昭和六年三月二十四日

蔚珍公立普通學校長神野修

第二八九號

1931년 울진 공립보통학교 졸업증서

1931 **3월** 울진공립보통학교를 우등으로 졸업하다. 함께 졸업한 동기생은 134명으로 대부분은 남학생이었다. 그 가운데에는 같은 1916년 출생으로서 독립운동가이자 사회주의운동가로 활약하다가 월북한 최학소(崔學韶, 1916-?)도 있다. 울진공립보통학교 제19회 졸업생으로 양조업에 종사했던 최만유와는 평생 가깝게 지냈다.

1931년 서울 상경 기념사진

3월 말 교사 및 학우 3명과 함께 상경 기념사진을 촬영하다.

4월 1일 경성 제2고등보통학교(이후 경성 제2고보로 약칭, 현 경복고등학교)에 입학하다. 경성 제2고보는 1921년, 총독부가 문화통치의 일환으로 설립한 5년제 고등학교로 일찍이 유영국의 둘째 형 유영숙이 제1기생으로 입학했으므로 그 선택은 자연스러운 일이었다. 입학 동기생으로는 화가 장욱진(張旭鎭), 미술사학자 황수영(黃壽永), 정치가 박병배(朴炳培) 등이 있다.

학교는 만주사변 등으로 군국주의적인 분위기가 지배하는 가운데 자유주의적 교육관과 예술관을 지닌 미술교사 사토 쿠니오(佐藤九二男, 1897-1945)를 만난 것은 행운이었다. 학생들에게 예술적 감화를 준 사토 쿠니오의 영향 아래 유영국을 비롯하여 장욱진, 임완규, 김창억, 이대원, 권옥연 등이 훗날 대한민국을 대표하는 화가들로 성장하였다. 1961년에는 경성 제2고보의 '2'와 사토 쿠니오의 '9'를 따서 2·9동인전을 결성하여 함께 활동하기도 했다. 유영국 이전에 사토 쿠니오의 지도를 받은 졸업생으로는 정현웅(제4회), 심형구(제4회) 등이 있다.

1933

10월 27일 미술교사 사토 쿠니오가 도상봉, 공진형, 이마동, 이시구로 요시카즈(石黑義保), 야마구치 다케오(山口長男), 도다 카즈오(遠田運雄) 등과《청구회(靑邱會) 창립전》(10. 27-30, 경성 미스코시백화점 화랑)을 개최하다. 이 중 야마구치 다케오는 몬드리안을 비롯한 추상미술을 소개한 인물로 잘 알려져 있다.

1934

1934년 경성제2고보시절 금강산 수학여행 중 총석정 앞에서

4월 초 경성 제2고보 4학년이 되어 학급 급장을 맡다.

5월 중순 금강산의 신계사(新溪寺), 만물상, 구룡연, 총석정과 원산항 등에 수학여행을 다녀오다.

연말 군국주의적인 분위기 속에서 학급장으로서 학생들의 비행과 동향을 밀고하라는 일본인 담임교사의 강권에 따르지 않자 수차례 구타를 당하다. 5학년 진급을 앞두고 자퇴를 결행하다(훗날 경복고등학교 제11회 졸업생으로 추인됨). 귀향하여 부모로부터 사후 승낙을 받았으며, 마도로스가 되어 오대양 육대주를 누비며 살고자 일본 요코하마 상선학교 유학을 꿈꾸기도 했다.

1935

2월 4일 일본 유학을 떠나기 전 강남스튜디오에서 친구들과 기념촬영을 하다.

2월 23일 경성 제2고보 미술교사 사토 쿠니오의 조언을 받아 도쿄에 있는 문화학원(文化學院)유화과에 지원하다.

3월 도쿄시 시부야구 센다가야 욘쵸메 719(東京市澁谷区千駄ヶ谷四丁目七一九 長崎様方)에 거처를 마련하다.

4월 초 문화학원 유화과에 입학하다. 입학 동기생은 평양 출신의 김병기(金秉騏), 가메야마 츠네코(亀山恒子), 츠카모토 시젠(塚本自然)등 모두 10명이었다.

박성규(朴性圭)는 이미 졸업한 뒤였으며, 한국인으로는 김종찬(金宗燦), 이철이(李哲伊)가 각각 3학년과 2학년에 재학 중이었다.

4월 유영국의 문화학원 입학 소식을 접한 경성 제2고보 미술교사 사토 쿠니오로부터 제5회《독립미술가협회전》출품작이 실린 격려의 엽서를 받다.

1937

3월 이전 도쿄시 세타가야구 교도쵸 프렌드 하우스(東京市世田ケ谷区 經堂町 フレンドハウス)로 거주지를 옮기다.

3월 13일 제7회《독립미술가협회전》(3. 13-4. 4, 도쿄부립미술관)에 유화작품 〈랩소디〉를 출품, 입선하여 미술계에 데뷔하다. 이 작품은 러시아 구축주의 화가 류보프 포포바(Lyubov Popova, 1889-1924)가 1922년에 제작한 〈Le Cocu magnifique〉 무대세트에 영향받은 것으로, 향후 그가 화가로서 평생에 걸쳐 지속했던 진취적이고 아방가르드적인 태도를 예고해 주고 있다.

4월 이중섭, 안기풍 등 한국인이 대거 문화학원에 입학하다.

7월 이전 도쿄 시바구 니시쿠보 토모에쵸 32 이마콘 댁(芝區西久保 巴町 三二今方)으로 거처를 옮기다.

7월 10일 제1회《자유미술가협회전》(7. 10-19, 도쿄 우에노·일본미술협회)에 릴리프 〈작품 B〉를 출품하여 입선하다. 이후 1943년 도쿄 생활을 접고 귀국하기까지 유영국은 자유미술가협회를 거점으로 작품 활동을 펼쳤다. 이와 더불어 N.B.G.(Neo Beaux-Arts Group) 동인으로도 활동하기 시작했다.

1938

1월 26일 제2회《N.B.G. 양화동인전》(1. 26-28, 도쿄 긴자·기노쿠니야화랑)에 〈릴리프 오브제〉를 출품하다.

3월 문화학원 미술과를 제11회로 졸업하다.

동창생 명부에 따르면, 졸업 동기생으로 한중근(韓仲根), 라티프 사프타리타(Latip Saptarita), 니시무라 소노(西村その, 교장 니시무라 이사쿠의 딸), 카메야마 츠네코(龜山恒子), 이시이 미후유(石井三冬, 미술교사 이시이 하쿠테이의 딸), 츠카모토 시젠(塚本自然) 등 9명이 있다.

문화학원 시절 유영국은 색채가 작렬하는 표현주의적이고 야수파적 기질을 드러내는 그림을 그렸다고 한다. 또한 문화학원은 자유로운 분위기였으나, 교수진의 취향은 보수적인 경향이 짙었다고 회고한다. 데생과 구상화 지도 담당인 이시이 하쿠테이의 경우가 특히 그러해서, 유영국과 갈등을 빚기도 했다. 유영국은 그와의 의견 충돌로 그리던 그림을 뒤집어 놓고 뛰쳐나온 후 그의 수업에 다시 참가하지 않았다고 회고하고 있다. 유영국에게 교수들보다도 깊은 영향을 준 사람은 문화학원 제1회 졸업생이자 10년 선배로서 프랑스 유학을 다녀와 왕성하게 활동하던 무라이 마사나리 등 진취적인 태도를 지닌 선배 및 동료들이었던 것으로 보인다.

한편, 유영국은 일본 유학 시기 데생 공부를 위해 다니던 SPA연구소에서 만난 선배 화가 김환기, 길진섭 등과 절친하게 지냈다.

4월 13일 제3회《N.B.G. 양화전》(4. 13-15, 도쿄 긴자·기노쿠니야화랑)에 〈습작〉 등을 출품하다.

5월 이전 오오모리구 아라이주쿠 4-1295 메카마 아파트(大森區新井宿四ノ一二九六目浦 アパート)로 이사하다.

5월 22일 제2회《자유미술가협회전》(5. 22-31, 도쿄 우에노·일본미술협회)에 〈작품 R2〉, 〈작품 R3〉, 〈작품 E1〉, 〈작품 G〉을 출품하여 문학수 등과 함께 자유미술가협회상을 수상하고 회우로 추대되다.

이때 받은 자유미술가협회상 상금과 부모에게 재산 상속분으로 받은 돈을 합쳐 라이카 카메라 한 대를 구입했다.

1930년대 말-1940년대 초 일본 유학 시기 카메라를 매고 있는 유영국

1940년대 거리를 걷고 있는 유영국과 김환기

6월 이후 무라이 마사나리 등 여러 선배 및 동료 화가들이 거주하는 도쿄만에 위치한 시나가와구 오오이 스지노모리의 아파드 아파트 '포플라의 집'(品川区鈴野ヶ森一九二八 ポプラの家)으로 거처를 옮겨 예술가들과 교류의 폭을 넓히다.

9월 22일 제4회《N.B.G. 양화전》(9. 22 - 24, 도쿄 긴자·기노쿠니야화랑)에 〈작품 LA - 101〉 등을 출품하다.

11월 22일 제5회《N.B.G. 양화전》(11. 22 - 25, 도쿄 긴자·기노쿠니야화랑)에 〈역정(歷程) 2〉 등을 출품하고, 전람회 안내 엽서 표지에 자신의 작품을 싣다.

1939

3월 27일 제6회《N.B.G. 양화전》(3. 27 - 29, 도쿄 긴자·기노쿠니야화랑)에 〈계도(計圖) D〉 등의 작품을 출품하다.

5월 21일 제3회《자유미술가협회전》(5. 21 - 30, 도쿄 우에노·일본미술협회)에 회우 자격으로 〈작품 1(L24 - 39.5)〉, 〈작품 4(L24 - 39.5)〉를 출품하다.

6월 15일 제3회《자유미술가협회 오사카전》(6. 15 - 21, 오사카시립미술관)에 〈작품 1(L24 - 39.5)〉, 〈작품 4(L24 - 39.5)〉를 출품하다.

10월 19일 제7회《N.B.G. 양화전》(10. 19 - 24, 도쿄 긴자·기노쿠니야화랑)이 열렸으나 현재로는 유영국의 출품 여부는 정확히 확인되지 않는다.

1940

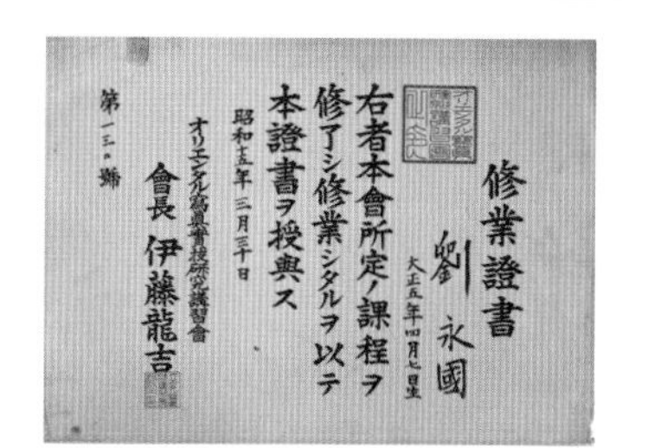

修業證書

劉永國

大正五年四月七日生

右者本會所定ノ課程ヲ修了シ修業シタルヲ以テ本證書ヲ授與ス

昭和十五年三月三十日

オリエンタル寫眞實技研究講習會

會長 伊藤龍吉

第一三〇號

1940년 오리엔탈 사진실기강습회 수료증서

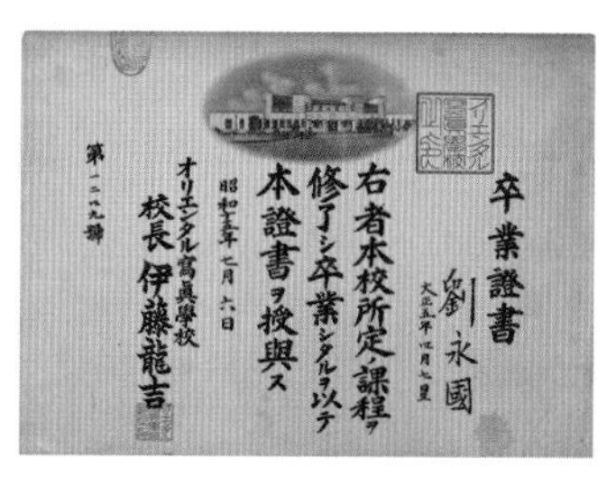

卒業證書

劉永國

大正五年四月七日生

右者本校所定ノ課程ヲ修了シ卒業シタルヲ以テ本證書ヲ授與ス

昭和十五年七月六日

オリエンタル寫眞學校

校長 伊藤龍吉

第一二九號

1940년 오리엔탈사진학교 졸업증서

3월 30일 사진현상소로 생계를 꾸리고 새로운 매체로서 사진의 조형적 가능성을 모색하고자 오리엔탈사진실기강습회에 참가하여 과정을 수료하다.

5월 22일 제4회《자유미술가협회전》(5. 22 - 31, 도쿄 우에노·일본미술협회)에 〈작품 404 - A〉, 〈작품 404 - B〉, 〈작품 404 - C〉, 〈작품 404 - D〉, 〈작품 404 - E〉 총 5점을 출품하다.

6월 15일 제4회《자유미술가협회 오사카전》(6. 15 - 21, 오사카시립미술관)에 〈작품 404 - A〉, 〈작품 404 - B〉, 〈작품 404 - C〉, 〈작품 404 - D〉, 〈작품 404 - E〉 총 5점을 출품하다.

전시회 개최시 간행된『자유미술』제2호에 자신의 작품 1점을 삽화로 게재하다. 이 전시가 종료된 직후 당국의 요구에 따라 명칭을 미술창작가협회로 바꾸다.

7월 6일 오리엔탈사진학교를 졸업하다.

10월 12일 《미술창작가협회 경성전》(10. 12 - 16, 경성·부민회관 소강당)에 〈릴리프 1〉, 〈릴리프 2〉, 〈릴리프 3〉, 〈작품〉 총 4점을 출품하여, 한국에 처음으로 유영국의 작품이 소개되고「조선일보」등 신문 매체를 통해 알려지다.

1941

4월 10일 제5회《미술창작가협회전》(4. 10 - 10. 21, 도쿄 우에노·일본미술협회)에 〈10 - 1〉, 〈10 - 2〉, 〈10 - 3〉, 〈10 - 4〉, 〈10 - 5〉, 〈10 - 6〉, 〈10 - 7〉, 〈10 - 8〉, 〈10 - 9〉 총 9점을 출품하다.

1942

1월 - 3월 오리엔탈사진학교에서 습득한 사진 기법을 바탕으로, 경주 남산, 불국사 등 경주 일원을 답사하며 불상·불탑·고분·고건축 등을 소재로 사진 작업을 하다.

4월 4일 제6회《미술창작가협회전》(4. 4 - 12, 도쿄 우에노·일본미술협회)에 경주 일원에서 찍은 사진 작품 〈사진 No.1〉, 〈사진 No.2〉, 〈사진 No.3〉, 〈사진 No.4〉, 〈사진 No.5〉, 〈보도사진 6〉, 〈보도사진 7〉 총 7점을 출품하다.

1943

3월 25일 태평양전쟁의 전운이 짙게 드리워진 가운데, 미술창작가협회가 '창작과제'로 '일본민족 번영의 아름다움'을 토픽으로 내걸고 제7회《미술창작가협회전》(3. 25 – 4. 2)를 열었으나, 이 전시에 출품하지 않고 활동을 멈추다. 귀국 후 아버지 소유의 어선으로 어업 활동을 시작하다.

4월 12일 문화학원 입학식 날 아침 문화학원의 설립자이자 교장 니시무라 이사쿠(西村伊作)가 '천황에 대한 불경죄 및 언론 출판 집회 결사 등 임시취체법 위반' 혐의로 자택에서 체포되다. 몇 달 후 징역 1년 형 판결을 받다.

8월경 8년여의 도쿄에서의 유학생활과 작품 활동을 접고, 고향 울진(울진읍 82 - 13)으로 돌아오다. 그동안 제작한 100여 점의 작품들 중 일부는 선배 무라이 마사나리에게 맡기고, 나머지 작품들은 배에 실어 가져오다.

8월 31일 유영국이 다니던 문화학원이 폐교 명령을 받아 일본 역사상 전무후무하게 국가권력에 의해 폐교된 수난 기록으로 남다.

1944

11월 15일 서울 YMCA에서 김기순과 결혼하고 금강산으로 신혼여행을 떠나다. 울진으로 돌아와 살림을 차리다.

1945년 평해 바닷가에서
부인 김기순 여사

1945

8월 17일 장녀 리지 태어나다. 유리지는 금속공예가로 성장하여 후에 서울미대 공예과 교수를 거쳤으며, 치우금속공예관(현재 '유리지기념관'으로 개칭됨)을 설립하고 관장으로 활동하였다.

1946

8월 1일 부친 유문종 작고하다.

1947

말 김환기로부터 서울미대 응용미술과 교수직 제안을 받다.

1948

3월 가족은 울진에 남겨두고, 유영국 혼자 먼저 서울 생활을 시작하다.

4월 15일 서울대학교 미술부 교수로 부임하다.

4월 21일 차녀 자야 태어나다.

11월 5일 해방 이후 각종 이데올로기 편향적 미술단체들에 가담하지 않던 유영국이 자유미술가협회에서 함께 활동했던 김환기, 이규상 등 추상작가를 중심으로 신사실파를 결성하다.

12월 7일 《신사실파 창립전》(12. 7 – 14, 서울·화신화랑)을 열고 〈회화 1〉, 〈회화 2〉, 〈회화 3〉, 〈회화 4〉, 〈회화 5〉, 〈회화 6〉, 〈회화 7〉, 〈회화 8〉, 〈회화 9〉, 〈회화 10〉 총 10점을 출품하다.

1948년 제1회《신사실파 창립전》
리플릿

1949

3월경 서울 성동구 약수동 366 – 4 번지의 집을 구입하여 울진에 거주하던 가족과 합류하다.

9월 제1회《대한민국미술전람회》(이하《국전》으로 약칭) 출품을 권유받았으나 거부하다.

11월 28일 제2회《신사실파전》(11. 28 – 12. 3, 서울·동화화랑)에 〈직선이 있는 구도 A〉, 〈직선이 있는 구도 B〉, 〈직선이 있는 구도 C〉, 〈직선이 있는 구도 D〉, 〈회화 A〉, 〈회화 B〉, 〈회화 C〉, 〈회화 D〉, 〈회화 E〉, 〈회화 F〉 총 10점을 출품하다.

1950	**1월 5일** 50년미술협회 창립총회에 참석하다. 이 협회는 유영국 뿐 아니라 김환기, 최재덕, 이쾌대, 장욱진, 남관, 김만형, 김병기, 김영주, 송혜수, 진환, 서강헌, 손응성, 이봉상 등이 준비위원으로 참여하였는데, "적극적인 예술정신에 의하여 전진코자 하는 진지한 미술가의 대동단결체로서 각자 예술의 자유로운 발전과 새로운 민족미술의 앙양을 도모하기 위하여" 30대의 역동적인 소장 작가들을 중심으로 결성된 단체이다.
	6월 중순 《50년미술협회 창립전》 개최를 2주 남짓 앞두고, 서울대학교 미술부장 장발이 전시 참여와 국립대 교수직 중 택일을 요구함에 따라 2년 3개월 동안 재직하던 서울대학교 미술부 교수직을 사퇴하다(행정적으로는 한국전쟁 발발로 서울 수복 후인 11월 20일자로 사표가 수리됨). 《50년미술협회 창립전》 출품을 위해 여러 점의 작품을 제작하였지만 경복궁미술관에서 7월 1일 개최될 예정이던 전시는 전쟁으로 무산되다.
	6월 25일 한국전쟁 발발. 인민군의 서울 점령 기간 중 생계를 위해 리어카를 빌려 교외에서 장작을 패다 파는 등 강인한 생활력을 발휘하다. 여러 동료 화가들과 미술가동맹에 차출되어 김일성, 스탈린 초상화 제작을 요구받고, 추상화가라는 핑계로 유영국은 의복을, 친구 장욱진은 넥타이를 분담하여 그리는 것으로 시간을 보내다.
	10월 30일 장남 진이 태어나다.
1951	**1월 4일** 1.4 후퇴 시 가족과 함께 고향 울진으로 피난을 떠나다.
	1월 말 생가에서 피난생활을 시작한지 약 3주 후, 거의 폐허가 다 된 부친 소유의 죽변 양조장을 수리하여 운영에 착수하다. 양조장 운영을 위한 원료 수급, 술 제조 배달 등 고된 노동에도 불구하고, 술지게미로 여러 마리의 돼지를 사육하는 등 강인한 생활력과 사업가 기질을 발휘하다. 철두철미한 양조 품질 관리와 신뢰를 바탕으로 양조장 운영은 큰 성공을 거두어 관동 지방의 대표적인 위치를 차지하게 되다. 여기엔 화가로서의 경험과 상상력도 한몫했다. 피난생활로 지친 사람들이 넘쳐나던 시절, 소주 이름을 줄리앙 뒤비비에르(Julien Duvivier) 감독의 「망향(望鄕)」으로 붙이는가 하면, 붉은색을 너무 많이 사용했다며 당국의 감찰을 받기도 했지만 스스로 디자인한 상표로 눈길을 끌었다.
1952	**4월** 맏딸 리지가 죽변국민학교에 입학하다. 책상을 제작하고, 능숙한 바느질 솜씨로 자신의 양복을 딸의 코트로 수선하여 입히는 등 아버지로서 솜씨 어린 애정을 표하다.
	이 해 양조장 한 모퉁이의 작은방을 화실로 쓰기 시작하다.
1953	**2월 6일** 차남 건 태어나다.
	5월 26일 제3회 《신사실파 부산전》(5. 26 - 6. 4, 부산·국립박물관)에 창립회원 김환기, 이규상, 제2회부터 가담한 장욱진에 이어 백영수와 이중섭이 합류한 가운데 〈산맥〉, 〈나무〉, 〈해변에서 A〉, 〈해변에서 B〉 총 4점의 작품을 출품하다. 제2회 《신사실파전》으로부터 3년 반 동안의 공백을 딛고 작품을 발표하고, 부산에 피난하여 밀집해 있던 여러 친구들을 만나 화가로서 고립감을 해소하다.

1954

1월 16일 부산 광복동의 피난지에서 환도하여 서울 남산에 자리 잡은 국립박물관에서 최순우가 기획한《한국현대회화 특별전》(1. 16 – 3. 31, 국립박물관)에 20여 명의 작가들과 더불어 출품하다.

6월경 약수동 집에 세 들어 있던 가족의 실수로, 보관 중이던 일본 체류기의 작품들, 신사실파 출품작들,《50년미술협회전》출품 준비 작품 등 그때까지 제작된 작품들 가운데 3점(제4회《자유미술가협회전》출품작 2점, 제2회《신사실파전》출품작 1점)을 제외한 모든 작품이 물에 잠겨 유실되는 뼈아픈 경험을 하다.

1955

5월 울진에서의 피난 생활을 접고, 서울 약수동 집으로 돌아와 화업을 본격적으로 재개하다. 이후 유영국은 직업 화가로서 태평양전쟁체제 속에서 1942년 제6회《자유미술가협회전》을 끝으로 작품 활동을 멈추고, 1948년《신사실파전》으로 재개했으나 다시 한국전쟁이 발발하면서 화업으로부터 멀어졌다. 그는 이 기간을 '잃어버린 10년'이라 명명하며, 그 결핍을 메우는 일이 자신의 업보라고 말하곤 했다.

5월 21일 서울로 돌아오자마자 대한미술협회 부회장을 맡던 중 1951년 미국으로 갔다가 돌아온 장발이 회장 선거에 입후보하자 그때까지 회장을 맡고 있던 고희동이 탈퇴하고 한국미술가협회를 창립하는 등 미학논쟁과는 무관한 미술인들의 분규를 목격하다.

5월 이후 양조장 운영은 타인에게 맡기고, 다만 관리를 위해 정기적으로 백두대간을 넘어 울진을 넘나드는 생활이 시작되다. 이때 경험한 거대한 자연은 유영국의 작품에 중요한 영감의 원천이 되다.

10월 도상봉을 중심으로 임원과 회원을 재정비한 대한미술협회에 입회하다.

11월 제4회《국전》(11. 1 – 30, 서울·경복궁미술관)에 처음으로 추천작가로〈산 있는 그림〉을 출품하다.

1956

9월 이항성이『신미술』을 창간하면서 자주 왕래하다.

10월 "현대회화의 문제를 기본이념으로 삼고, 그 회화운동의 전위체로서 독자적인 활동을 하기 위하여," 박고석, 이규상, 한묵, 황염수 등과 모던 아트협회를 창립하다. 미술인이 주체가 되는 그룹전 시대가 열려, 창작미술협회, 현대미술가협회 등이 연이어 창립되는 등 답보상태에 있던 한국미술계에 새로운 전기가 마련되다.

11월『신미술』제2호,「좌담회: 미술인의 당면과제」에 참여하여, 현대미술, 전위, 외국문화 수용과 교류 등 당면 과제에 대하여 다음과 같이 말하다; "흡수할 수 있으면 많이 흡수하되 개성과 유사성의 혼돈은 배척해야지요. (중략) 흡수할 것과 내면에서 자아낸 것과는 차질점(差質點)이 있다고 생각됩니다." "영향과 교류의 경향 역시 어떤 '백그라운드'를 지니고 있어야 온전히 이루어질 것이라고 생각합니다."

11월 제5회《국전》초대작가로 다시 초청되었으나 출품을 거부하다.

1957

1957년 제1회《모던 아트협회전》리플릿

4월 9일 제1회《모던 아트협회전》(4. 9 – 15, 서울·동화화랑)에〈산맥〉,〈산과 구름〉,〈호수〉,〈가을〉,〈생선〉,〈노을〉,〈새〉총 7점을 출품하다.

10월 제6회《국전》에 추천작가로 초대되었으나 출품을 거부하다.

11월 홍익대학교 미술학부 전임강사에 취임하다.

11월「조선일보」주최 제1회《현대작가초대전》에 모던 아트협회가 재야 작가단체로 초대되었으나 협회 차원에서 출품을 거부하여 출품하지 않다.

11월 16일 제2회《모던 아트협회전》(11. 16 - 22, 서울·화신화랑)에 대구의 정점식과 마산의 문신이 신입회원으로 참여한 가운데, 〈계곡〉, 〈사람〉, 〈산〉, 〈해변〉 총 4점을 출품하다.

1958년 제2회
《현대작가초대전》 리플릿

1958

3월 15일 《반공미술전》(3. 15 - 4. 15, 반공회관)에 초청작가로 출품하다.

3월 31일 홍익대학교 미술학부 전임강사를 퇴임하다.

6월 3일 제3회《모던 아트협회전》(6. 3 - 9, 서울·화신화랑)에 〈산맥〉, 〈구름〉, 〈바다에서〉, 〈비(雨)〉, 〈나무〉, 〈언덕〉 총 6점을 출품하다.

6월 14일 「조선일보」 주최 제2회《현대작가초대전》(6. 14 - 7. 13, 서울·덕수궁미술관)에 〈산〉, 〈새〉, 〈아침〉, 〈Stream〉, 〈산수〉 총 5점을 출품하다.

10월 제7회《국전》에 추천작가로 초대되었으나 출품을 거부하다.

11월 1일 제4회《모던 아트협회전》(11. 1 - 8, 동화백화점 화랑)에 정규, 김창억이 신입회원으로 가담한 가운데 〈계곡〉, 〈노을〉, 〈산〉, 〈호수〉 총 4점을 출품하다. 이 전시를 마지막으로《현대작가초대전》 참여 여부를 둘러싼 회원들과의 입장 차이로 인해 자신이 주도하여 결성한 모던 아트협회를 탈퇴하고,《현대작가초대전》에 주력하다.

1959

4월 24일 제3회《현대작가초대전》(4. 24 - 5.13, 서울·경복궁미술관)에 초대작가로 〈지형〉, 〈단층〉, 〈계곡〉, 〈바다〉, 〈바다풀〉 총 5점을 출품하다.

9월 5일 서울 세종로 감리빌딩에 현대미술연구소를 열고 김병기, 한봉덕과 함께 지도위원으로 활동을 시작하다.

10월 제8회《국전》에 추천작가로 초대되었으나 출품을 거부하다.

제3회《모던아트협회》 전시장 앞에서 회우들과 함께
(왼쪽부터 문신, 이규상, 유영국, 박고석, 한묵)

1960

3월 4일 제1회《현대미술연구소습작전》(3. 4 - 5, 감리회관 현대미술연구소)에 찬조출품하다. 당시 학생 출품자로는 방혜자, 권영숙, 김옥녀, 황덕성, 표경국 등이 있다.

4월 11일 제4회《현대작가초대전》(4. 11 - 5.10, 서울·경복궁미술관)의 조직을 주도하고 〈영(嶺)〉, 〈숲〉, 〈바다〉, 〈해토(解土)〉, 〈산〉 총 5점을 출품하다.

6월 『사상계』 6월호 특집 「4월혁명화첩」에 작품 〈4월〉을 게재하다.

6월 3일 4·19혁명을 계기로 대한미술협회가 미술계 혁신을 모색하고자 20여 명의 미술인을 초청하여 개최한 미술인좌담회에 참가하다.

8월 23일 「조선일보」에 작품 〈산〉과 에세이를 게재하다.

10월 제9회《국전》에 추천작가로 초대되었으나 출품을 거부하다.

10월 무대윤리위원회 위원으로 참가하다.

10월 4·19혁명에도 불구하고, 제9회《국전》이 개혁과 담을 쌓고 구태를 반복하자 미술계 혁신을 도모하려는 이들과 함께 60년현대미술가연합을 결성하고 대표로 추대되어 국전 개혁, 현대미술관 건립 등의 내용이 포함된 9개 조항의 선언문을 발표하다.

12월 현대미술연구소가 서울 세종로에서 명륜동으로 자리를 옮기다.

12월 14일 4월민주혁명순국학생위령탑 심사위원으로 활동하다.

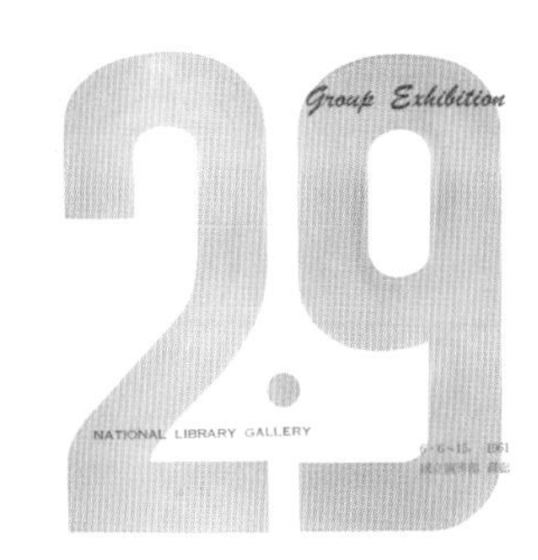

1961년 제1회《2·9 동인전》리플릿

1960년대 약수동 자택 앞마당에서 작업중인 유영국

1961

2월 2·9 동인회를 창립하다. 2·9는 장욱진, 김창억, 임완규, 이대원, 권옥연 등 경성 제2고보 미술교사 사토 쿠니오의 가르침을 받은 제자들 6인이 모여 제2고보의 '2'와 사토 쿠니오의 '9'를 딴 명칭이다.

4월 1일 제4회《현대작가초대전》(4. 1–23, 서울·경복궁미술관)에 권옥연, 김영주, 이세득, 홍종인 등과 함께 심사위원으로 참여하고, 초대작가 자격으로 〈산〉을 출품하다.

4월 22일 국제자유문화연합회 주최《국제자유미술 동경전》(4. 22–5. 7, 일본 도쿄·국립경기장 미술관)에 출품하다. 당국으로부터 여권이 발급되지 않아 도쿄 방문은 무산되다.

6월 《파리국제청년작가비엔날레》초청작가 선정위원으로 활동하다.

6월 6일 제1회《2·9 동인전》(6. 6–15, 서울·국립도서관화랑)에 〈영(嶺)〉이라는 제목의 작품 4점을 출품하다.

6월 22일 5.16 군사쿠데타 정부가 6월 12일 공포한 사회단체 등록에 관한 법률에 따라 추진된 미술단체 통합을 위한 합동준비위원회에 현대미술가연합 준비위원으로 위촉되다. 수도여자사범대학에서 개최된 회의에는 불참하다. 두 차례에 걸친 회의에서 다시 현대미술가연합측 실행위원으로 위촉되다.

9월 15일 현대미술연구소 개소 2주년을 기념하여 자축회와 습작전을 열다.

10월 17일 문교부에 의해 국전 규정이 제정됨에 따라 구성된 추천작가모임에서 유화부 심사위원으로 위촉되다.

11월 이른바 '개혁 국전'으로 평가되는 제10회《국전》(11. 1–20)에 화가 권옥연, 김영주, 김흥수, 미술평론가 이경성, 방근택 등과 심사위원으로 참여하였으나 출품은 거부하다.

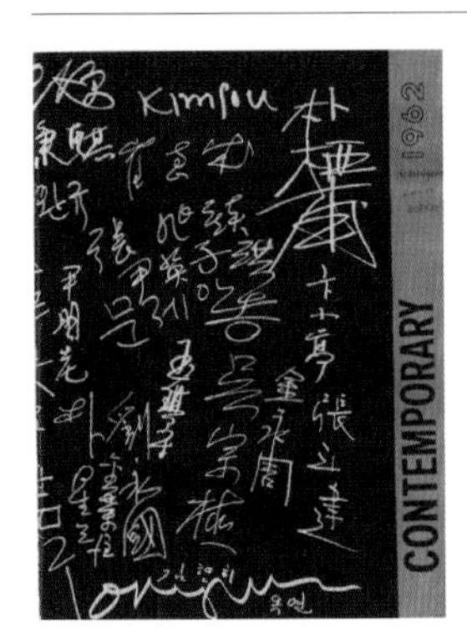

1962년 제1회《세계문화자유초대전》리플릿

1962년 제1회《신상회 창립전》리플릿

1962

6월 21일 제1회《세계문화자유초대전》(6. 21–27, 서울·중앙공보관)에 출품하다.

11월 제10회《국전》이 '개혁 국전'으로 평가받았음에도 불구하고, 제11회《국전》이 다시 복고적 양상을 보이자 국가 문화정책으로부터 자유로운 미술계의 자립에 뜻을 같이 하는 강록사, 김종휘, 김창억, 문우식, 박석호, 이대원, 이봉상, 정문규, 임완규, 조병현, 한봉덕, 황규백 등 중진 미술인들이 모여 신상회를 결성하다. 이로써 민간 후원을 유치하는 등 새로운 시도를 통해 미술인들에 의한 공모전이 처음으로 개최되다.

11월 16일 《신상회 창립전》(11. 16–25, 서울·경복궁미술관)에 〈작품 1〉, 〈작품 2〉, 〈작품 3〉, 〈작품 4〉, 〈작품 5〉, 〈작품 6〉, 〈작품 7〉 총 7점을 출품하다.

11월 27일 제2회《2·9 동인전》(11. 27–12. 3, 서울·국립도서관화랑)에 〈작품 A〉, 〈작품 B〉, 〈작품 C〉, 〈작품 D〉 총 4점을 출품하다.

1963

4월 19일 제2회《신상회전》(5. 19–31, 서울·경복궁미술관)에 〈구름〉, 〈산〉, 〈양지(陽地)〉, 〈눈〉 총 4점을 출품하다.

5월 6일 제2회《세계문화자유초대전》(5. 6–12, 중앙공보관화랑)에 〈산〉, 〈작품〉 총 2점을 출품하다.

6월 14일 제7회《상파울로비엔날레출품작 한국전》(6. 14-16, 국립공보관)에 작품 〈숲〉, 〈산1〉, 〈산2〉 총 3점을 출품하다.

9월 28일 제7회《상파울로비엔날레》(9. 28 - 12. 22, 브라질·상파울로)에 작품 〈숲〉, 〈산1〉, 〈산2〉 총 3점을 출품하다.

12월 6일 제3회《2·9 동인전》(12. 6-11, 서울·국립도서관화랑)에 작품을 출품하다.

劉永國
Exhibition
Yoo Young kuk
PRESS CENTER GALLERY (3rd Floor)
1964 作品展
11·14-19
新聞会館 大講堂(三層)

1964년 유영국의 제1회 개인전 포스터

1964

6월 28일 제3회《신상회전》(6. 28-7. 7, 서울·경복궁미술관)에 〈작품 1〉, 〈작품 2〉, 〈작품 3〉, 〈작품 4〉 등 총 4점을 출품하다. 이 전시를 마지막으로 운동 차원의 모든 그룹활동을 중단하고, 자신의 작업에 몰입하고자 결심하다.

10월 18일 「조선일보」의 '네 전문가 지상 심포지움' 「국전론」에서 다음과 같이 언급하다:" 현재 국전을 지배하고 있는 것은 고루한 사실" 뿐이며, 그것은" 파벌적 심사위원 구성과 그에 따른 편파적 심사 때문이다."" 심사위원에 젊은 작가들의 대폭적인 참여가 필요하다."

11월 14일 49세에 처음으로 개인전(11. 14-19, 서울·신문회관 특설화랑)을 개최하다. 대작 중심의 〈작품 1-15〉 총 15점을 출품하다. 이후 매 2년을 주기로 개인전을 개최하다.

12월 16일 제4회《2·9 동인전》(12. 16-20, 중앙공보관화랑)에 〈작품 A〉를 출품하다.

1965

2월 제9회《현대작가초대전》의 운영위원을 김영주, 김중업, 이경성, 최순우와 함께 맡다.

6월 제9회《현대작가초대전》에 초대작가로 작품을 출품하다.

11월 14일 《문화자유초대전》(11. 14-20, 서울 예총회관화랑)에 〈콤포지숀 65-11〉 등 3점을 출품하다.

1966

5월 24일 제2회 개인전(5. 24-29, 서울·중앙공보관)을 개최하다.

9월 4일 제10회《현대작가초대전》(9. 4-13, 경복궁미술관)에 초대작가로 〈양(陽)〉을 출품하다.

홍익대학교 미술대학에 정교수로 부임하고 서양화과장을 맡다.

1967

9월 1일 제2회《한국현대회화 10인전》(9. 1-8, 서울·신세계전시장, 「중앙일보」 주최)에 출품하다.

韓国現代絵画展
CONTEMPORARY KOREAN PAINTING

1968년《한국현대회화전》
(동경국립근대미술관) 브로슈어

1968

7월 19일 《한국현대회화전》(7. 19-9. 1, 일본·도쿄국립근대미술관)에 〈원 A〉, 〈원 B〉, 〈원 C〉, 〈산 A〉, 〈산 B〉를 출품하고, 개막식 및 좌담회에 참석하다.

9월 10일 제3회《한국현대회화 10인전》(9. 10-17, 서울·신세계전시장, 「중앙일보」 주최)에 〈산 東〉, 〈산 西〉, 〈산 南〉 총 3점을 출품하다.

9월 28일 문화공보부에 의해 제17회 국전심사위원으로 위촉되다.

11월 11일 제3회 개인전(11. 11-24, 서울·신세계화랑)을 개최하다.

1969

1월 이후 1971년까지 도쿄 국립근대미술관 주최《한국현대회화전》(1968. 7. 19-9. 1, 도쿄 국립근대미술관) 출품작들이 인도, 파키스탄, 네팔 순회전을 하다.

1960년대 홍익대학교 재직시절 유영국

6월 이탈리아 피스토이아에서 열리는 제1회《국제회화비엔날레》에 서세옥, 안동숙, 정창섭, 박서보과 함께 초청받다.

11월 11일 경희대학교 미술교육과에 1970년 2월 28일까지 출강하다.

1970

3월 19일 《초대작가전》(3. 19 - 26, 서울·신세계화랑)에 작품 1점을 출품하다.

6월 9일 「한국일보」 주최 제1회《한국미술대상전》(6. 9 - 7. 9, 서울·경복궁 국립현대미술관)에 출품하다.

11월 14일 제4회 개인전(11. 14 – 20, 서울·신세계화랑)을 개최하다.

스튜디오제 전환에 따라 학교 근무일 수가 주 3일에서 주 6일로 바뀜에 따라 전업화가로서의 정체성을 지키기 위해 홍익대학교 미술대학 교수직을 사직하다.

1971

5월 2일 경복고등학교동창회 주최《경복고등학교 개교 50주년 기념 동문미술전》(5. 2 - 8, 서울·문예회관)에 작품 2점을 출품하다.

9월 28일 제20회《국전》운영위원회에 의해 서양화 비구상부문 심사위원장으로 위촉되다.

1972

6월 유네스코한국위원회 발간『Modern Korean Painting 한국현대화집』에 작품 5점이 수록 간행되다.

7월 5일 국립현대미술관 주최《한국근대미술 60년전》(서울·덕수궁 국립현대미술관)의 추진위원으로 활동하고, 〈산 A〉, 〈산 B〉를 출품하다.

9월 제21회《국전》서양화 비구상부문 심사위원장으로 위촉되다.

1973

7월 5일 국립현대미술관 주최《한국현역화가 100인전》(7. 5 - 8. 4, 서울·덕수궁 국립현대미술관) 추진위원으로 활동하고, 작품을 출품하다.

1975

11월 14일 제5회 개인전(11. 14 - 22, 서울·현대화랑)에 〈산〉, 〈지붕〉 등의 제목으로 1972년부터 제작된 소품들을 중심으로 50여 점을 출품하다. 예술 활동 이후 처음으로 작품 1점을 판매하다.

1976

1970년대 말 등촌동 화실에서 작업중인 유영국

4월 6일 제6회 초대 개인전(4. 6 - 11, 서울·신세계미술관)에 1971년 이후 제작된 작품 중 〈산〉, 〈산사〉 제목의 137x137cm 크기의 작품 7점, 135x135cm 크기의 작품 10점, 134x134cm 크기의 작품 14점, 162x135cm 크기의 작품 3점, 105x105cm 크기의 작품 7점 등 미발표작 총 40점을 출품하다.

이 해 「한국일보」 주최 제7회《한국미술대상전》 심사위원, 제25회《국전》운영위원으로 활동하다.

대한민국예술원상 미술본상을 수상하다.

1977

2월 심근경색으로 서울대병원에 입원하다.

3월 14일 《한국현대서양화대전》(3. 14 - 4. 2, 덕수궁 국립현대미술관)에 〈산〉을 출품하다.

6월 21일 《6월 초대전》(6. 21 - 30, 서울·선화랑)에 〈산〉 연작 36점을 출품하다.

10월 서울대병원에 다시 입원하여 심장 박동기 부착 시술을 받다.

10월 21일 제7회 개인전(10. 21 - 29, 서울 진화랑)에 〈산〉 연작 36점을 출품하다.

11월 서울 등촌동에 새집을 짓기 위해 서울 중구 약수동에서 떠나 집을 임대하여 세 들다.

1978

5월 6개월 간 셋집살이를 마감하고, "겨울 아침 해 뜨는 풍경이 아름다운" 서울시 양천구 등촌동 186 - 1 번지 2층 양옥집을 지어 이사하여, '등촌동 시대'를 열다.

8월 12일 《서울갤러리 개관전》(8. 12 - 21, 서울·서울갤러리)에 〈산사(山寺)〉, 〈산〉 등 3점을 출품하다.

9월 23일 《신사실파 회고전》(9. 23 - 30, 서울·원화랑)에 〈거리에서〉, 〈바다에서〉, 〈사람〉을 출품하다.

1979

1979년 유영국 초대전 당시 덕수궁 국립현대미술관 앞에서

6월 1일 국립현대미술관 주최 《유영국초대전》(6. 4 - 17, 서울·덕수궁 국립현대미술관) 기념 도록 《YOO YOUNG - KUK》이 대영문화사에서 발행되다.

6월 4일 국립현대미술관 주최 《유영국초대전》(6. 4 - 17, 서울·덕수궁 국립현대미술관)에 장녀 리지에 의해 재제작된 1930년대 후반 초기 릴리프 작품을 포함하여, 1957년부터 1977년 사이에 제작된 작품들을 출품하여 제8회 개인전을 열다.

9월 1일 《한국현대미술 50년대전》(9. 1 - 14, 서울·국립현대미술관)에 출품하다.

9월 17일 대한민국예술원 회원에 위촉되어, 제1회 《예술원미술분과회원작품전》(9. 17 - 29, 서울· 예술원 전시실)에 〈산〉을 출품하다.

1980

9월 17일 제2회 《예술원미술분과회원작품전》(9. 17 - 27, 서울·예술원전시실)에 〈작품〉 3점을 출품하다.

10월 7일 제9회 개인전(10. 7 - 13, 서울·현대화랑)에 아침 해와 노을, 동산의 나무를 소재로 한 작품들을 출품하다.

제10회 개인전(기간 미상, 서울·공간화랑)에 소품 위주의 작품을 출품하다.

1981

4월 17일 《한국미술 '81전》(4. 17 - 5. 7, 서울·국립현대미술관)에 출품하다.

5월 2일 《경복인미술전》(5. 2 - 8, 서울·경복고등학교미술관, 경복고등학교동창회 주최)에 〈산〉을 출품하다.

12월 7일 제3회 《예술원미술분과회원작품전》(12. 7 - 13, 서울·현대화랑)에 〈작품 1〉을 출품하다.

1982

6월 28일 《국제화랑 개관기념 10인전》(6. 28 - 7. 10, 서울·국제화랑)에 〈산〉 연작을 출품하다.

10월 19일 《오늘의 회화전》(10. 19 - 29, 서울·진화랑)에 〈산〉을 출품하다.

11월 12일 제4회 《예술원미술분과회원작품전》(11. 12 - 18, 서울·현대화랑)에 〈작품 B〉를 출품하다.

1983

1월 12일 《한국현대미술전》(1. 18 - 2. 13, 이태리·밀라노 비스콘티홀)에 〈작품〉을 출품하다. 전시 개막 참석차 약 1달 동안 부부 동반으로 이태리 밀라노, 파리 등 유럽을 여행하다.

4월 12일 제11회 개인전(4. 12-17, 서울·신세계미술관)을 개최하다.

9월 5일 《유영국·올리비에 드브르(Olivier Debre) 초대 2인전》(9. 5-24, 서울·주한불란서문화원)에 작품 5점을 출품하다.

1984

5월 18일 《'84 현대미술초대전》(5. 18-6. 17, 서울·국립현대미술관) 초대작가 선정위원으로 위촉되어 활동하고, 〈작품〉을 출품하다.

6월 8일 《진우회전》(6. 8-16, 서울·선화랑)에 〈작품〉을 출품하다.

12월 5일 《한국근대미술자료전》(12. 5-30, 서울·국립현대미술관 서관 2층) 자문위원으로 위촉되다.

보관문화훈장을 수상하다.

1980년대 사진을 찍는 유영국

1985

10월 4일 광복40주년기념 《현대미술 40년전》(10. 4-18, 서울·국립현대미술관)에 국립현대미술관 소장 〈산〉(1962)이 전시되다.

1986

8월 26일 국립현대미술관 과천관 개관기념 《한국현대미술전》에 출품하다.

1987

3월 2일 《4주년 개관기념전》(3. 2-29, 서울·가나화랑) 〈산〉 2점을 출품하다.

5월 23일 《'87 현대미술초대전》(5. 23-6. 21, 과천·국립현대미술관)에 〈작품〉을 출품하다.

6월 건축을 전공한 차남 건이 설계하여 신축한 서울 서초구 방배동 12-34번지 집으로 거주지와 작업실을 옮기다.

8월 24일 《서울미술대전》(8. 24-9. 13, 서울·국립현대미술관)에 3년 전에 시작하여 마감한 100호 규모의 신작을 출품하다.

10월 16일 제9회 《예술원미술분과회원작품전》(10. 16-22, 서울·예술원미술관)에 〈작품 1〉을 출품하다.

1988

8월 17일 88올림픽기념 《세계현대미술제》(8. 17-10. 5, 과천·국립현대미술관)에 〈무제〉(1968) 5점과 신작 〈무제〉(1987) 1점, 총 6점을 출품하다.

1989

8월 21일 제5회 《서울미술대전》(8. 21-9. 20, 서울·서울시립미술관)에 〈산〉을 출품하다.

1990

8월 2일 《'90 현대미술초대전》(8. 2-31, 과천·국립현대미술관)에 〈작품〉을 출품하다.

1991

3월 15일 《현대미술 25인전》(3. 15-30, 서울·현대화랑)에 〈무제〉(1971) 2점을 출품하다.

5월 14일 《한국근대회화 7인전》(5. 14-26, 서울·현대백화점미술관)에 〈작품 A〉, 〈작품 B〉, 〈작품 C〉를 출품하다.

6월 1일 제1회 《경복동문미술전》(6. 1-8, 서울·가나화랑)에 〈산〉(1989), 〈산〉(1991)을 출품하다.

1990년대 방배동 화실에서 작업중인 유영국

1993

3월 22일 《현대미술의 기호와 형상전》(3. 22-30, 서울·현대화랑) 〈작품〉(1970) 2점을 출품하다.

1995

4월 12일 제12회 개인전(4. 12-26, 서울·갤러리 현대)에 1965년에서 1990년 사이 제작된 작품들을 출품하다.

1996	6월 12일 제27회 《바젤(Basel) 아트페어》(6. 12-17, 스위스·바젤국제전시장)에 〈산〉 시리즈 2점을 출품하다.
	10월 16일 「중앙일보」 주최 《유영국전》(10. 16-11. 24, 서울·호암갤러리)에 초기부터 1990년대까지 제작된 작품 60여 점을 출품하여 제13회 개인전을 열다. 삼성문화재단·「중앙일보」 발행 도록 『YOO YOUNGKUK』이 발간되다.
1997	도록 『YOO YOUNG-KUK』(이수정, 오영은(미술과 삶) 편집) 발행되다.
1998	10월 14일 제14회 개인전(10. 13 -23, 서울·갤러리 현대)에 약 40점을 출품하다.
1999	4월 10일 《동아시아 회화의 근대-유화의 탄생과 그 전개》(4. 10-5. 23, 일본·시즈오카 미술관 외 일본 내 4개 미술관)에 〈10-7〉(1940)와 〈작품〉(1940) 등 2점을 출품하다.
	10월 11일 제21회 《예술원미술전》(10. 11-31, 서울·예술원미술관)에 절필작 〈작품〉을 출품하다.
2000	4월 7일 《갤러리현대개관 30주년기념전》(4. 7-25, 서울·갤러리현대)에 〈산〉 3점을 출품하다.
	12월 29일 이인범 저 『유영국과 초기 추상』이 한국예술종합학교 한국예술연구소에 의해 발행되다.
2001	9월 26일 《한국현대미술의 전개》(9. 26-10. 7, 서울·갤러리현대)에 출품하다.
2002	3월 1일 《격조와 해학: 근대의 한국미술》(3. 1-5. 12, 서울·호암갤러리, 「중앙일보」 주최)에 출품하다.
	4월 17일 《한국 근대회화100선전》(4. 17-6. 30, 서울·덕수궁 국립현대미술관)에 〈산〉(1959)을 출품하다.
	5월 17일 《서울시립미술관 개관전-한민족의 빛과 색》전 (5. 17-7. 5, 서울시립미술관)에 〈작품〉을 출품하다.
	8월 30일 《유영국-한국추상미술의 기원과 정점전》(8. 30-10. 6, 서울·가나아트센터)에 작품 50여 점을 출품하고 제 15회 개인전을 열다.
	9월 14일 《유영국-한국추상미술의 기원과 정점전》기념 학술세미나 '유영국, 한국 추상미술 해석의 쟁점'이 이인범 발제, 김병기, 이구열 증언 및 대담, 김영나 사회로 가나아트센터 아카데미 홀에서 개최되다.
	11월 11일 오후 8시 서울대병원에서 지병인 심장병으로 투병 중 승천하다.
	11월 13일 오전 9시 삼성서울병원에서 김병기, 황염수, 이대원, 권옥연, 문학진, 최종태, 오광수, 김인환 등 지인과 예술인들이 참석한 가운데 영결식을 개최하고, 경기도 여주군 강천면 걸은리에 묻히다.
2003	5월 12일 재단법인 유영국미술문화재단이 설립되다. (주소 :서울시 서초구 방배동 12-34, 이사장: 윤명로, 이사: 김종량, 서용선, 서희석, 유건, 유진, 이인범, 최종태, 홍석현, 감사: 홍정희, 노일봉)
	11월 5일 유영국미술문화재단 갤러리현대 주최로 《유영국 1주기전》(11. 5-11. 23, 서울·갤러리현대)이 열리고 사진, 릴리프, 회화 작품 등 총 43점이 출품되다.

『유영국 저널』 창간호	2004	11월 11일 2주기 기념사업으로 『유영국 저널』이 창간되다. 이후 2012년까지 총 8집의 저널이 발간되다.
		이 해 경기도 여주군 강천면 걸은리 산 59-1, 산 58번지 산소 앞에 유영국의 예술관을 압축적으로 말해 주는 화가 자신의 언명, "산은 내 앞에 있는것이 아니라 내 안에 있다"는 글귀가 새겨진 화비(畵碑)가 세워지다.
	2005	8월 24일 《오지호·유영국 2인선》(8. 24-9. 11, 광주 신세계 갤러리) 에 총 10점의 작품을 출품하다.
		10월 26일 유영국 화백의 드로잉 60점을 수록한 『유영국전작 드로잉집』이 발간되다.
		11월 4일 《유영국 3주기전-유영국 드로잉유영국 드로잉 전》(11. 4 -11. 27, 서울·가나아트센터)이 열리다.
		11월 5일 한국미술이론학회에서 주관하고 유영국미술문화재단에서 주최한 심포지엄: 〈한국의 초기 추상미술〉이 국민대학교에서 열리다.
	2007	11월 29일 《신사실파 창립 60주년 기념전-리얼리티의 성좌》(11.9-08. 1.13, 서울·환기미술관)에 김환기, 이규상, 장욱진, 백영수, 이중섭과 함께 출품하다.
	2008	1월 13일 《신사실파 창립 60주년 기념전- 리얼리티의 성좌》전 개최 기념으로 이인범 편저 『한국 최초의 순수 화가동인 신사실파』가 유영국문화재단에 의해 도서출판 미술문화에서 발행되다.
	2009	12월 정하윤의 글 「유영국(劉永國, 1916-2002) 회화 연구: 동·양의 예술관을 통한 서양미술의 수용」이 이화여자대학교 대학원 석사학위청구논문으로 제출되다.
	2010	2월 유영아의 글 「유영국(劉永國,)의 초기 추상 연구-일본 유학기 구성주의의 영향을 중심으로」가 서울대학교 대학원 서양화가 미술이론전공 석사학위청구논문으로 제출되다.
		11월 11일 《유영국의 1950년대와 1세대 모더니스트들》(11. 11-12. 5, 서울·가나아트센터)에 유화 28점이 출품하다.
	2012	5월 7일 화집 『Yoo Youngkuk』이 유영국미술문화재단·(주)갤러리현대·마로니에북스 기획으로 마로니에북스에서 발행되다.
		5월 17일 유영국 평전, 오광수 저 『유영국-삶과 창조의 지평』이 마로니에북스에 의해 발행되다.
		5월 18일 《한국 추상미술의 선구자 유영국 10주기전》(5. 18-6. 17, 서울·갤러리 현대)에 〈Work〉외 총 45점을 출품하다.
	2016	11월 4일 유영국 탄생 100주년 기념전《유영국, 절대와 자유》(2016. 11. 4 -2017. 3. 1, 국립현대미술관 덕수궁관 / 2017.3.29 - 6. 25, 부산시립미술관)이 열리다.

1968년경 사진가 임응식이 촬영한 유영국의 작업 광경 사진, 국립현대미술관 소장

출품작 목록

※ 출품작 목록은 국립현대미술관 전시 기준으로 작성되었습니다.
(부산시립미술관 전시의 경우, 변경될 수 있음)

001 **릴리프 오브제** ***Relief Object,***
1937(유리지 재제작 Reproduced by Yoo Lizzy 2002), 혼합재료 Mixed media, 53×40cm, 유영국미술문화재단 소장

002 **습작**(習作) ***Study***
1937(유리지 재제작 Reproduced by Yoo Lizzy 2003), 혼합재료 Mixed media, 49.5×37cm, 유영국미술문화재단 소장

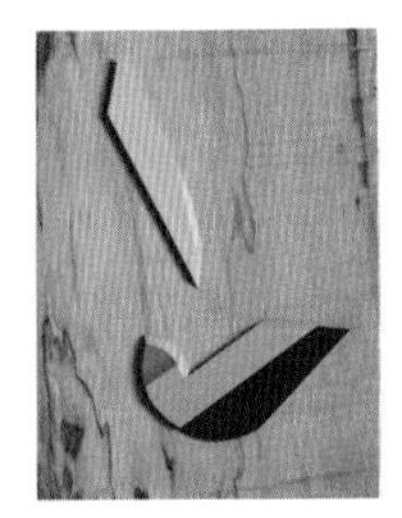

003 ***Work***
1938(유리지 재제작 Reproduced by Yoo Lizzy 2003), 혼합재료 Mixed media, 40×52.5cm, 유영국미술문화재단 소장

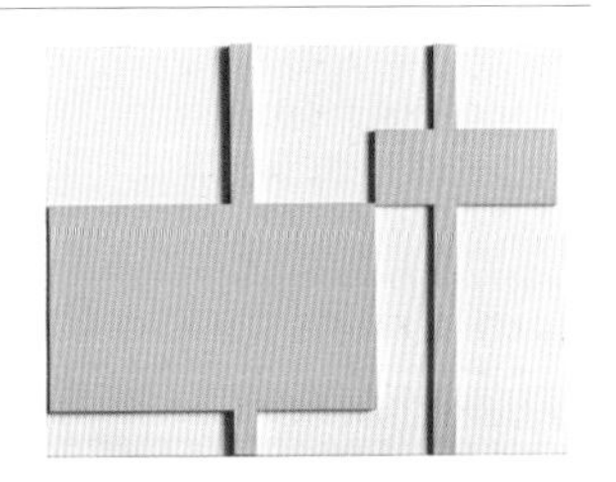

004 **작품 LA-101** ***Work LA-101***
1938(유리지 재제작 Reproduced by Yoo Lizzy 2003), 혼합재료 Mixed media, 40×51cm, 유영국미술문화재단 소장

005 **역정 2**(歷程 2) ***Journey 2***
1938(유리지 재제작 Reproduced by Yoo Lizzy 2002), 혼합재료 Mixed media, 81×90.5cm, 유영국미술문화재단 소장

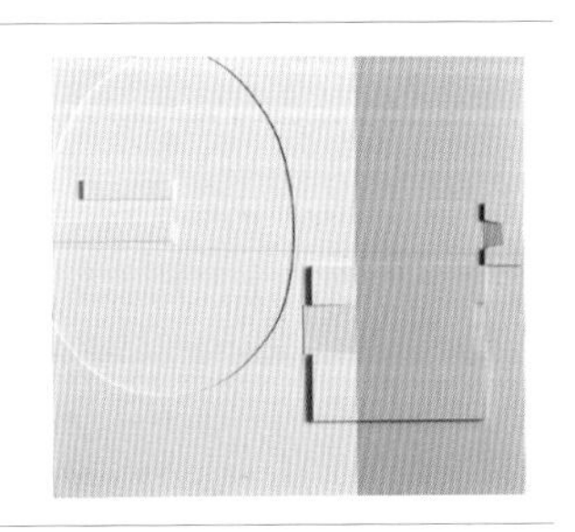

006 **계도**(計圖) **D** ***Design (D)***
1939(유리지 재제작 Reproduced by Yoo Lizzy 2002), 혼합재료 Mixed media, 51×90cm, 유영국미술문화재단 소장

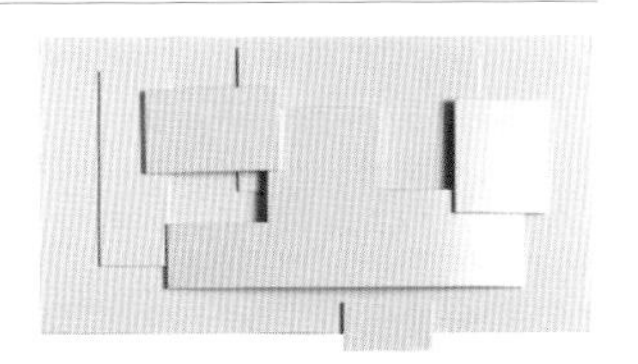

007 **작품 R3** ***Work R3***
1938(유리지 재제작 Reproduced by Yoo Lizzy 1979), 혼합재료 Mixed media, 65×90cm, 유영국미술문화재단 소장

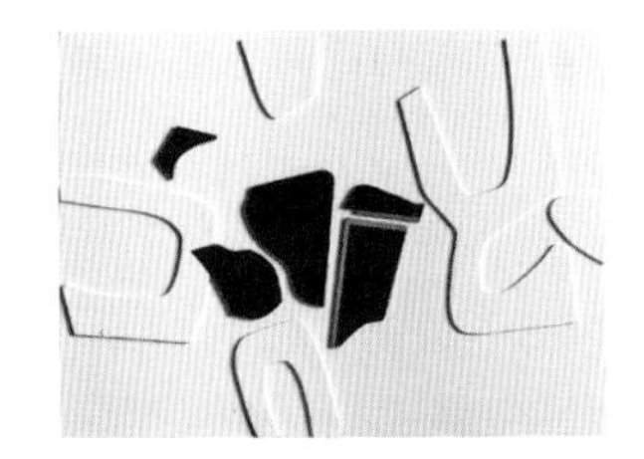

008 **작품 1(L24-39.5)**
Work 1(L24-39.5)
1939(유리지 재제작 Reproduced by Yoo Lizzy 1979), 혼합재료 Mixed media, 70×90cm, 유영국미술문화재단 소장

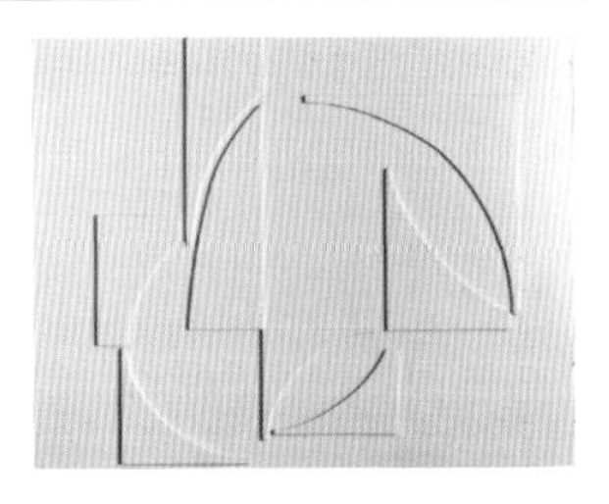

009 **작품 4(L24-39.5)**
Work 4(L24-39.5)
1939(유리지 재제작 Reproduced by Yoo Lizzy 2003), 혼합재료 Mixed media, 62×90cm, 유영국미술문화재단 소장

010 **작품 404-C** ***Work 404-C***
1940(유리지 재제작 Reproduced by Yoo Lizzy 2003), 혼합재료 Mixed media, 48×40cm, 유영국미술문화재단 소장

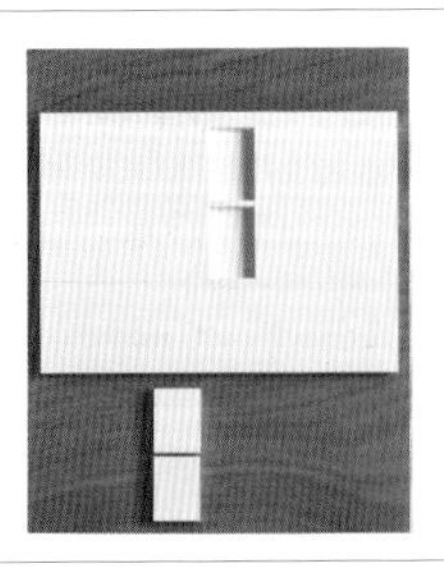

011 **작품 404-D *Work 404-D***
1940(유리지 재제작 Reproduced by Yoo Lizzy 2002), 혼합재료 Mixed media, 90×74cm, 유영국미술문화재단 소장

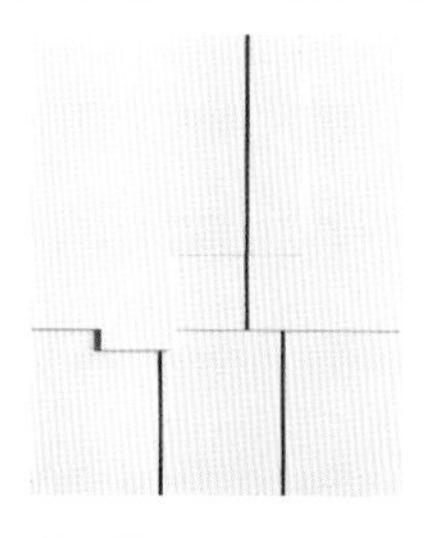

012 ***10-7***
1940, 캔버스에 유채 Oil on canvas, 38×45cm, 유영국미술문화재단 소장

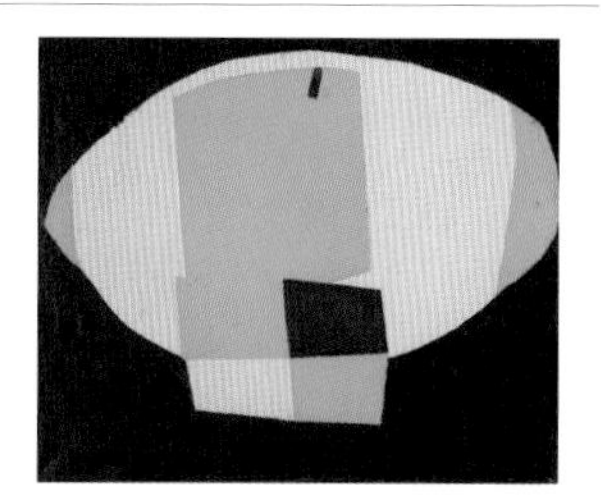

013 **작품 *Work***
1940, 캔버스에 유채 Oil on canvas, 45×37.7cm, 유영국미술문화재단 소장

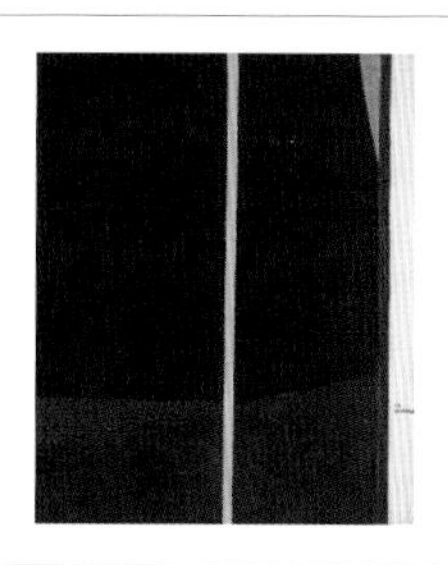

014 **경주 불국사 대웅전 불상 *Gyeongju Bulguksa Daewungjeon Buddha***
1941-1942년 경, 젤라틴 실버 프린트 Gelatin silver print, 10.6×15.6cm, 유영국미술문화재단 소장

015 **경주 탑골 석불 동면 불상 *Gyeongju Nsmsan Tapgok Buddhist Sculpture***
1941-1942년경, 젤라틴 실버 프린트 Gelatin silver print, 10.8×15.1cm, 유영국미술문화재단 소장

016 **경주 동남산 계곡 마애삼존불 *Gyeongju Eastnamsan Maaeseokbul***
1941-1942년경, 젤라틴 실버 프린트 Gelatin silver print, 15×10.6cm, 유영국미술문화재단 소장

017 **경주 산신암(産神庵) 대마애불 *Gyeongju Westnamsan Sanshinamdaemaaebul***
1941-1942년경, 젤라틴 실버 프린트 Gelatin silver print, 15.1x×10.7cm, 유영국미술문화재단 소장

018 **경주 서남산 마애삼존불 *Gyeongju Westnamsan Maaebul***
1941-1942년경, 젤라틴 실버 프린트 Gelatin silver print, 15.1×10.8cm, 유영국미술문화재단 소장

019 **경주 석굴암 내부 불상 *Gyeongju Seokguram Buddhist Sculture***
1941-1942년경, 젤라틴 실버 프린트 Gelatin silver print, 10.7×15.2cm, 유영국미술문화재단 소장

020 **경주 오릉묘(伍陵墓) *Gyeongju Oreung***
1941-1942년경, 젤라틴 실버 프린트 Gelatin silver print, 10.2×15.2cm, 유영국미술문화재단 소장

021 **경주 불국사 대웅전 *Gyeongju Bulguksa Daewungjeon***
1941-1942년경, 젤라틴 실버 프린트 Gelatin silver print, 10.6×15cm, 유영국미술문화재단 소장

022 **경주 분황사탑 *Gyeongju Bunhwangsa Pagoda***
1941-1942년경, 젤라틴 실버 프린트 Gelatin silver print, 15.3×10.6cm, 유영국미술문화재단 소장

023 **경주 서남산석탑**
Gyeongju Westnamsan Pagoda
1941–1942년경, 젤라틴 실버 프린트 Gelatin silver print, 15.3×10.6cm, 유영국미술문화재단 소장

024 **경주 박물관 내 귀부**(龜趺)
Turtle-Shape Base in Gyeongju Museum
1941–1942년경, 젤라틴 실버 프린트 Gelatin silver print, 10.5×15.5cm, 유영국미술문화재단 소장

025 **박물관 내 사초석**(寺礎石)
Foundation Stones in Gyeongju Museum
1941–1942년경, 젤라틴 실버 프린트 Gelatin silver print, 15.4×10.7cm, 유영국미술문화재단 소장

026 **직선이 있는 구도** ***Composition***
1949, 캔버스에 유채 Oil on canvas, 45.5×53cm, 유영국미술문화재단 소장

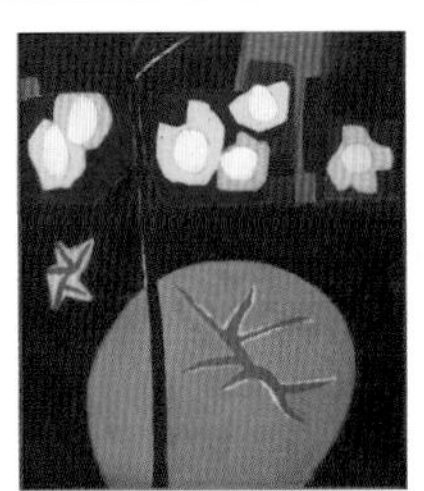

027 **작품** ***Work***
1953, 캔버스에 유채 Oil on canvas, 65×50cm, 유영국미술문화재단 소장

028 **작품** ***Work***
1953, 캔버스에 유채 Oil on canvas, 65×52cm, 유영국미술문화재단 소장

029 **바다에서** ***On the Sea***
1957, 캔버스에 유채 Oil on canvas, 130×97cm, 개인 소장

030 **작품** ***Work***
1957, 캔버스에 유채 Oil on canvas, 101×101cm, 개인소장

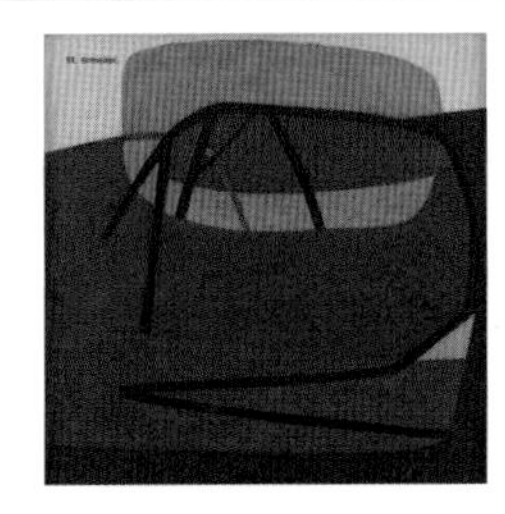

031 **산** ***Mountain***
1957, 캔버스에 유채 Oil on canvas, 100×81cm, 개인소장

032 **사람** ***A Man***
1957, 캔버스에 유채 Oil on canvas, 59×48cm, 개인소장

033 **바다에서** ***On the Sea***
1957, 캔버스에 유채 Oil on canvas, 61×53cm, 개인소장

034 **작품** ***Work***
1957, 캔버스에 유채 Oil on canvas, 100×100cm, 개인소장

035 산 *Mountain*
1957, 캔버스에 유채 Oil on canvas, 97×130cm, Museum SAN 소장

036 작품 *Work*
1957, 캔버스에 유채 Oil on canvas, 73×100cm, 개인소장

037 작품 *Work*
1958, 캔버스에 유채 Oil on canvas, 102×130cm, 개인소장

038 작품 *Work*
1958, 캔버스에 유채 Oil on canvas, 102×102cm, 개인소장

039 새 *Bird*
1958, 캔버스에 유채 Oil on canvas, 100×73cm, 개인소장

040 아침 *Morning*
1958, 캔버스에 유채 Oil on canvas, 100×73cm, 개인소장

041 계곡 *Valley*
1958, 캔버스에 유채 Oil on canvas, 162×130cm, Museum SAN 소장

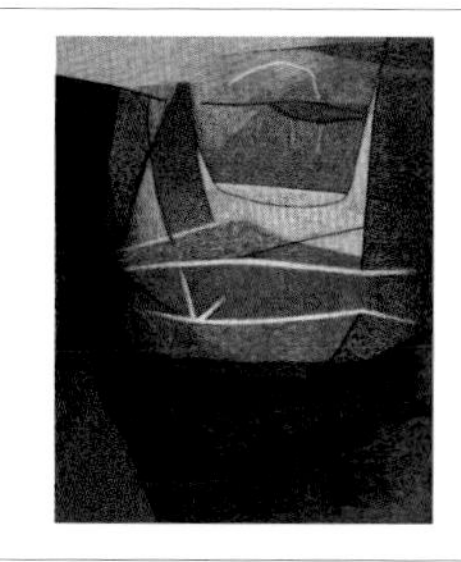

042 바다풀 *Sea Plant*
1959, 캔버스에 유채 Oil on canvas, 130.2×96.1cm, 개인소장

043 산(흙) *Mountain(Soil),* 1959, 캔버스에 유채 Oil on canvas, 130.6×194cm, 국립현대미술관 소장

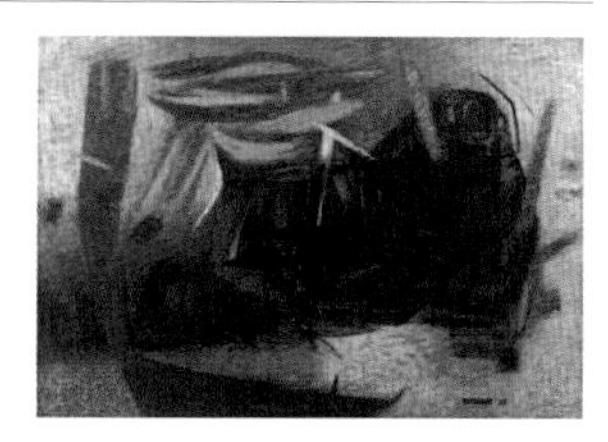

044 산(지형) *Mountain(Topography)*
1959, 캔버스에 유채 Oil on canvas, 130.8×193cm, 국립현대미술관 소장

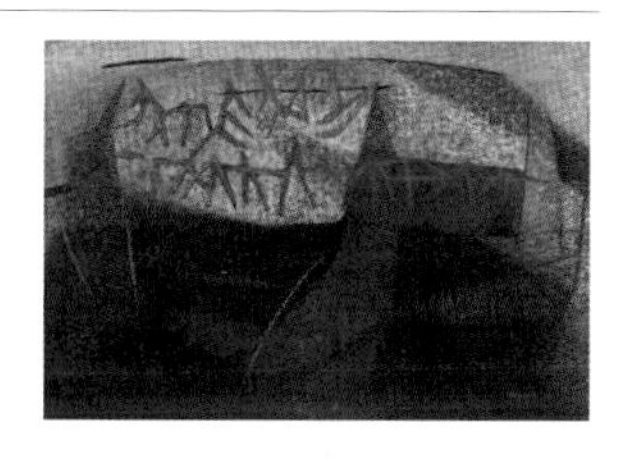

045 작품 *Work*
1959, 캔버스에 유채 Oil on canvas, 130×102cm, 개인소장

046 작품 *Work*
1960, 캔버스에 유채 Oil on canvas, 162×130cm, 개인소장

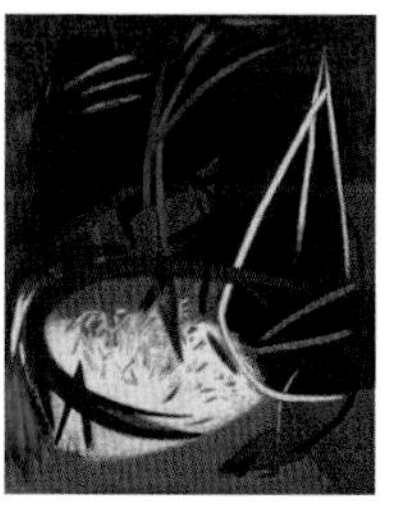

047 **산 *Mountain***
1960, 캔버스에 유채 Oil on canvas, 100×100cm, 개인소장

048 **작품 *Work***
1961-2, 캔버스에 유채 Oil on canvas, 161×129cm, 개인소장

049 **산 *Mountain***
1960, 캔버스에 유채 Oil on canvas, 136×211cm, 개인소장

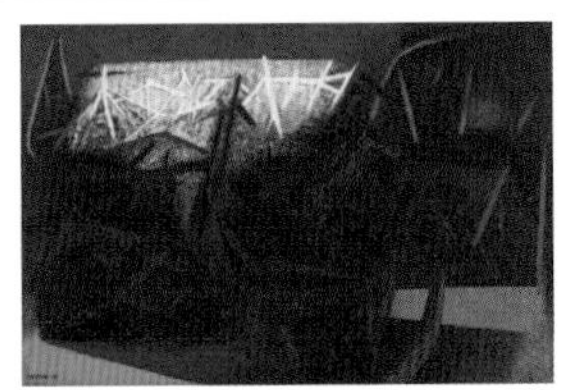

050 **산 *Mountain***
1961, 캔버스에 유채 Oil on canvas, 136×194.3cm, 개인소장

051 **작품 *Work***
1963, 캔버스에 유채 Oil on canvas, 130×162cm, 개인소장

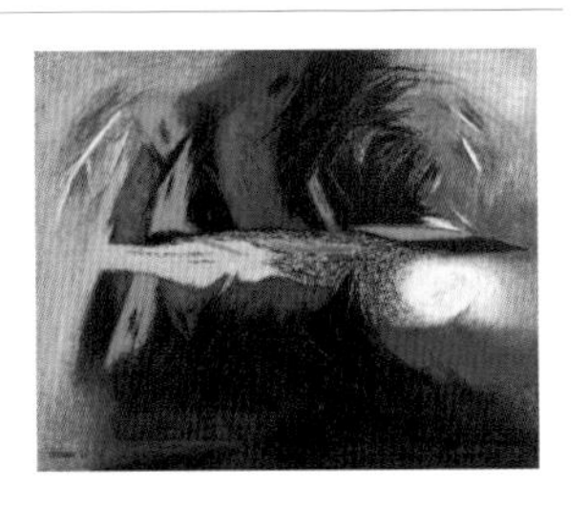

052 **산 *Mountain***
1962, 캔버스에 유채 Oil on canvas, 130×194cm, 개인소장

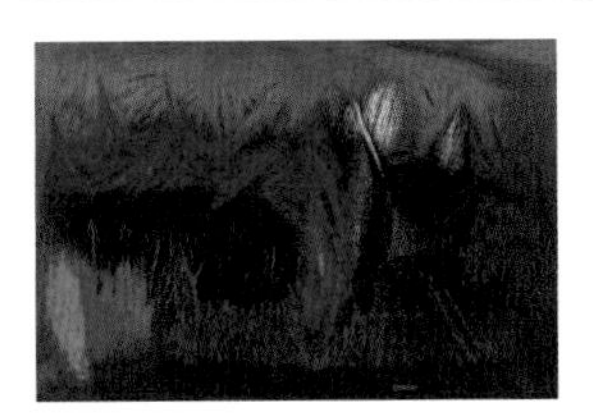

053 **작품 *Work***
1962, 캔버스에 유채 Oil on canvas, 130×194cm, 개인소장

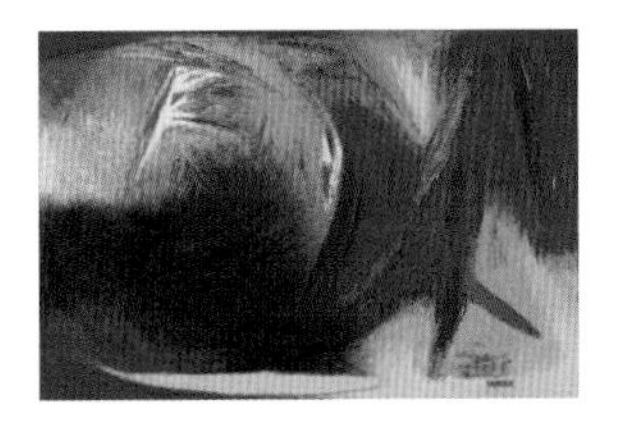

054 **해토**(解土)
Thawing of the Ground
1961, 캔버스에 유채 Oil on canvas, 130×162cm, 개인소장

055 **작품 *Work***
1964, 캔버스에 유채 Oil on canvas, 130×194cm, 개인소장

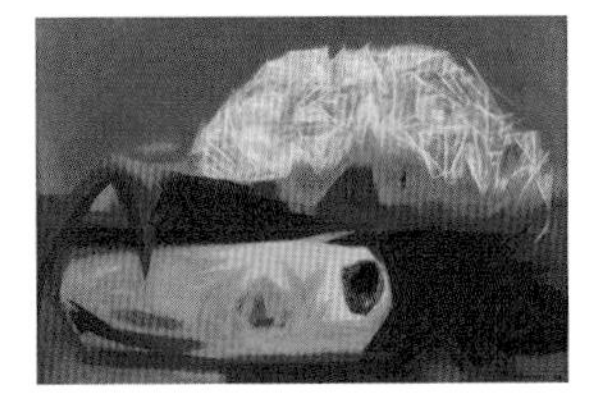

056 **작품 *Work***
1964, 캔버스에 유채 Oil on canvas, 129×161cm, 개인소장

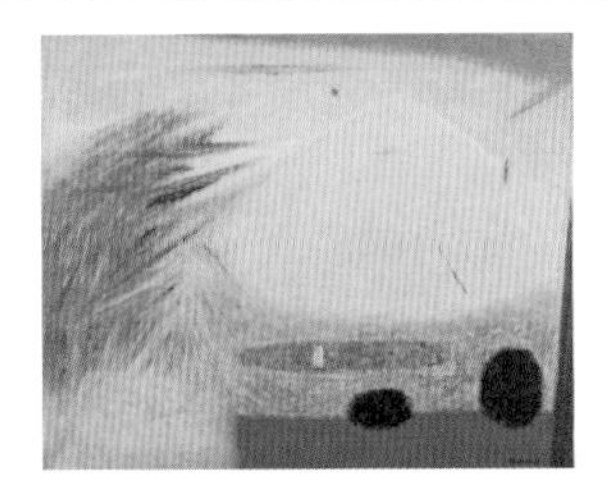

057 **작품 *Work***
1964, 캔버스에 유채 Oil on canvas, 130×194cm, 개인소장

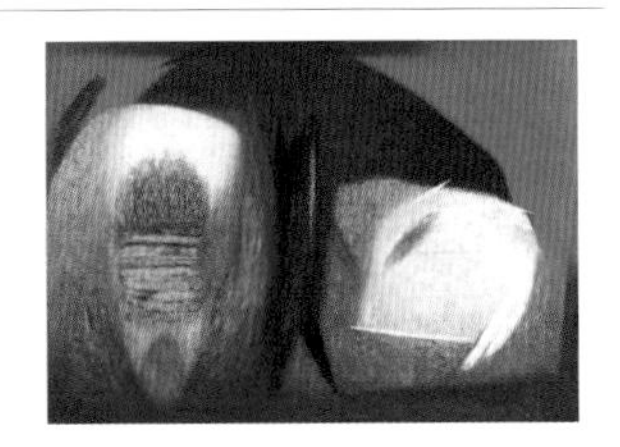

058 **작품 *Work***
1964, 캔버스에 유채 Oil on canvas, 130×194cm, 개인소장

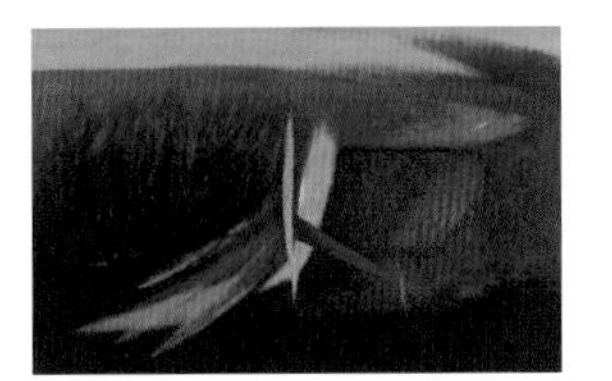

059 작품 *Work*
1964, 캔버스에 유채 Oil on canvas, 215×139cm, 개인소장

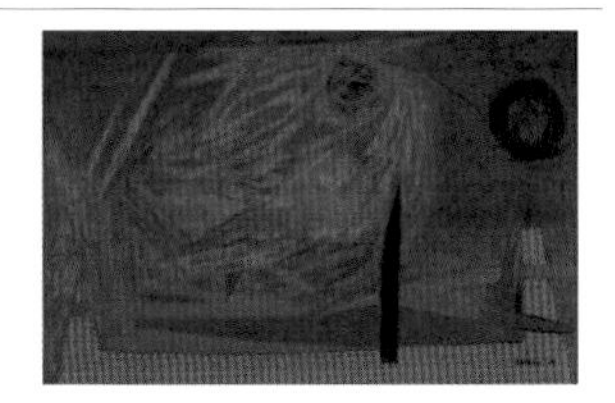

060 작품 *Work*
1964, 캔버스에 유채 Oil on canvas, 130×194cm, 개인소장

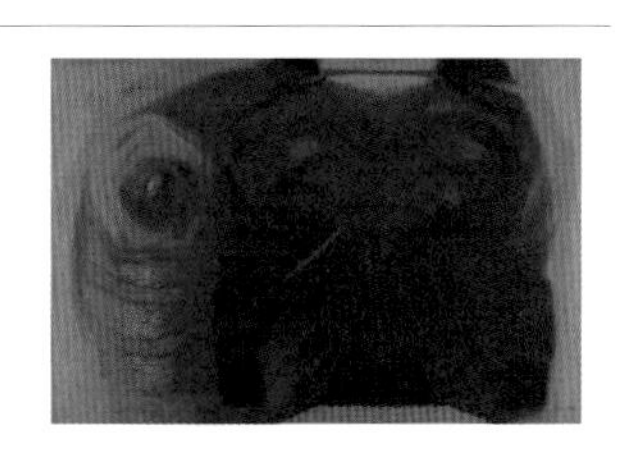

061 작품 *Work*
1964, 캔버스에 유채 Oil on canvas, 130×195cm, 개인소장

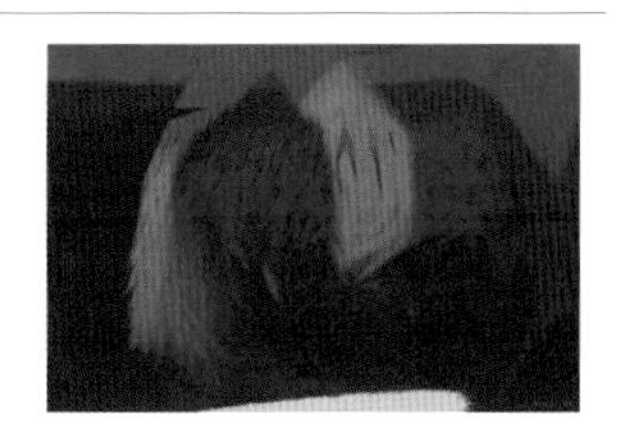

062 작품 *Work*
1963, 캔버스에 유채 Oil on canvas, 130×162cm, 개인소장

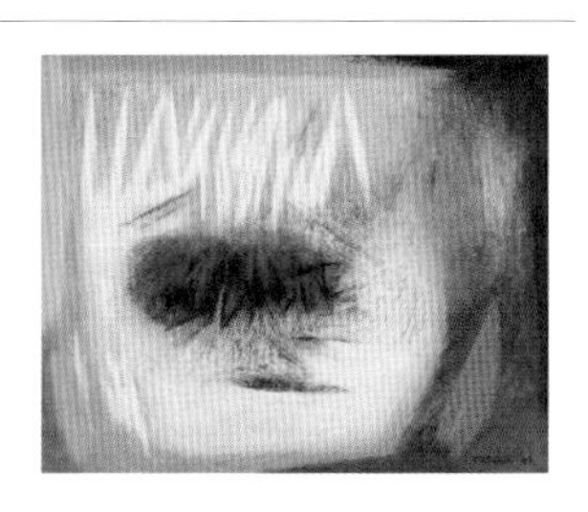

063 무제 *Untitled*
1965, 캔버스에 유채 Oil on canvas, 130×162cm, 개인소장

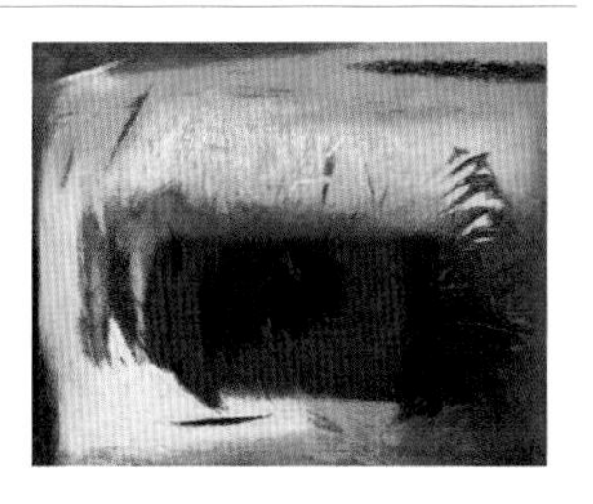

064 작품 *Work*
1967, 캔버스에 유채 Oil on canvas, 130×130cm, 개인소장

065 작품 *Work*
1966, 캔버스에 유채 Oil on canvas, 162.3×129.7cm, 개인소장

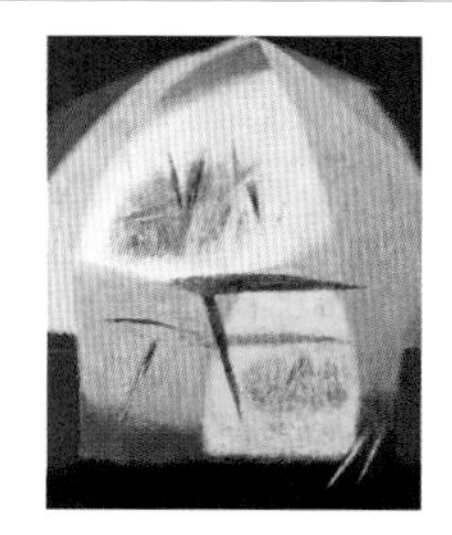

066 작품 *Work*
1968, 캔버스에 유채 Oil on canvas, 81×81cm, 개인소장

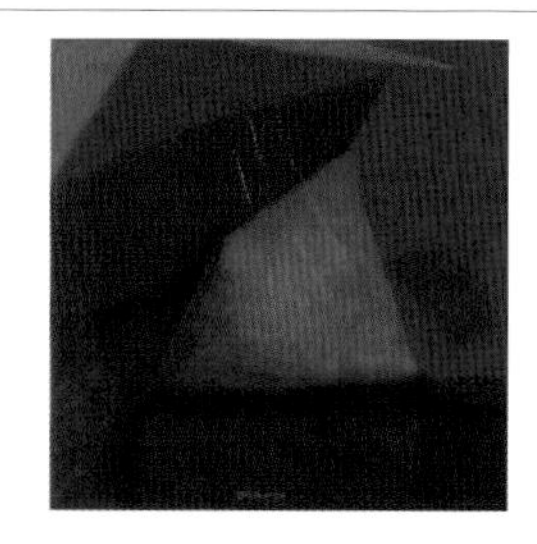

067 산 *Mountain*
1966, 캔버스에 유채 Oil on canvas, 130×162cm, 삼성미술관 리움 소장

068 무제 *Untitled*
1965, 캔버스에 유채 Oil on canvas, 159.5×128.5cm, 삼성미술관 리움 소장

069 작품 *Work*
1965, 캔버스에 유채 Oil on canvas, 130×162cm, 개인소장

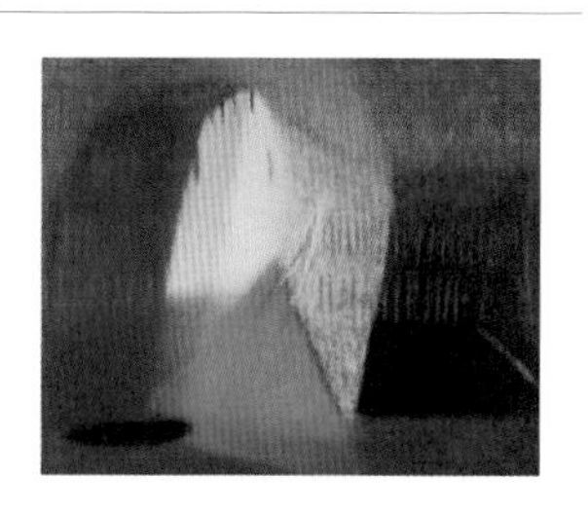

070 작품 *Work*
1967, 캔버스에 유채 Oil on canvas, 130×130cm, 서울시립미술관 소장

071 **산 *Mountain***
1968, 캔버스에 유채 Oil on canvas, 129×129cm, 개인소장

072 **산 *Mountain***
1968, 캔버스에 유채 Oil on canvas, 136×136cm, 개인소장

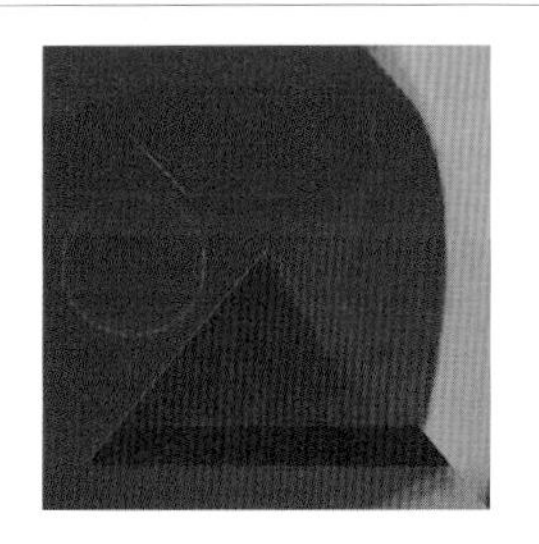

073 **작품 *Work***
1968, 캔버스에 유채 Oil on canvas, 136×136cm, 개인소장

074 **원(円)-A *Circle-A***
1968, 캔버스에 유채 Oil on canvas, 136×136cm, 유영국미술문화재단 소장

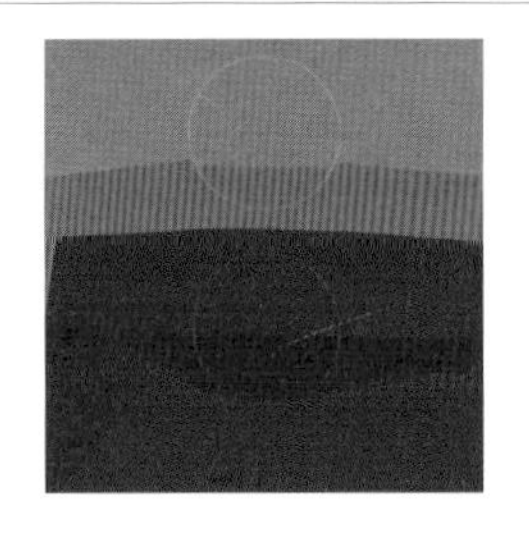

075 **원(円)-C *Circle-C***
1968, 캔버스에 유채 Oil on canvas, 135×135cm, 개인소장

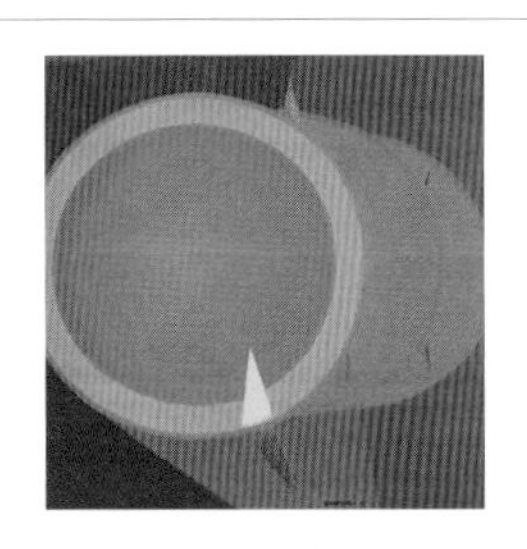

076 **작품 *Work***
1968, 캔버스에 유채 Oil on canvas, 136×136cm, 개인소장

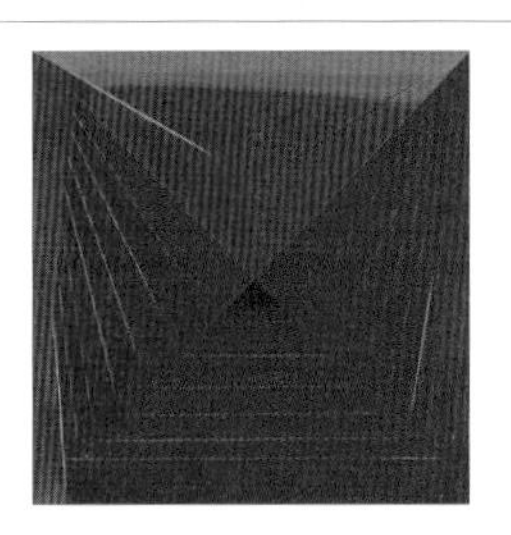

077 **산 *Mountain***
1974, 캔버스에 유채 Oil on canvas, 106×106cm, 개인 소장

078 **산 *Mountain***
1977, 캔버스에 유채 Oil on canvas, 130x130cm, 개인소장

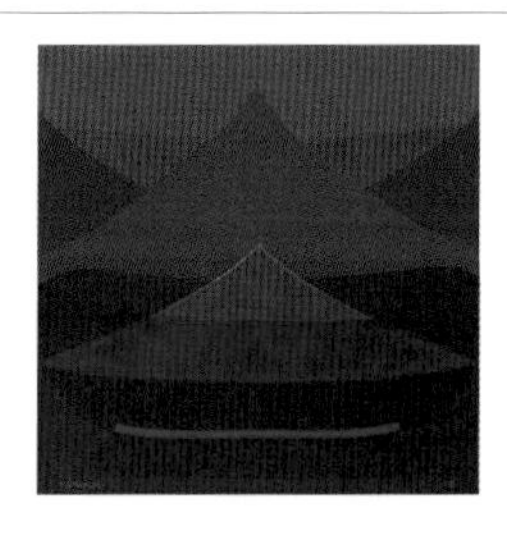

079 **작품 *Work***
1969, 캔버스에 유채 Oil on canvas, 136×136cm, Museum SAN 소장

080 **산 *Mountain***
1968, 캔버스에 유채 Oil on canvas, 136×136cm, 개인소장

081 **작품 *Work***
1969, 캔버스에 유채 Oil on canvas, 136×136cm, 개인소장

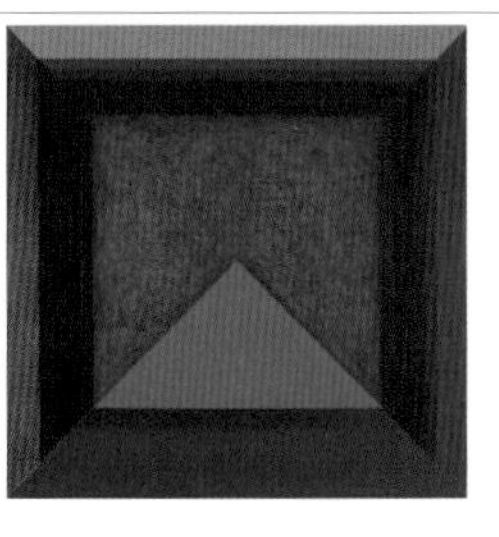

082 **작품 *Work***
1970, 캔버스에 유채 Oil on canvas, 136×136cm, 유영국미술문화재단 소장

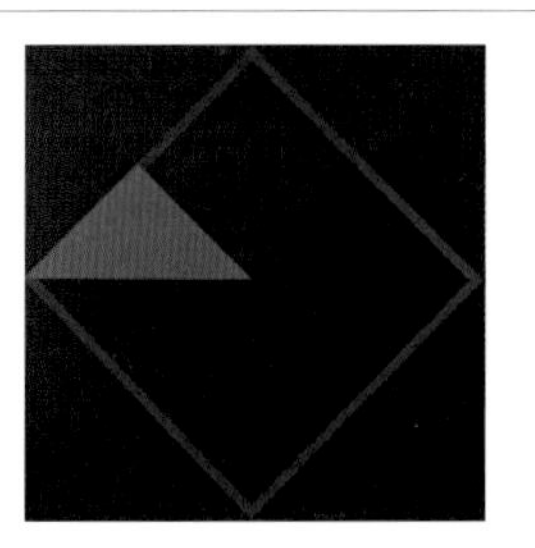

083 산 ***Mountain***
1968, 캔버스에 유채 Oil on canvas, 135×135cm, 개인소장

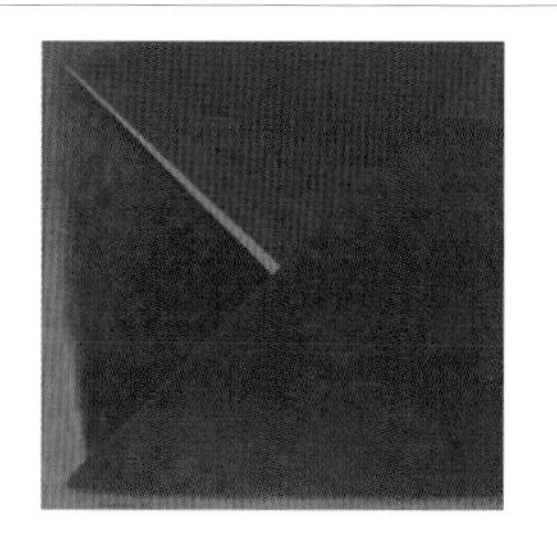

084 산 ***Mountain***
1968, 캔버스에 유채 Oil on canvas, 136×136cm, 개인소장

085 작품 ***Work***
1979, 캔버스에 유채 Oil on canvas, 135×135cm, 서울시립미술관 소장

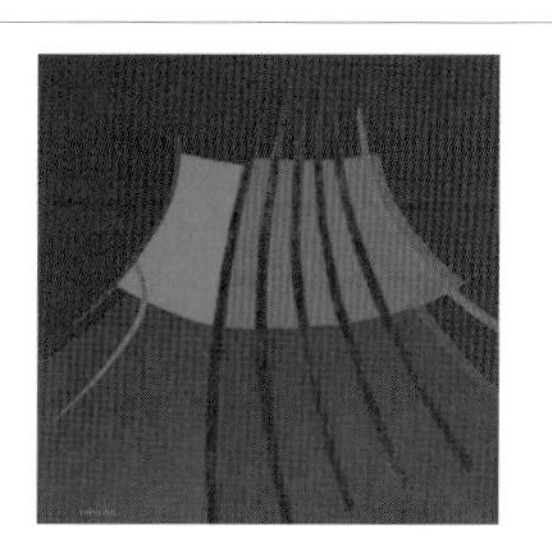

086 작품 ***Work***
1979, 캔버스에 유채 Oil on canvas, 106×106cm, 개인소장

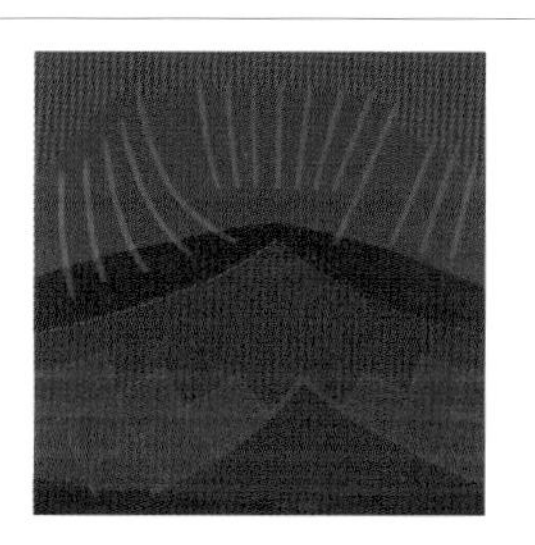

087 산 ***Mountain***
1972, 캔버스에 유채 Oil on canvas, 133×133cm, 개인소장

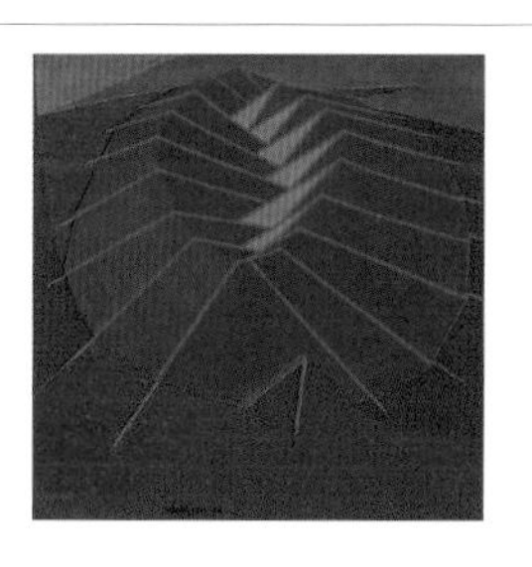

088 작품 ***Work***
1970, 캔버스에 유채 Oil on canvas, 136×136cm, 유영국미술문화재단 소장

089 작품 ***Work***
1970, 캔버스에 유채 Oil on canvas, 136×136cm, 유영국미술문화재단 소장

090 산-Red ***Mountain-Red***
1994, 캔버스에 유채 Oil on canvas, 126×96cm, 유영국미술문화재단 소장

091 산-Blue ***Mountain-Blue***
1994, 캔버스에 유채 Oil on canvas, 126×96cm, 유영국미술문화재단 소장

092 작품 ***Work***
1973, 캔버스에 유채 Oil on canvas, 53×65cm, 개인소장

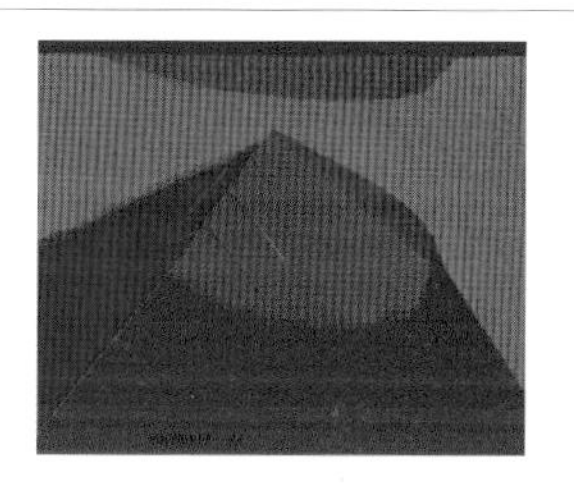

093 작품 ***Work***
1980, 캔버스에 유채 Oil on canvas, 53×65 cm, 개인소장

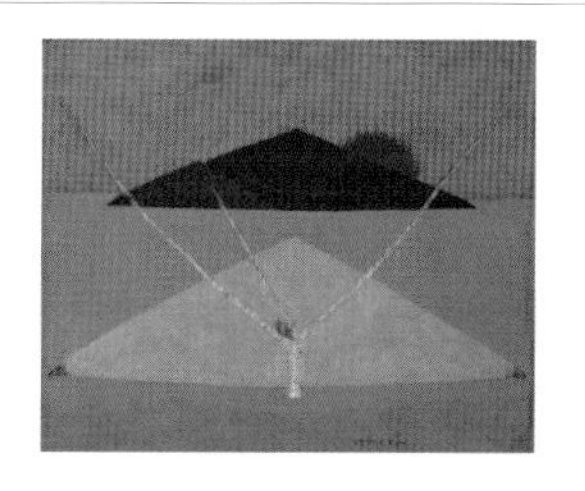

094 작품 ***Work***
1979, 캔버스에 유채 Oil on canvas, 105×105cm, 개인소장

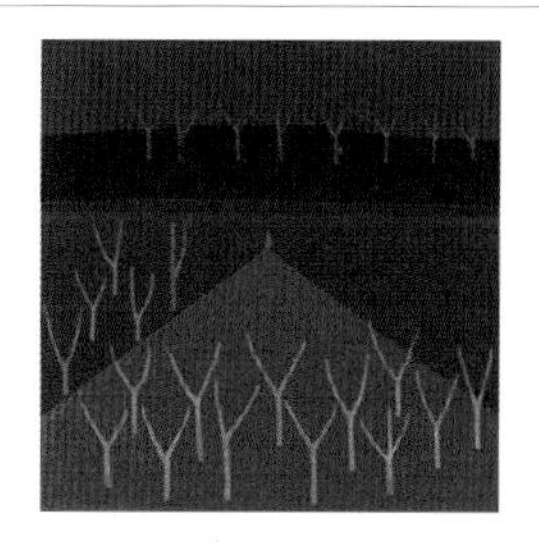

095 작품 *Work*
1989, 캔버스에 유채 Oil on canvas, 135×135cm, 서울미술관 소장

096 작품 *Work*
1988, 캔버스에 유채 Oil on canvas, 130×194cm, 개인소장

097 작품 *Work*
1987, 캔버스에 유채 Oil on canvas, 135×135cm, 개인소장

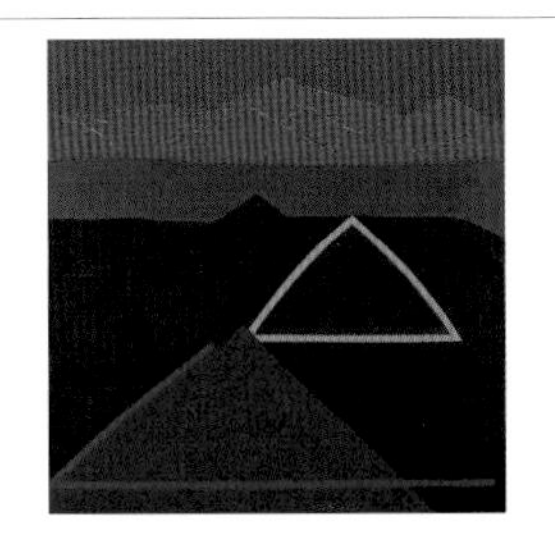

098 무제 *Untitled*
1984, 캔버스에 유채 Oil on canvas, 130×162cm, 개인소장

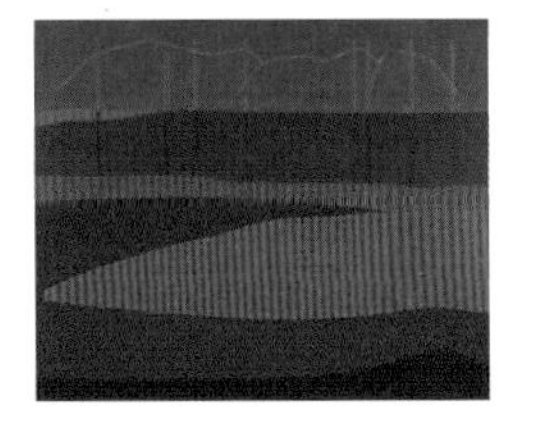

099 작품 *Work*
1981, 캔버스에 유채 Oil on canvas, 91×73cm, 개인소장

100 산과 호수 *Mountain and Lake*
1979, 캔버스에 유채 Oil on canvas, 53×65cm, 개인소장

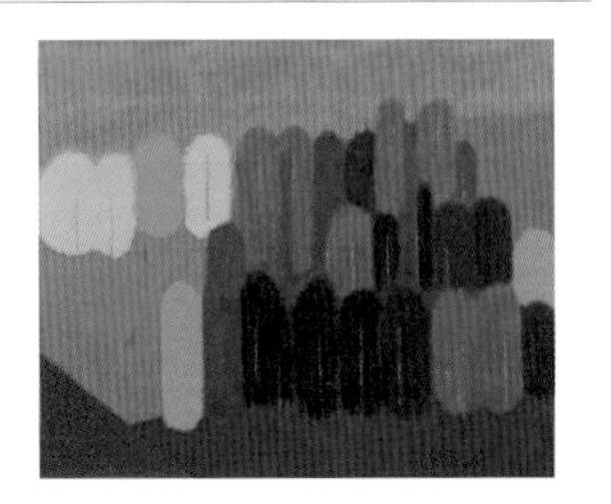

101 작품 *Work*
1989, 캔버스에 유채 Oil on canvas, 105×105cm, 개인소장

102 산 *Mountain*
1980, 캔버스에 유채 Oil on canvas, 106×106cm, 개인소장

103 작품 *Work*
1982, 캔버스에 유채 Oil on canvas, 73×100cm, 개인소장

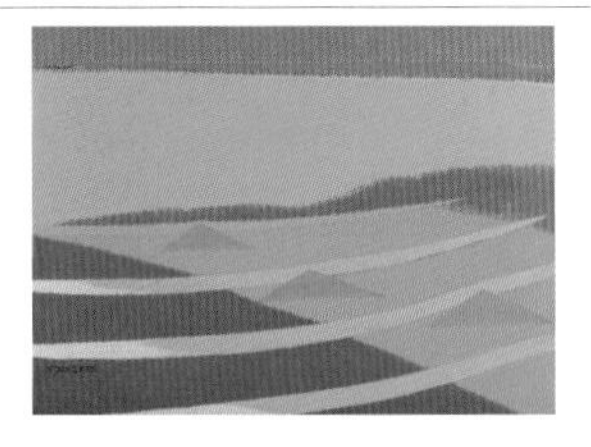

104 작품 *Work*
1981, 캔버스에 유채 Oil on canvas, 73×100cm, 개인소장

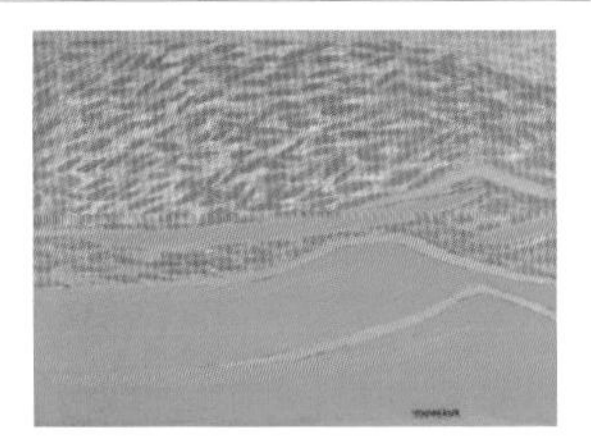

105 작품 *Work*
1989, 캔버스에 유채 Oil on canvas, 65.4×91cm, 개인소장

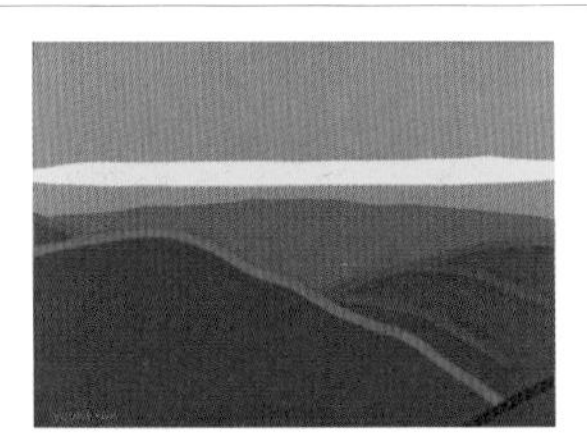

106 작품 *Work*
1994, 캔버스에 유채 Oil on canvas, 66×91cm, 개인소장

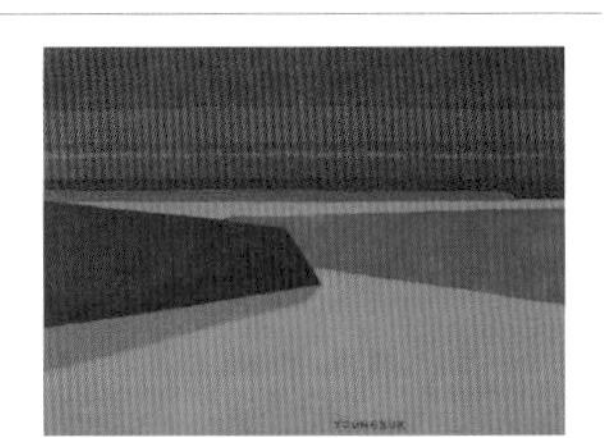

107 **산 *Mountain***
1970, 캔버스에 유채 Oil on canvas, 104×104cm, 개인소장

108 **무제 *Untitled***
1993, 캔버스에 유채 Oil on canvas, 105×105cm, 개인소장

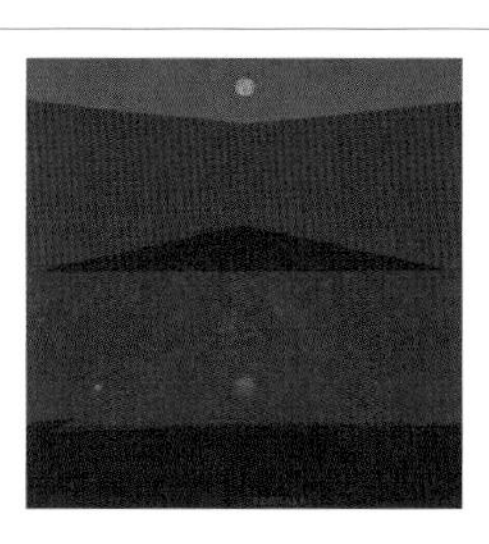

109 **작품 *Work***
1999, 캔버스에 유채 Oil on canvas, 105×105cm, 유영국미술문화재단 소장

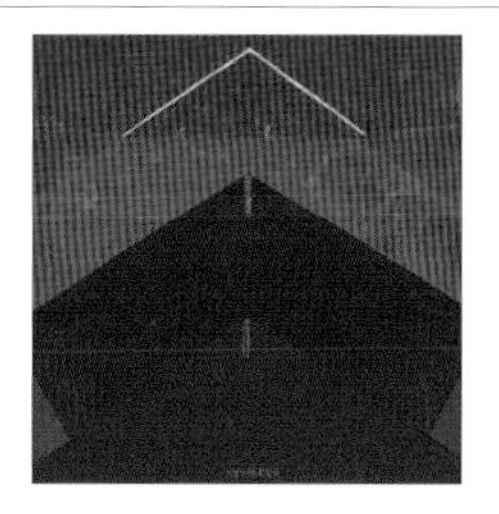

유영국 탄생 100주년 기념전

유영국, 절대와 자유

발행일 2016. 11. 3
초판 3쇄 2022. 6. 30

펴낸이 지미정
편집 김인혜
디자인 f205
번역 박명숙

펴낸곳 미술문화 | 주소 경기도 고양시 고양대로1021번길 33 402호
전화 02)335-2964 | 팩스 031)901-2965 | 홈페이지 www.misulmun.co.kr
등록번호 제2012-000142호 | 등록일 1994. 3. 30.
인쇄 동화인쇄

이 도서의 국립중앙도서관 출판시도서목록(CIP)은 서지정보유통지원시스템 홈페이지(http://seoji.nl.go.kr)와 국가자료공동목록시스템(http://nl.go.kr/kolisnet)에서 이용하실 수 있습니다. (CIP제어번호: 2016025049)

가격 38,000원

ISBN 979-11-85954-18-9 03600